Performance In

Series Editors: Bryan Reynolds,
University of

Performance In ssay collections on theatre, performance, and visual culture that share an underlying commitment to the radical and political potential of the arts in our contemporary moment, or give consideration to performance and to visual culture from the past deemed crucial to a social and political present. *Performance Interventions* moves transversally across artistic and ideological boundaries to publish work that promotes dialogue between practitioners and academics, and interactions between performance communities, educational institutions, and academic disciplines.

Titles include:

Alan Ackerman and Martin Puchner (*editors*)
AGAINST THEATRE
Creative Destructions on the Modernist Stage

Elaine Aston and Geraldine Harris (*editors*)
FEMINIST FUTURES?
Theatre, Performance, Theory

Elaine Aston and Geraldine Harris
A GOOD NIGHT OUT FOR THE GIRLS
Popular Feminisms in Contemporary Theatre and Performance

Anna Birch and Joanne Tompkins (*editors*)
PERFORMING SITE-SPECIFIC THEATRE
Politics, Place, Practice

Maaike Bleeker
VISUALITY IN THE THEATRE
The Locus of Looking

Sara Brady
PERFORMANCE, POLITICS AND THE WAR ON TERROR
'Whatever it Takes'

Clare Finburgh and Carl Lavery (*editors*)
CONTEMPORARY FRENCH THEATRE AND PERFORMANCE

James Frieze
NAMING THEATRE
Demonstrative Diagnosis in Performance

Lynette Goddard
STAGING BLACK FEMINISMS
Identity, Politics, Performance

Alison Forsyth and Chris Megson (*editors*)
GET REAL
Documentary Theatre Past and Present

Jen Harvie
FAIR PLAY – ART, PERFORMANCE AND NEOLIBERALISM

Leslie Hill and Helen Paris (*editors*)
PERFORMANCE AND PLACE

D.J. Hopkins, Shelley Orr and Kim Solga (*editors*)
PERFORMANCE AND THE CITY

Amelia Howe Kritzer
POLITICAL THEATRE IN POST-THATCHER BRITAIN
New Writing: 1995–2005

Alison Jeffers
REFUGEES, THEATRE AND CRISIS
Performing Global Identities

Stephen Greer
CONTEMPORARY BRITISH QUEER PERFORMANCE

Marcela Kostihová
SHAKESPEARE IN TRANSITION
Political Appropriations in the Post-Communist Czech Republic

Jon McKenzie, Heike Roms and C.J W.-L. Wee (*editors*)
CONTESTING PERFORMANCE
Emerging Sites of Research

Jennifer Parker-Starbuck
CYBORG THEATRE
Corporeal/Technological Intersections in Multimedia Performance

Ramón H. Rivera-Servera and Harvey Young
PERFORMANCE IN THE BORDERLANDS

Mike Sell (*editor*)
AVANT-GARDE PERFORMANCE AND MATERIAL EXCHANGE
Vectors of the Radical

Melissa Sihra (*editor*)
WOMEN IN IRISH DRAMA
A Century of Authorship and Representation

Brian Singleton
MASCULINITIES AND THE CONTEMPORARY IRISH THEATRE

Performance Interventions
Series Standing Order ISBN 978–1–403–94443–6 Hardback
978–1–403–94444–3 Paperback
(*outside North America only*)

You can receive future titles in this series as they are published by placing a standing order. Please contact your bookseller or, in case of difficulty, write to us at the address below with your name and address, the title of the series and the ISBN quoted above.

Customer Services Department, Macmillan Distribution Ltd, Houndmills, Basingstoke, Hampshire RG21 6XS, England

---

Fair Play – Art, Performance and Neoliberalism

Jen Harvie

palgrave
macmillan

First published 2013 by
PALGRAVE MACMILLAN

Palgrave Macmillan in the UK is an imprint of Macmillan Publishers Limited, registered in England, company number 785998, of Houndmills, Basingstoke, Hampshire RG21 6XS.

Palgrave Macmillan in the US is a division of St Martin's Press LLC, 175 Fifth Avenue, New York, NY 10010.

Palgrave Macmillan is the global academic imprint of the above companies and has companies and representatives throughout the world.

Palgrave® and Macmillan® are registered trademarks in the United States, the United Kingdom, Europe and other countries.

ISBN 978–1–137–02728–3 hardback
ISBN 978–1–137–02727–6 paperback

This book is printed on paper suitable for recycling and made from fully managed and sustained forest sources. Logging, pulping and manufacturing processes are expected to conform to the environmental regulations of the country of origin.

A catalogue record for this book is available from the British Library.

A catalog record for this book is available from the Library of Congress.

Typeset by MPS Limited, Chennai, India.

Dedicated with love and gratitude to three
inspiring women:
my mum, Judy Harvie,
our dear friend, Barbara Rowe,
and my dear friend and colleague, Lois Weaver.

Contents

Acknowledgements

I am enormously grateful to Erin Hurley for reading draft elements of this book and returning extensive, detailed, insightful, encouraging and prompt feedback. I have not been able to do justice to it all – but I am thankful for it, and for having Erin as a fellow traveller and friend.

Thanks also to my colleagues in Drama at Queen Mary, University of London (QMUL), who have supported this research, especially Catherine Silverstone, Dominic Johnson, Lois Weaver, Maria Delgado, Bridget Escolme and successive Heads of Drama, Michael McKinnie and Nicholas Ridout, as well as Caoimhe McAvinchey, Keren Zaiontz, Kim Solga, Martin Welton, Ali Campbell, Nadia Davids, Rose Sharp and Tiffany Watt-Smith. Sincere thanks also to the many students at QMUL who have worked on ideas in this book with me, including MA students of Contemporary Theatre and Performance and Contemporary Performance; BA students on Offstage London and London/Culture/Performance; and PhD students in Drama. Particular thanks to Charlotte Bell for excellent and efficient research assistance.

I am grateful to the many academics, artists, writers and friends who have helped me think through ideas in this book and otherwise supported its completion. Alongside those mentioned elsewhere in these acknowledgements, these include: Maria Agiomyrgiannaki, Paul Allain, Oreet Ashery, Lis Austin, Bobby Baker, Nick Baker, Shahidha Bari, Simon Bayly, Dave Beech, Gianna Bouchard, Alan Braidwood, Sarahleigh Castelyn, Minty Donald, Markman Ellis, Kate Elswit, Michael Elwyn, Camilla Gibb, Siobhain Gibson, Sarah Gorman, Simone Hancox, Dee Heddon, Robert Hewison, Katja Hilevaara, Leslie Hill, Edd Hobbs, D.J. Hopkins, David Horovitch, Cressida Hubbard, Wendy Hubbard, Shannon Jackson, Nora Jaffary, Lois Keidan, Joe Kelleher, Andy Lavender, Stephen Lawson, Laura Levin, Johanna Linsley, Elyssa Livergant, Brian Lobel, Hari Marini, Lynne McCarthy, Nick Millar, Russell Miller, Aoife Monks, Britt Oldenburg, Daniel Oliver, Louise Owen, Shelley Orr, Lou Palmer, Helen Paris, Owen Glyndwr Parry, David Pinder, Aaron Pollard, Paul Rae, Alan Read, Dan Rebellato, Theron Schmidt, Bill Schwarz, Jane Sillars, Gini Simpson, Alison Steadman, Patrick Thoburn, Sarah Thomasson, Joanne Tompkins, Rebecca Trowler, Fintan Walsh, Helena Walsh and Lee White.

I am grateful to Queen Mary, University of London, for granting me a period of research leave, and to successive Heads of the School of

English and Drama, Michèle Barrett and Julia Boffey, for ongoing support. Many thanks to the School administrative team, including Jenny Gault, Huw Marsh, Daphne Rayment, Patricia Hamilton, Jenn Chenkin, Richard Coulton, Matthew Mauger, Suzi Lewis, Harriet Taylor, Rob Ellis, Faisal Abul and Bev Stewart.

Thanks too to colleagues at Palgrave Macmillan, especially Paula Kennedy, Sacha Lake, Ben Doyle, Alice Tomlinson and series editors Elaine Aston and Bryan Reynolds. Thanks to copy editor Penny Simmons. Thanks to an anonymous reader of my proposal for constructive feedback, and to Ric Knowles, whom I learned was a reader for the press and who gave very valuable feedback and support.

Many, many thanks to artist Marcus Coates and filmmaker Michael Smythe of NOMAD for permission to use a photo (by Nick David) from *Vision Quest – A Ritual for Elephant & Castle* for the book cover. Thanks also to Chrome Hoof, who appear in the photo, and to Paul Moss of Workplace Gallery, Gateshead, for help in establishing communication with Marcus and Michael.

Thanks to colleagues who invited me to present material that has informed my thinking for this book and/or appears in this book: Olga Celda and Manuel Molins, who organized the International Congress on European Contemporary Dramaturgy in Valencia, Spain (2010); Zoë Svendsen, who convened the Cambridge University Graduate Drama Seminar (2010); organizers of Performance Studies international (PSi) 16, 'Performing Publics', in Toronto (2010); Fiona Curran, Leah Lovett and Henrietta Simson who curated the symposium 'Surplus to Requirements?' at the Slade, University College London (2011); Peter W. Marx, Alexandra Portmann and colleagues who organized the 'Cultural Mobility' International Workshop at the Institut für Theaterwissenschaft, University of Bern, Switzerland (2011); Lara Shalson and colleagues at King's College London, who convened the 'Public Investments' seminar series (2011); Susan Bennett and Karen Fricker, who convened the 'Economies of Place and Performance' Working Group at the American Society for Theatre Research, Montreal (2011); Lionel Pilkington and colleagues who ran 'Archives, Historiography, Politics – Ten Years On – Performance, Memory, Futures' at the National University of Ireland, Galway (2011); Adam Alston, Virginia Elgar and Michael Pearce who convened the 'Theatre and Alternative Value' Theatre and Performance Research Association Postgraduate Symposium, London (2012); Faye Woods, Simone Knox, John Bull and Graham Saunders at the University of Reading (2012); organizers of PSi 18, 'Performance :: Culture :: Industry', at the University of Leeds (2012); and colleagues from the Victoria and Albert Museum and the University of Reading who organized 'Subsidy, Patronage & Sponsorship: Theatre and Performance Culture in Uncertain Times' (2012).

The London Centre for Arts and Cultural Exchange (as of 2012 renamed The Cultural Capital Exchange) contributed seed funding towards research on arts and cultural value (2009). Thanks to them, and to Louisa Pearson and Sophie Leighton-Kelly who assisted me with work on that project and to participants in our two-day symposium at QMUL on 'The Excellence Agenda' (2010).

Minor elements of my discussion of Roger Hiorns's *Seizure* were previously published in my article, 'Democracy and Neoliberalism in Art's Social Turn and Roger Hiorns's *Seizure*', *Performance Research: A Journal of the Performing Arts* 16.2 (2011), pp. 113–23. (available at <http://www.tandfonline.com/doi/full/10.1080/13528165.2011.578842>). Some elements of my discussion of Michael Landy's *Break Down* were previously published in my article, 'Witnessing Michael Landy's *Break Down*: Metonymy, Affect, and Politicised Performance in an Age of Global Consumer Capitalism', *Contemporary Theatre Review* 16.1 (2006), pp. 62–72 (available at <http://www.tandfonline.com/doi/full/10.1080/10486800500451013#.UbyxK9jDJI4>).

Thanks too to staff at the British Library and at the London Fields Lido. Thanks for respectful camaraderie in Montreal to Alice and Biscuit.

My family has supported my work enormously. Thanks to my sister and family: Juju, David, Orillia and Quinte Vail. Thanks to my cousins, including Pat Harvie and George Garlock, and Aykroyds, Dan, Donna, Danielle, Stella and Belle. Thanks to Peter and Lorraine Aykroyd. Thanks to the Kilbride clan: Rosemary Kilbride and Ray Maciocia; Ann, John, Charlotte, Hannah, Joe and Frank Robinson; and Francis Kilbride. Thanks and fair play to you too, Frank Kilbride, for endorsing my choice of title. Many, many thanks to my mum, Judy Harvie.

Thanks to Deb Kilbride, for everything.

Introduction: Fair Play

Fair play?

I was inspired to write this book in response to the recent proliferation of performance and art practices that engage audiences *socially* – by inviting those audiences to participate, act, work and create together; observe one another; or simply be together. This trend has been growing exponentially since the 1990s in, for example, much public art, immersive theatre, one-to-one theatre, and relational and delegated art. In performance and theatre, practices of immersing audiences within theatrical worlds and inviting them to participate there are no longer principally confined to their usual manifestations in applied performance contexts such as theatre-in-education. In sculpture and art installation, audiences are increasingly welcomed to interact with the works at least spatially, and sometimes through touch or more vigorous participation. They are also encouraged to interact with each other, for example through looking at one another, or moving or speaking together, in a trend which art curator and critic Nicolas Bourriaud has famously termed socially 'relational' (Bourriaud, 2002) and art theorist Claire Bishop has called 'the social turn' in contemporary art (Bishop, 2006b). The enormity and spread of this trend raises questions about why these practices are proliferating, what they say about contemporary culture, what they can actually do for audiences, and what they can offer contemporary social relations.

This last question interests me most, because these practices appear to hold out the heady promise of enormous social value in two important ways. First, they seem to offer widespread constructive social engagement, with participants communicating, collaborating, co-creating and mutually supporting one another. Second, they appear to extend this invitation to engage socially very widely, across all audiences equitably, perhaps even democratically. These two features – social engagement and fair, democratic opportunity – are what most inspire me about the possibilities of these socially engaged trends in contemporary art and performance. They inspire me because I believe in and am committed to them, and because so many other features of contemporary culture – globally, and notably in the United Kingdom, where I am writing – threaten at least to diminish them and possibly, horribly, to obliterate them.

I believe in and want social engagement because people are, need to be and benefit from being socially interdependent. We need to learn from and about each other, to be able to rely on and support each other and to negotiate our similarities and differences if not always, if ever, to resolve them. We need some 'fellow feeling', some social sympathy, to check unreserved self-interest.[1] We also need social engagement to sustain democracy, people's shared exercise of power. All of these essentials of social life are jeopardized by contemporary cultural trends which damage communication and prioritize self-interest. Communication may appear to be enhanced by contemporary technologies, for example, but in many ways they inhibit it, isolating individuals in silos of blinkered attention to personal mobile communication devices. The kind of self-interest evident in that scenario is actively cultivated by dominant neoliberal capitalist ideologies which aggressively promote individualism and entrepreneurialism and pour scorn on anyone unfortunate enough to need to draw on the safety net of welfare support.

I believe in and want fair, democratic opportunity because I support principles of human rights, equality, equality of opportunity, social justice and the fair distribution of resources, including when that necessitates their redistribution, for example through just taxation and welfare settlements. These principles too are at risk in neoliberal capitalist conditions which I explore in more detail below, and which continue to favour exclusivity rather than inclusivity, further concentrating privilege with those who are already privileged. These two features of social life – social engagement and equality of opportunity – are, for me, two of its most precious possibilities. I invoke them in my title, *Fair Play*. The fact that they are under threat worries me deeply. That art and performance might help to retrieve, protect, sustain and extend them gives me hope.

But I am also a sceptic. I have to ask whether art and performance can ever achieve such heroic social feats. And I have to question how on earth they could ever do so in the kinds of existing compromised social and political circumstances that I alluded to above. The sceptic in me asks whether these trends in art and performance are not, in fact, complicit with the agendas of neoliberal capitalist culture like so much else is, passed off as critical social interventions when they are actually nourishing to neoliberalism's inequalities. As Michel Foucault and others have argued, political ideologies such as neoliberalism are not principally imposed through top-down government 'controls', but rather through 'governmentality' – the dissemination of knowledge that people internalize so that they become self-governing (Burchell, Gordon and Miller, 1991; Foucault, 1991). Neoliberalism's particular commitment to minimizing state regulation and 'interference' means that its survival and expansion are especially dependent on the operations of dispersed, naturalized governmentality. Might these proliferating forms of socially turned art contribute to neoliberal governmentality? Might they sometimes offer a spectacle of communication and social engagement rather more than a qualitatively and sustainably rich and even critical engagement? Might they exacerbate inequalities more than they diminish them, for example by effectively limiting how much agency they actually divest to their audiences? And might they operate insidiously as a distraction, offering pleasantly diverting opportunities for social engagement and equality but ones which can only ever be temporary and limited, and which cannot remotely begin to compensate for the larger and would-be secure structures of social welfare that are simultaneously being dismantled and potentially destroyed? In the United Kingdom, during the Conservative-led Cameron administration in which I am writing, examples of this kind of erosion of social welfare structures include the ever less sufficient provision of social housing, the increasing privatization of formerly state-supported healthcare and schooling, and the accelerating withdrawal of state-support for higher education teaching and for the arts. In the context of such a bonfire of social welfare's principles and structures, what could any arts possibly do to quench the flames or, indeed, to prevent themselves inadvertently adding fuel to the fire?

In this pressured context, *Fair Play* explores what this expansion of socially engaged art and performance practice can actually offer audiences and what it can offer social relations. Who gets to do what, where, when and how in this cultural practice, and how does this affect people? What are this practice's relationships to social engagement, communication, social justice, equality and democracy; how might it contribute to or weaken them? If it invites participation, who can participate and on what terms? What is the quality of that participation and how does it vary for different participants in changing contexts? How do these artistic trends articulate contemporary social understandings of the individual and the social? What are the relationships between these trends and the historically coinciding social, economic and political expansion of neoliberal capitalism? What happens to social relations in a context of neoliberal capitalism, with its emphases on deregulation, the primacy of the individual and meritocracy, which is ostensibly the power of anyone who earns it, but is effectively the power of those who have the skills, resources and contacts – the cultural capital, in other words – to do so, effectively becoming plutocracy, the power of the wealthy? How do these potentially socially democratic art practices and neoliberal capitalist ideologies produce, inform, challenge and/or undermine each other?

By exploring the significant trend of socially turned art and performance, *Fair Play* aims to contribute to a better understanding of current social tensions between, on the one hand, principles of social equality, social justice and democracy and, on the other, neoliberal capitalism, merit/plutocracy and selfish individualism. It seeks strategies for preserving fairness, constructive social relations and individual agency while diminishing inequality and selfish individualism, despite the massive power and insidious spread of global neoliberal capitalism. *Fair Play* also argues that in order properly to answer questions about these art and performance practices' social effects, it cannot treat these practices in isolation, as though unattached to and unaffected by broader social and material contexts. The book's first chapter therefore offers a close analysis of participation in this art and performance, considering it especially as and in relation to labour. As I elaborate further below, ensuing chapters then explore the various ways qualities of participation are affected by the broader contexts of, in particular: British cultural policy's emphasis on entrepreneurialism, especially in the New Labour era; contemporary spatial practices, including how they are affected by current shifts in urban and housing policies; and arts funding, especially as the Cameron government withdraws more and more state funding and puts arts organizations under increasing pressure to secure private, philanthropic funding. In these explorations, I seek to depict and examine some of the complex, dynamic, networked connections that produce the social and political potentials of contemporary participatory art and performance.

Socially turned art and performance

In this section, I offer a brief overview of currently proliferating socially turned art and performance and the main critical discourses that respond to them, with the proviso that Chapter 1 of this book opens with an expanded discussion of the kinds of art and performance work which might be understood under this rubric and explores in detail a number of examples, including many cited only briefly here. Broadly speaking, socially turned art and performance practices work, first, actively to engage others who are not the artists (so principally, but not always, audiences), and in so doing, second, to enhance their social engagement. They rarely invite individual audience members to contemplate in silent solitude a static art object hung on a wall. They engage audiences in active participation with an environment and/or process that compels those audiences to interact socially with each other.

This kind of engagement is clearly demonstrated in what Bourriaud has called 'relational' art which has burgeoned since the early 1990s and sets up situations for active social encounter; for example, the café installations of an artist such as Rirkrit Tiravanija, where visitors eat meals together.[2] However, even artworks which do not engage audiences in a familiar social setting such as a mealtime, also often engage them socially. For example, many large-scale installations – including all those produced in Tate Modern's Turbine Hall since it opened in 2000 and up to the time of writing in 2012 – could be considered relational, given that their immersion of audiences in a shared environment requires those audiences to experience the artwork in relation not only to 'itself' but also to each other. For example, all Turbine Hall visitors were immersed in the otherworldly environment of Olafur Eliasson's *The weather project* (2003), as they were all overshadowed by the red 'skin' of Anish Kapoor's vaulting installation *Marsyas* (2002) and as they were all literally undermined by the long fissure in the Hall's concrete floor of Doris Salcedo's *Shibboleth* (2007). Similarly, audiences are immersed in installations in Tate Britain's also large Duveen Galleries; for example, in Martin Creed's *Work No. 850* (2008) where runners sprinted the length of these galleries at set intervals, and Michael Landy's *Semi-Detached* (2004) where he installed to-scale front and back replica elevations of his parents' suburban home. Some art in outdoor spaces can also effectively 'capture' audiences in shared social contexts, as many of the installations on Trafalgar Square's Fourth Plinth have been doing since it opened as a site of new artworks in central London in 1998 (Fourth Plinth), and as Antony Gormley's vast *Angel of the North* (1998) near Gateshead in northeast England might be seen to do. Art can also be considered 'socially turned' when it actively engages not principally, or not only, audiences, but other delegated makers. Santiago Sierra and Phil Collins, for example, often hire others to execute their works, drawing explicit attention to the social relations between the works' various participant/makers.

Socially turned theatre and performance, likewise, actively engage their audiences. Here, audiences do not sit in darkness, in silence, contemplating moving performers on a stage set apart in the light. Audiences are invited effectively to become performers, roaming at will through fully designed environments in immersive theatre such as the work of Punchdrunk and Shunt. Audience interaction is actively solicited in such immersive performance as *You Me Bum Bum Train* and in one-to-one performances and audience-addressing live art by the likes of, for example, Adrian Howells, Brian Lobel, Oreet Ashery, Bobby Baker and Lois Weaver as Tammy Whynot.

As these forms of art and performance are proliferating, so are the critical literatures around them and the critical claims made for them by, for example, Nicholas Bourriaud, Jessica Morgan, Claire Bishop and Shannon Jackson. Bourriaud became an early and influential critic of what he termed 'relational aesthetics' with the 1998 French publication and 2002 English translation of his eponymously titled short book. He claims that in relational aesthetics, 'art tak[es] as its theoretical horizon the realm of human interactions and its social context' (Bourriaud, 2002, p. 14).[3] Its role is 'to actually be ways of living and models of action within the existing real' (p. 13). It is not principally about object and ownership, but about process, 'a period of time to be lived through, like an opening to unlimited discussion' (p. 15). 'The artwork is presented as a *social interstice*' (p. 45, italics original) that 'encourages an inter-human commerce' (p. 16) not dictated by capitalist economic contexts. It emphasizes that art's meaning 'only exists in the encounter and in the dynamic relationship enjoyed by an artistic proposition with other formations, artistic or otherwise', including social formations (p. 21). A relational artwork 'thus creates, within its method of production and then at the moment of its exhibition, a momentary grouping of participating viewers' (p. 58). For Bourriaud, these artworks 'construct models of sociability suitable for producing human relations, the same way an architecture literally "produces" the itineraries of those presiding in it' (p. 70). They also often take the form of 'convivial, user-friendly artistic projects, festive, collective and participatory, exploring the varied potential in the relationship to the other' (p. 61). Distinguishing them from earlier socially engaged models of artistic practice such as those of Joseph Beuys, however, Bourriaud claims that this art is 'no longer seeking to represent utopias'. Rather, he claims that it attempts to 'create various forms of *modus vivendi* permitting fairer social relations' (p. 46) in what he terms 'everyday micro-utopias' (p. 31).

Bourriaud makes several very important contributions to understandings of the form in *Relational Aesthetics*. He enumerates and details the trend in visual, sculptural and installation art, discussing many vivid examples in detail. He sets it within art historical and theoretical contexts. And he argues for what he sees it achieving. While it does not seek to demonstrate future-oriented utopias, he proposes, it is informed by '*democratic* concerns' (p. 57, italics original) and it aims instead to provide, in everyday activities at the moment of encounter, modest but pervasive communication, provisional social consensus and micro-utopias. Recognizing the hegemonic constraints of, for example, the society of the spectacle and capitalist relations, it nevertheless strives to stimulate positive social encounters that might include features of 'neighbourliness' (p. 47), 'harmony and cohabitation' (p. 53). It forms audiences as a public with political agency and ethical responsibility in a modest consensual democracy.

For some critics, including Tate Modern curator Jessica Morgan and critic Claire Bishop, Bourriaud's approach and his claims risk, themselves, being utopian, naïve and unrealistic. In her introduction to a 2003 Tate Modern group exhibition of often-participatory work in the 'expanded field of sculpture' (Morgan, 2003),[4] Morgan warns,

> The question of the significance of participation, though vital to much contemporary work, is one that should be treated with some suspicion. The mere involvement of the actions of audience members is not enough to assume a vital or direct relationship to the work of art .... How the exchange of participation takes place must be carefully framed, so that the interaction itself brings about awareness not only of the pleasure or discomfort of social interchange but a consciousness of the workings of a larger political, economic or psychological framework as evidenced in these relations.
>
> (2003, p. 24)

'What is missing from a theory of relational aesthetics based entirely in the social', she concludes, 'is an acknowledgement of the role of context, not merely as a source of reference in art, but as a determining force in the meaning of objects' (ibid., p. 25) and, I would add, in the meaning of other art and performance events and acts. As well as advocating for consideration of its contexts, Morgan argues that relational artwork can make evident an understanding of community as pluralist. A pluralist community is neither a fully unified singular public, which would be impossible and also undesirable because it would repress and disavow difference; nor is it a fully dispersed multitude, which would be undesirable because it would permit extreme and ultimately violent self-interest. The type of pluralist community relational art might offer, Morgan suggests, is that evoked by philosopher Jean-Luc Nancy's terms 'being-with', 'being-in-common' and 'being-with-each-other', which accommodate difference in mutuality (ibid., pp. 16 and 26; see, for example, Nancy, 2000).

Bishop has been most fulsome and vehement in her criticism of Bourriaud's arguments. In a 2004 article in *October* entitled 'Antagonism and Relational Aesthetics', she argues that the kind of work Bourriaud admires – and that he and other influential curators produce in the 'laboratories' they often curate for this artwork – risks 'becom[ing] marketable as a space of leisure and entertainment', 'dovetail[ing] with an "experience economy", the marketing strategy that seeks to replace goods and services with scripted and staged personal experiences'[5] in order to produce what experience economy gurus Joe Pine and Jim Gilmore hail as not only 'consumer allegiance, but also a more profitable bottom line' (Pine and Gilmore, 2011, back cover). In other words, this artwork stands to be not democratic and socially empowering, as Bourriaud would have it, but, instead, part of what Theodor Adorno scornfully called 'the culture industry', an entertainment market that offers its audiences no real power and actually deadens their awareness of the ways dominant economies enfold and exploit them (Adorno, 1991).

Bishop does claim that relational art can have strong political power, and can produce democratic relations, but for her this happens when it cultivates situations that are not socially benign and consensual, like those Bourriaud tends to focus on and potentially to celebrate. For Bishop, democracy is enacted through art practices that cultivate socially antagonistic and dissonant relations, in recognition that 'a democratic society is one in which relations of conflict are *sustained*, not erased. Without antagonism there is only the imposed consensus of authoritarian order – a total suppression of debate and discussion, which is inimical to democracy.'[6] Furthermore, for Bishop, politically powerful dissonant relational artwork draws attention to its place not in some soft and fuzzy, undifferentiated social space which might aim to cast identities and relations as equally undifferentiated and shared. It sets it visibly in institutional contexts – such as galleries and biennales – where differences in identities and relations – such as hierarchies of class and ethnicity – are rendered acutely apparent (Bishop, 2004, pp. 70ff.). The 'relational antagonism' that she identifies in the work of artists Santiago Sierra and Thomas Hirschhorn, for example, is 'predicated not on social harmony, but on exposing that which is repressed in sustaining the semblance of this harmony', thereby providing 'a more concrete and polemical grounds for rethinking our relationship to the work and to one another' (ibid., p. 79). The artwork emphasizes social differences and dissonances not to endorse or celebrate them, but to recognize and acknowledge rather than disavow them, and effectively to cite their inequalities as motivating grounds for social interrogation and possible change.

Bishop followed up the arguments of 2004's 'Antagonism and Relational Aesthetics' with 'The Social Turn: Collaboration and Its Discontents' in *ArtForum* in 2006, which appears in a revised version in her compendious 2012 tome of history and analysis, *Artificial Hells: Participatory Art and the Politics of Spectatorship* (see also Bishop, 2005; Bishop, 2006a; and Bishop and Tramontana, 2008). In these contexts, as well as arguing for explorations of relational art's dissonance, she advocates for critical approaches which assess not simply its ethical achievements, but its aesthetics. Analysis which focuses on its ethical achievements, she argues, plays into 'soft social engineering' (Bishop, 2012, p. 5), political agendas for the arts such as those of Tony Blair's New Labour government (ibid., pp. 13ff.; see also Bishop, 2006b, p. 180), which risk 'instrumentali[zing] art to fulfil policies of social inclusion – a cost-effective way of justifying public spending on the arts while diverting attention away from the structural causes of decreased social participation, which are political and economic (welfare, transport, education, healthcare, etc.)' (Bishop in Roche, 2006). Building her case on the work of philosopher Jacques Rancière, she argues that aesthetic analysis can be political analysis; that the aesthetic is not intrinsically '(at best) merely visual and (at worst) an elitist realm of unbridled seduction complicit with spectacle' (Bishop, 2012, pp. 26–7); and that '[a]esthetics and politics ... overlap in their concern for the distribution and sharing out of ideas, abilities and experiences' amongst people (ibid., p. 27).

Shannon Jackson has become the most influential analyst of the participatory trend within the field of performance studies. Her 2011 monograph, *Social Works: Performing Art, Supporting Publics*, examines a range of socially engaged art and performance practices to explore not only their apparent 'aesthetic conviviality' but also the social systems on which they – and so much else – depend (Jackson, 2011, p. 6). Supportive social systems, she argues, 'usually occupy the background of experience' (ibid., p. 6) and, when noticed, are often considered inconvenient, or downright suspect; consider the example of that familiar villain, the corrupt bureaucracy. Jackson seeks 'art forms that help us to imagine sustainable social institutions', and a political art discourse that advocates for not only social disruption (like Bishop's celebrated dissensus) but also 'social coordination', to get a better understanding of 'how art practices contribute to inter-dependent social imagining' (ibid., p. 14).

What does *Fair Play* have in common with this range of responses to, and arguments about, socially engaged art and performance practices? Like the authors referred to above, I too want to explore and evaluate the social and political potential of these practices. I agree with Morgan that participation is not intrinsically politically progressive. Thus, though I seek these practices' democratic potential and look for ways they extend equal opportunities for social engagement, I also pay attention to ways they constrain or suppress those opportunities. I explore what models of social relation and community these practices can produce, while I remain wary of models that either fetishize a myth of a unified singularity and thereby obliterate difference, or propose an unresolved multitude. I seek models of community that recognize people's social interdependence without assimilating their distinctiveness. I am less concerned about debates over consensus and dissensus than Bishop is because I am interested in exploring the political potentials of practices that stimulate either and/or both. Like Jackson, I am wary of prioritizing dissenting art practices as Bishop does, because we need some agreement, but also because pleasurable fun can constructively engage audiences while dissent's bad feeling can risk alienating them. Like Bishop, I am keen to pay careful attention to the conditions – often to do with class and wealth – that might prevent some people from participating and that might thereby limit the Rancièrian 'distribution of the sensible', in other words, who gets to sense/experience what, where and how. Finally, and importantly, I respond to Bishop's and Morgan's appeal to *contextualize* these practices.

This is the greatest contribution this book aims to make: to contextualize these socially engaged art and performance practices in broader social and material contexts in order to consider not only what kinds of opportunities for what qualitative experiences of participation the art practices 'themselves' offer audiences, but also, importantly, how those opportunities are affected by the practices' social and material contexts. The book's first chapter attempts to assess the qualitative effects for audiences of participation in art and performance practices as far as is possible 'in isolation'. Subsequent chapters, however, go on to assess how participation is affected by broader social and material conditions that delimit – or enhance – what kinds of participation are possible. These conditions include cultural policy in Chapter 2, urban spatial practices and housing policy in Chapter 3 and arts funding policies in Chapter 4. These subsequent chapters often look at a greater range of art and performance beyond the participatory forms outlined above and in Chapter 1, because they ask how participation in culture is more broadly and fundamentally affected not just by artistic practices but also by policy-making, spatial organization and arts funding.

The contexts I aim to delineate and evaluate focus on the United Kingdom – particularly England, and particularly London for reasons I elaborate below – roughly from the beginning of New Labour's term in 1997 to the present, during the term of the Conservative-led coalition government that took power in 2010. This UK context distinguishes *Fair Play* from Jackson's *Social Works*, given that she focuses more on art and performance practices in the United States but also, more importantly, is writing from the United States (more precisely, California). I say more importantly because a key distinction between Jackson's approach and mine is that she depicts a landscape which looks to me to be broadly intolerant of welfare state support and, even, to perceive the welfare state as effectively redundant. By contrast, my feeling writing in the United Kingdom is that though many here may distrust and malign the welfare state, and though it is certainly engaged in a tough fight to preserve itself against the onslaughts of neoliberal capitalism which would dismantle it and privatize its services, the welfare state does survive and is fiercely defended. This defence is patently obvious in such large-scale, highly visible events and activities as public protests against cuts to the public sector (for example, on 20 October, 2012, in Belfast, Glasgow and London where, reportedly, 100,000 protesters marched) (Press Association, 2012a); the work of campaigning group UK Uncut, 'a grassroots movement taking action to highlight alternatives to the government's spending cuts' (UK Uncut, 2012); and the stunning homage to the National Health Service performed in the 2012 London Olympics opening ceremony, *Isles of Wonder*, directed by Danny Boyle when 'GOSH' (for Great Ormond Street children's hospital) and 'NHS' were spelt out consecutively in gigantic, stadium-filling letters formed of dozens of glowing hospital beds (Boyle, 2012). But this backing for the welfare state – and for its principles of the availability of social support at the point of need – is also quietly evident in less spectacular but more pervasive ways, such as the persistence of its institutions in the United Kingdom despite collusive government and business efforts to dismantle them, as well as the naturalization of neoliberal governmentality that I discussed above.

I highlight this contextual difference between where Jackson was writing from and where I write from because it indicates different contextual attitudes towards social relations for me and her to consider and for the art practices we write about to engage with and model. In other words, part of what I seek to investigate in *Fair Play* is how the persistence of an admittedly embattled UK welfare state – with its principles of social support, the redistribution of wealth to reduce poverty and a fundamental commitment to social equality – makes the performance of genuinely equitable socially engaged models of participatory performance any more or less viable in the United Kingdom in the second decade of the twenty-first century.

Neoliberal capitalism

Though I claim and take pride and comfort in the persistence of the UK welfare state, I am by no means complacent about either its current vitality or its future longevity. It is under significant threat, posed by the continued ascendency of neoliberal capitalism and the expanding naturalization of neoliberal governmentality. Neoliberalism is the revived form of liberalism which thrived first in Britain in the seventeenth century and which recognizes and prioritizes the individual's right to seek self-fulfilment and to do so in conditions unrestricted by state-instituted regulations, such as the requirements to pay appropriate taxes, to heed trade restrictions or to observe employment laws pertaining to hiring, firing and paying workers. In neoliberal capitalism, these principles of diminished state intervention and enhanced individual liberty to seek self-reward work in the service of maximizing private profit. Simultaneously, the welfare state is diminished as taxation shrinks and government 'intervention' – which in some contexts might instead be seen as support, for example of workers' rights – is rolled back.

The British 'cradle to grave' welfare state was informed by recommendations for eradicating what William Beveridge identified in his famous 1942 report to government as the five 'Giant Evils' of 'want, disease, ignorance, squalor and idleness' (Beveridge, 1942). Founded in measures introduced by Clement Atlee's Labour government elected in 1945, it was informed by Keynesian economics' advocacy for government intervention during times of recession and included the creation of the National Health Service in 1948; various enhancements to state pensions and other insurance benefits; a programme of local authority house-building; and the nationalization of various industries and utilities, including the Bank of England and coal mining. It suffered serious erosion under consecutive Conservative governments led by Margaret Thatcher and John Major from 1979 to 1997. In this 'golden age' of neoliberal capitalism, business thrived and social support nosedived: Thatcher, the 'Milk Snatcher', withdrew the provision of milk to school children; she introduced the infamous Poll Tax, a local government tax that charged every adult the same amount, regardless of property value or location (and therefore taxed the poorest disproportionately); and she supported industry at the expense of workers by, for example, closing dozens of coal mines in cuts that devastated the livelihoods of thousands of miners and their families. She famously claimed, 'There is no such thing as society' (Thatcher in Keay, 1987). Between 1979 and 1995, poverty almost doubled. At the start of that period, 5.5 per cent of the working-age UK population lived in poverty; by its end, the figure was 10.9 per cent. In the same period, the percentage of single mothers living in poverty rose from 11 to 28 per cent (Huber and Stephens, 2001, p. 280). In Chapter 3, I explore the serious long-term consequences of Thatcherite legislation introduced in 1980 which allowed occupants of council housing the Right to Buy those properties, severely and enduringly depleting social housing stock and principles of social housing provision.

Tony Blair's New Labour government elected in 1997 did little to reverse the entrenchment of neoliberal capitalist ideology and government in the United Kingdom. Political commentators Andrew Glyn and Stewart Wood observe that though, on one hand, Blair was importantly committed to reducing the poverty that had grown so quickly under Conservative governments, on the other hand, like Tory governments before it, his government remained keen to support business competitiveness by keeping 'intervention and regulatory burdens to a minimum' and constraining taxation and spending (Glyn and Wood, 2001, pp. 220–1). New Labour's principle strategies for eradicating poverty relied on '"trickle-down" effects resulting from improved incentives for entrepreneurs at the top end' (ibid., p. 221); hence the fact that New Labour chief strategist Peter Mandelson could claim with apparent reasonableness when speaking with Californian computer executives in 1998 that he was 'intensely relaxed about people getting filthy rich' (quoted in Toynbee and Walker, 2009, p. 17; see also Mandelson, 2008). There were at least two large social problems with New Labour's approach. First, it neither necessarily reduced let alone eradicated poverty if the passive 'trickle-down' failed to happen; where Blair pledged to eradicate child poverty in the United Kingdom by 2020 and to halve it by 2010, the target was missed, with over two million children still living in poverty in 2012 (BBC News, 2012a).[7] Second, though New Labour's approach might have reflected their commitment to eradicating poverty, its invitation to the rich to get richer also demonstrated their comfort with and cultivation of increased *inequality*. As journalists Polly Toynbee and David Walker warn, inequality damages social welfare and democracy. 'Growing inequality in income and wealth undermines democracy. Grandiose promises of equal human rights and civic equality dissipate when it is money that secures power' (Toynbee and Walker, 2009, p. 15), as was the case, they argue, in Blairite Britain. In *The Spirit Level: Why Equality is Better for Everyone*, Richard Wilkinson and Kate Pickett influentially argue that two of the main 'costs of inequality' are 'community life and social relations' and 'social mobility' (Wilkinson and Pickett, 2010).

In Chapter 1, I look in more detail at the neoliberalism of cultural policy under successive New Labour governments led by Blair and then Gordon Brown and the ways that those governments worked to embed and naturalize neoliberal ideologies rather than to eliminate, challenge or at least problematize them.

The increasingly neoliberal state cultivated by New Labour has of course been extended by the Conservative-led coalition government under David Cameron that came to power in 2010 in the face of enormous state debt, ostensibly caused by the financial crises of 2007 on, but more broadly brought about by capitalism's self-interest, risk-taking and auto-regenerative propensity to cultivate destruction, which I explore in Chapter 2. Like other conservative governments elsewhere at this time, Cameron's government has implemented what economic geographer David Harvey has identified as 'draconian austerity measures', actively dismantling various aspects of the UK welfare state, including aspects of healthcare provision and support for early childhood development, thereby 'threatening public well-being' (Harvey, 2011, p. 262). 'Throughout much of the advanced capitalist world', Harvey writes, 'following an initial flirtation with a revival of Keynesianism, the sovereign debt crisis has become an excuse for the capitalist class to dismantle what is left of the welfare state through a politics of austerity' (ibid., p. 265). Harvey argues that '[t]he present economic difficulties in both the US and Britain, as well as throughout Europe, are essentially being deepened for a political reason rather than out of economic necessity. That political reason is the desire to have done with capital's responsibility to cover costs of social reproduction' (ibid., p. 269), or of what I am calling here, social welfare or social support.

The Conservative-led government's claim that 'We are all in this together'[8] aims to persuade Britons that all cultures, classes and industries across the nation are equally sharing and bearing the burden of the austerity cuts it is imposing. But this rhetorical claim is patently untrue.

Cameron's government has widely withdrawn state funding to social services that support those most in need, including older people and young people including students, and it has enhanced support to only particular industries. In Higher Education, it has withdrawn state funding for teaching in arts and humanities, it has reduced funding in all other teaching areas and it has overseen an exponential rise in tuition fees that is bound to increase the exclusiveness of access to higher education in England at least.[9] As I explore in Chapter 3, despite acute shortages in social housing, and despite all of the negative effects on health and wellbeing that housing insecurity brings with it, the Cameron government is eroding housing support allowances and the provision of social housing itself at the same time as it is introducing planning policy that serves both business (property developers) and the comparatively wealthy (by reducing requirements on developers to include affordable housing provision in developments, allowing them to concentrate on the more lucrative provision of private stock). As I explore in Chapter 4, in the arts, Cameron's government is withdrawing over 30 per cent of state funding to the arts in 'austerity measures' that are definitely threatening both the creativity and the survival of many arts organizations and pressuring them to rely increasingly on free labour – the privilege of those who can support themselves independently. By simultaneously promoting a culture of philanthropy, Cameron's government is also threatening the independence of arts organizations, requiring them to bend to the priorities of business in order to survive.

Do these widespread and deep cuts to the welfare state indicate a wholesale rejection by Cameron's government of its responsibility 'to cover costs of social reproduction', as Harvey puts it? Cameron would certainly not like people to think so. Because alongside these and many other extensive cuts to public services, he has actively promoted his vision of the 'Big Society', with its three-pronged commitment to community empowerment, the opening up of public services and social action (Cabinet Office, 2012), creating 'the impression that the Conservative Party has truly changed, to the extent that it now discusses the mythic banned entity of Mrs Thatcher, for whom "society" was a term altogether too close to the great enemy, "social-ism"' (Szreter and Iskhanian, 2012, p. 10). But the ostensible commitment to social welfare invoked in the Big Society's name and rhetoric is, principally, rhetoric rather than action let alone pragmatic, material support. The Big Society delegates responsibility for welfare to individuals in a move that 'diverts attention away from government' and its cuts and simultaneously bolsters neoliberal ideology by rejecting 'Big Government and the tax-hungry state ... in favour of the heroic, autonomous individual and their liberty to act economically and socially as they see fit' (ibid., p. 10).

In these conflicting contexts – where the welfare state and its principles of democratic social support endures but faces ever more sustained and aggressive erosion by neoliberal capitalism – I am particularly concerned to investigate how participatory art and performance practices might productively resist but also, damagingly, contribute to neoliberal governmentality.

Multidisciplinary methods

My critical methodologies in this book are multidisciplinary. This is necessary given that my aim is to examine participatory art and performance practices in relation to, first, issues of welfare, equality of opportunity and democracy; second, trends in work, economics, industry and urban spatial practices; and third, governments' and government agencies' policies related to culture, urban development, arts funding, housing and housing support. This range of concerns requires both a multidisciplinary method – which draws on cultural materialism, actor-network theory and hybrid strategies in, for example, economic and social geography – and expertise from a range of disciplinary areas, including art and performance theories but also sociology, geography, urban studies, curatorial studies, political theory, cultural economy, cultural studies, literary theory and studies in housing, philanthropy and gentrification.

Cultural materialism fundamentally informed my training in theatre and performance analysis.[10] Through it, I understand culture as always enmeshed in social, material and historical conditions; contributing to the production of ideologies; and therefore important to consider in the construction of social relations, especially hierarchies of class. A cultural materialist approach emphasizes that cultural practices such as art and performance do not exist in some kind of material and historical vacuum, hovering in an idealized realm outside of time, political signification, social relations and material processes and conditions. Its examination of cultural practices as processes in material contexts consistently aims to explore culture as a site of ideological contest, and to consider the ways that culture participates in the dissemination of ideologies and may be complicit with or offer challenges to hegemonic ideologies. My critical approach to understanding contemporary participatory art and performance practices is cultural materialist in that it relates those practices to broader material networks (of, for example, funding, labour, social and cultural policy, economics and urban development) as well as to wider social discourses (for example, of journalism, policy documentation and think tank analysis) and broader social issues (of inclusion and exclusion, class privilege and democracy).

Cultural materialism is guided by a set of practical and ethical-political priorities: to examine cultural practices and processes in material contexts in order to assess their political and ideological effects, especially on class-based social relations. But cultural materialism is not, perhaps, a system. A system which has loosely informed (though by no means dictated) my methods in this book is actor-network theory (or ANT). ANT was initially developed in science and technology studies (see Callon, Law and Rip, 1986; Latour, 1995), but it has become influential in numerous disciplines including sociology, geography and economics. It is a systemic approach to identifying relations between things and ideas and to understanding infrastructures that contribute to the development of, for example, industries, new technologies, ecologies and, for my purposes, cultural objects, events, processes and practices. ANT sees all things as operating in networks, infrastructures or assemblages made up of many, heterogeneous actors. In ANT, the term 'actor' is not intended to signify a professional performer. ANT actors include people, but other things besides, such as objects, animals and organizations, and elements that both are obviously social and may appear technological. No person and no thing acts alone; all actors are important in the network and all contribute to developments and may also contribute to network breakdowns. For example, a theatre performance is part of an actor-network that includes its performers and audience, but also the theatre's technical crew, directors and designers; the materials that make up its set, costumes, building and auditorium; its technologies of lighting, sound, power and plumbing; the actors' training; conventions of communication; the theatre's funding; its advertising; local transport networks; financial systems that manage payments; relevant policy makers (such as, in England, Arts Council England and the Department of Culture, Media and Sport); and so on and on and on. The performance 'works' given the integration of all of these functioning actors; it risks breaking down if any actor does not function 'properly', for example, if local transport is suspended, mains power is interrupted, the lighting system's computer programme is accidentally deleted, would-be audiences do not buy tickets or the theatre's funding is cut. What I aim to explore in this book are the actor-networks that affect access to and qualities of social engagement in contemporary culture, including in participatory art and performance but also apparently 'beyond' it, in cultural policy, social policy and economic conditions.

There are several aspects of ANT that I find helpful for multidisciplinary analysis and that resonate with the values and aims of cultural materialism. These include: its constructivist understanding of all things and relations as made rather than essential or given; the importance it attributes to a complex network of multiple actors/determinants in making meaning; the sense that all actors (including people, things and institutions) are relational and importantly connected to each other; and its emphasis on all actors as potentially equally important, so that what might initially appear to be of only 'background' significance (such as arts funding to what is apparently the 'main event' of the art object/performance) can be seen, where appropriate, as a main actor (Latour, 1998a, 1998b). I do not apply a rigorous or consistent ANT approach in this book. For example, I do not approach all actors as potentially equally important; I focus instead on particular actors' effects. And although I am keen to explore the agency of multiple actors (including artists but also audiences, policies and spatial practices), I generally focus on *human* agency. This is because I am also keen to attribute outcomes – such as the post-2007 economic crisis and austerity cuts – not as inevitable 'given the circumstances' (a phrase which implies those circumstances were unavoidable), but as *produced* through the will of particular, powerful human actors as well as the ideologies their actions help to perpetuate.

My methods are also empirical. Each chapter describes and draws on a number of art and performance case studies, aiming to build a picture of the landscape of current artistic work in participatory art and performance practices and to indicate the range of possibilities for engagement – or non-engagement – that they present.

Overall, I am methodologically concerned to trace the multiple, networked ways that art and performance practices' significations and political effects are currently produced. I am politically motivated to track who gets to do what, how and with what effects in these art and performance practices and to explore their roles as bearers of or defenders against neoliberal governmentality. I also aim to explore how neoliberal governmentality might operate through not just economic policy, but also other aspects of policy including housing policy and cultural policy, as well as through other means, such as government and industry methods of cultivating new industries (such as the creative industries).

Art and performance now

The art and performance I examine in this book is contemporary, socially turned and has, in the vast majority of cases, been produced or exhibited in London. I will address each of these qualifying parameters in turn. Most of the art and performance I look at has been produced between the mid-1990s and 2012. The starting point of my time period is set by the increase in socially engaged art practice I see at that time, for example in the work of Rachel Whiteread, Michael Landy and Grayson Perry, and in the curatorial work of agencies such as Artangel, which dates its most important work from 1992 (see Artangel, 2012), and Tate Modern, which opened in 2000. The book tracks a period of sustained growth in socially engaged art and performance through to the time of writing, up to the end of 2012.

This period also, of course, coincides politically and significantly with the last years of the Thatcher-legacy Conservative government under John Major, 13 years of New Labour, and the first years of Conservative-led coalition government under David Cameron. This is significant for a number of reasons. First, it is relevant to my particular concern with the relationships of these art and performance trends to ideologies of democratic social welfare and neoliberal capitalism because these ideologies have been engaged in an often fierce contest during this period. Furthermore, this contest has been fought over issues which particularly concern me here: changing patterns of labour, including increasing labour precarity; the role of the artist as entrepreneur and/or as craftsperson; the public and private distribution of space, especially housing; and the public and private funding of the arts. Second, these political contexts are significant because they directly and indirectly influence these artists' work, much of which speaks explicitly to those contexts. The book aims to diagnose the present – what trends are happening in art and performance from the 1980s to the 2010s, how they are nurtured and/or constrained by contemporary circumstances (political, economic, social and cultural) and what they say about those circumstances, especially contemporary social relations.

The art and performance I examine in this book is socially turned or socially engaged. It engages audiences in ways outlined by Bourriaud, in relation *to each other,* not just to what is apparently the artwork. I write 'apparently' because much of this practice proposes no autonomous artwork; the artwork includes the audience and its relations. I recognize that my terminology around socially engaged art and performance in this paragraph thus far and in the rest of the book is somewhat loose; this is deliberate. I neither utilize nor propose a set terminology for socially engaged art and performance practices because I want to recognize and explore their variety, dynamism and hybridity. I also want to examine both theatre/performance and visual/sculptural art, recognizing that both use a shared repertoire of practices of engagement and that, in some instances, it is difficult or unproductive to distinguish between them.

I do not generally focus on applied art or performance projects. To generalize somewhat crudely for the sake of brevity, the primary aim of applied projects is to collaborate artistically and socially with a particular (often socially marginalized) group of people. Applied projects tend to emphasize socially meaningful (and usually 'positive') processes, sometimes more than artistic outcomes. By contrast, the work I focus on commonly emphasizes artistic output, and its social 'agenda' is often ambiguous or at least more open than applied agendas tend to be. I also do not focus on artistically informed activism or protest, though these too could be seen to fall within the remit of socially engaged contemporary art and performance. Their practice has grown exponentially in the period I am concerned with, starting, perhaps, with protests against the World Trade Organization meeting in Seattle in 1998 and subsequent G8 summits in, for example, Genoa in 2001, and continuing through protests against the war in Iraq, especially in February 2003; against austerity cuts (2012); against London Olympics policies (relating to, for example, exclusion zones, branding, the colonizing of government funding, security, spectacle and more from about 2010 on); and against economic inequality and corporate greed in the Occupy movement of 2011 on. I do not focus on activism and protest partly because there is too much of this kind of practice satisfactorily to address it alongside my main focus on practices which are principally more artistically inclined. That will have to be the project for another book.

The work I do focus on could perhaps best be identified as 'aesthetically turned' socially turned art and performance. That said, part of what this book aims to demonstrate and explore is that boundaries between contemporary 'applied' and 'fine' art practices, and between art and activism, are very porous, or have broad overlaps, and that much art and performance which is apparently 'aesthetically turned', or that appears to prioritize its art practices and outcomes, is vigorously engaged in complex social work.

The art and performance I examine in this book has principally – though not exclusively – been produced and/or exhibited in London, in the United Kingdom, and is usually the work of British artists. I am keenly aware that the book and I stand to be accused of metropolitan bias, of maintaining a myopic and narcissistic focus on metropolitan activities which reproduces rather than questions metropolitan cultural hegemony both within the United Kingdom and globally. Though I want to be sensitive to the possibility that I might reproduce metropolitan cultural hegemony, even if unwittingly, and though I have aimed to include in this book examples of cultural practice from beyond London where appropriate (without being simply tokenistic), I also want to defend the book's London focus on two main counts.

First, the book documents and analyses a cultural trend which is particularly strong in, though by no means exclusive to, London. The kind of work that I am examining is being made and exhibited by many artists and companies in London, partly because London is home to so many artists; partly because London has so many relevant resources – of funding, sponsorship, resident and visiting audiences, specialist collaborators, infrastructures such as venues and agencies, and more; and partly for other reasons, such as the fact that acute political stresses in London (on, for example, housing and wealth inequality) provoke critical artistic response. Though I report on this concentration of activity in London, therefore, I also recognize that this concentration itself is partly an effect of the sometimes biased distribution of resources such as arts funding and appropriate (though not necessarily purpose-built) arts venues, and it is also bound to be somewhat self-perpetuating, as the well-resourced metropolis draws more artists in, who draw more resources in, and so on. *Achieving Great Art for Everyone* (ACE, 2010a) is the title of Arts Council England's (ACE's) 2011–21 strategic vision document, but even ACE recognizes there are many areas of the United Kingdom that have comparatively poor access to cultural resources.[11] Meanwhile, London-based organizations (many of which admittedly are also expected to fulfil a national remit) received 49 per cent of ACE'S secure (as distinct from project-based) National Portfolio funding in 2012 (ACE, n.d. p. 1). Furthermore, the majority of the UK's major exhibiting venues, producing companies and promoting agencies are in London. Major ones that I cite in this book include, for example, Tate Modern, Tate Britain, the Hayward Gallery, the British Museum, the National Theatre, the Barbican, the Live Art Development Agency (LADA), ACE itself and that monumental arts apparatus of 2012, the London Cultural Olympiad. With resources such as these, the metropolis becomes something of a vortex, drawing in artists from across the United Kingdom and the world. I am examining this art and performance trend principally in London, therefore, because it has a very rich seam here and because it is important to evaluate what this comparatively resource-rich area of activity achieves.

Second, as noted above in relation to my temporal focus, concentrating on practices in London helps me to identify and engage with the vivid tensions between welfare state socialism and neoliberal capitalism that are also – and in some respects, especially – acute in London and that make up the terrain in which I want to consider this cultural practice. London is a centre of global finance, the biggest financial sector in Europe, with a vast, rich finance industry predictably dominated by neoliberal capitalism (Jenkins and Masters, 2012). It has a huge wealthy population but also some of the UK's greatest concentrations of poverty and, therefore, of reliance on state support. By some accounts, it has the greatest wealth inequality in the Western world (see Dorling, 2011). In relation to some of the specific contexts I consider later in the book, particularly in Chapter 3, though there are housing shortages in many places in the United Kingdom, such shortages are exceptionally acute in the overheated housing bubble and densely populated city that is London. These shortages put particular strains on the ways people use space in London, whether they are artists, residents and/or business people, and on the ways that space is understood as ostensibly public or private, inclusive or exclusive, residential, industrial, cultural or something else besides. Similarly, though many UK cities are seeking to repurpose themselves as 'creative cities', this ambition is being both realized and extended in London in ways that increasingly affect its population (by potentially privileging already-privileged educated workers) and that are cautionary for other cities seeking to develop as creative cities. More positively, London's concentration of cultural infrastructures means its artists can have comparatively good access to networks of support – perhaps a kind of artistic welfare system – that are, frankly, exceptional. In Chapter 2, I consider the ways that sets of connections facilitated with the support of agencies such as LADA help artists to sustain shared social networks of communication, ethics and practices despite cultural policy directives that exhort them to work as entrepreneurial free agents. And in Chapter 4, in the aftermath of ACE's significantly reduced post-2010 budget, I consider the success of ACE's enhanced instruction to large arts organizations which continue to receive substantial ACE funding, such as the National Theatre, that they must actively support other organizations as a condition for receiving ACE funding.

I focus on London, therefore, because it is a site of significant contrasts. For residents, London holds huge disparities of wealth and poverty, health and illness, support and neglect and opportunities for education, work and more. For artists, it offers the advantages of dozens of well-funded arts organizations and agencies, but also the challenges of enormous competition and, for many, of not being able to earn a living from their art. Though London may have metropolitan privilege, in other words, this privilege is absolutely not homogeneous, and part of the remit of this project is to trace these unevenly distributed advantages and disadvantages across the experiences of London's residents, visitors, audiences and artists, and art and performance in London (see Harvie, 2009a).

The book unfolds

Chapter 1, 'Labour: Participation, Delegation and Deregulation', opens with an expanded account of the kinds of art and performance practices I focus on in this book and then begins my evaluation of the potential social value of contemporary art and performance's participatory trend. It considers the positive potentials of this trend's invitation to everyone to be an artist, as well as the damage it risks by casting everyone as the kind of precarious, insecure labourers whom critics, including Richard Sennett and Ulrich Beck, have identified as symptomatic of work in an age of what I am calling neoliberal capitalism and Sennett (2006) calls 'the new capitalism'.

Chapter 2, 'The "Artrepreneur": Artists and Entrepreneurialism', asks what it means now to be an artist, particularly given shifts in UK cultural policy from the New Labour era on that increasingly put artists under pressure to be entrepreneurs, and indeed, to model entrepreneurialism. It delineates some of the particular problems of this pressure: its emphasis on and celebration of self-interested individualism; its implicit acceptance that an inevitable by-product of innovation is creative destruction (a concept I unpack in more detail in Chapter 2); and its emphasis on productivity over other potential values. It also explores some of the ways that artists have constructively responded to and challenged these problems, by forming horizontal networks of support that defy individualism, by pursuing the putative logic of creative destruction to its demonstrably disastrous conclusions, and by exploring the counter-arguments of craftsmanship to neoliberalism's emphases on growth, productivity and profit.

Chapter 3 focuses on some of the pressures on, and creative opportunities in, urban space that are emerging in this era of 'the new capitalism'. It traces the cultural policy initiatives of so-called 'creative cities' that aim to expand creative and cultural industries and the potential impacts these initiatives can have on urban demographics, attracting comparatively privileged, well-educated workers and reinforcing hierarchical stratifications in the urban labour force. It explores the huge emergent trend for pop-up, temporary art and performance venues and practices, examining the creative potentials pop-ups offer, but also their potential complicity with gentrification, which can admittedly contribute to urban development but also risks displacing comparatively poor urban populations. It contextualizes this risk by examining the many ways that Cameron government policies – to do with social housing provision, housing support and development planning – are critically eroding the availability in London (and elsewhere) of affordable housing, contributing to what Conservative London Mayor Boris Johnson trenchantly identified as a 'Kosovo-style ethnic cleansing' because their measures will effectively expel the poor from London (Johnson, 2010). The chapter then examines a selection of socially engaged art and performance practices that respond to their complicity with processes of gentrification, explore the complex and contested meanings of home and model critical practices of social gathering, engagement and collaboration in the face of neoliberalism's menacing propensity to separate and stratify.

Where Chapter 3 reflects on tensions between a sense of democratic public entitlement to urban space and that space's ever-increasing privatization and class-based segregation, the final chapter reflects on tensions between public and private financing of the arts. In the year of its election, 2010, Cameron's government announced swingeing cuts of 30 per cent to arts funding and, simultaneously, a programme of advocacy for a new philanthropic (private) culture of arts funding. This chapter explores the effects of this shift on the arts and the strategies arts organizations have pursued to build mixed economies of funding for their work, including crowdfunding and cross-subsidy. This is not, in general, an optimistic chapter; I see the Cameron government's arts funding cuts as symptomatic of its violently destructive approach to apparatuses of shared social resource, welfare, art and sociability. But I also seek to identify and enumerate the many resourceful, resilient, inventive strategies that artists and arts organizations have created, activated and exploited in order to survive and thrive in this ferociously hostile climate.

Fair play

This book aims to offer a number of things. It aims to contribute to understandings of contemporary socially engaged art and performance and to debates about that art and performance's social and aesthetic potentials. It aims to delineate some of the insistent, fierce pressures that neoliberal capitalism exerts, not just in what might be seen as its 'proper' domains of business and politics, but also across cultural practices. And it aims to chart some of the myriad strategies that artistic networks and practices of social, interdependent participation, collaboration and welfare demonstrate for resisting and challenging those pressures. I do not conclude that these strategies trounce, eradicate or even always seriously destabilize contemporary neoliberal capitalism. But I do seek and find in them many, subtle, partial and effective responses to neoliberal capitalism's support for self-interested individualism. I find in them models of fairness and constructive social engagement that give me hope for fair play.

1
Labour: Participation, Delegation and Deregulation

Introduction

In 2010 artists Kate Bond and Morgan Lloyd opened the original London version of the deeply immersive theatrical event *You Me Bum Bum Train* (*YMBBT*) in a disused building in Bethnal Green.[1] Individual audience members started out at timed intervals on journeys that took them through dozens of carefully produced immersive scenarios where they were the only audience, they were invited to perform and they became 'the star of the show' (Hemming, 2011). Bond and Lloyd request that volunteers, audiences and reviewers keep the scenarios secret so that future audiences can be surprised, but some of the scenes have gradually been disclosed: a kebab shop; a chat show, where the audience is the host; and an American football team's changing room, where the audience is the coach (ibid.). *Financial Times* reviewer Sarah Hemming revealed,

> By the time I reeled out, elated, I had delivered a sermon, burgled a house, given a pep talk to a team of American footballers and been thrown down a chute with the rubbish sacks .... In a typical journey on the You Me Bum Bum Train, every scene is fitted out in precise and loving detail, down to the institutional lighting in a job centre, the oily car parts in a garage or the smell of a football changing room.
>
> (2011)

Audiences and reviewers raved. *Daily Mail* reviewer Patrick Marmion enthused, 'People emerge high with excitement', and, 'this must be one of the most amazing, must-see events of the summer' (Marmion, 2010). Hemming (2011) described the show as 'inspiring, liberating and exhilarating'. Bond and Lloyd won an Oxford Samuel Beckett Theatre Trust Award.

YMBBT returned in modified form in 2011 in an old postal sorting office in Holborn, central London, and in another incarnation in Stratford, East London, as part of the London Cultural Olympiad in summer 2012. By now, it was a huge cause célèbre, partly because its tickets were piping-hot commodities and sold out speedily, but also because its practices of employment – or more precisely unpaid employment – were garnering increasingly high-profile scrutiny, including with actors' union Equity. *You Me Bum Bum Train*'s inventors Bond and Lloyd claimed that, to achieve its deeply immersive experience, the show required thousands of volunteers as cast and crew. In one incarnation, says Lloyd, '4000 people took part because they wanted to contribute for unknown strangers – it's kind of like a big surprise party' (*Time Out*, 2012). Bond and Lloyd have argued that tickets would be prohibitively expensive if all volunteers received Equity wages. 'Our last show involved 450 people', Bond explained in 2012. 'If we paid everyone at Equity rates, it would cost between £2.5 and £3m to stage. It's just not possible' (quoted in Barnett, 2012a). All *YMBBT*'s cast and crew are volunteers and unpaid, and even Bond and Lloyd do not take a wage from the show, reportedly surviving on working tax credits and sleeping in the venues (Chandrasekhar, 2012). Furthermore, Lloyd claims that it is not only impossible to pay volunteers, but undesirable. 'Even if we could pay people', he has said, 'it would completely change the dynamic. The whole point is to create an exciting, inclusive experience – for the audience and the performers .... It's really special' (quoted in Barnett, 2012a).

'A row is brewing', the *Guardian* reported before the show opened in 2012. 'The performers' union Equity is considering taking legal action against the company's two artistic directors, Kate Bond and Morgan Lloyd, on the grounds that none of the small army of actors and crew involved in the show – which costs £20 a ticket – gets paid' (Barnett, 2012a). In 2011, the blog Actorsminimumwage (AMW) had launched a campaign encouraging *YMBBT* volunteers to claim National Minimum Wage and to collaborate with Equity in pressuring *YMBBT* producers to pay that wage (AMW, 2011). AMW pointed out that the *YMBBT* company received £40,000 in Arts Council funding. The show's various co-producers have included other ACE-funded organizations such as the Barbican, Theatre Royal Stratford East and the Cultural Olympiad. Bond and Lloyd argue that *YMBBT* both requires and thrives on free labour; others counter that *YMBBT* ravenously devours free labour, mocks the principle that labour should be paid and risks making acting the privileged domain of the independently wealthy. Interviewed by the *Guardian*, actor, director and Equity member Samuel West, for example, said, 'no matter how good the artistic results, I can't support a working model where actors aren't paid at all. Otherwise the only people who can afford to be in those shows are those who have other jobs or savings or private incomes – and that alters the demographic of actors you can use, and eventually the demographic of the profession' (in Barnett, 2012a).

You Me Bum Bum Train offers a notorious example of some of the acute pressures on human labour – and humans ourselves – in contemporary art and performance cultures. In insecure contemporary economies, people are persuaded to undersell themselves by taking underpaid and unpaid work in the hope that it will lead to future paid work – as well as for the thrill of the work itself. But while *YMBBT* makes this potential for exploitation starkly visible through the headline-grabbing example of its thousands of unpaid volunteers, it could be argued that such worker exploitation is pervasive – if usually less acute and less frequently noted – across much contemporary art and performance, where audiences are increasingly regularly called on to participate in, contribute to and at least co-create the performance also for free and sometimes, more precisely, at the *cost* of a fee. Even in immersive theatre events where all *professional* performers are paid, audiences often contribute their labour for free by, for example, peopling crowd scenes. In one-to-one performances, the audience member is often invited to act – to be in bed with Oreet Ashery in *Say Cheese* (from 2001) or to have one's feet bathed by Adrian Howells in *Foot-Washing for the Sole* (2009) (see Zerihan, 2009). Likewise, in many audio walks – such as, in London alone, Janet Cardiff's *The Missing Voice (Case Study B)* (1999), Graeme Miller's *Linked* (2003) and Platform's *And While London Burns* (2006) – the listener becomes the performer of the walk, the 'real' actors long gone. Similarly, in relational and installation art, the audience co-creates the event – by having a social encounter in a work by Tino Sehgal (for example in *These Associations* in the Tate Modern Turbine Hall, 2012), sliding down a slide in Carsten Höller's *Test Site* (Turbine Hall, 2006) or inhabiting the microclimate of Olafur Eliasson's *The weather project* (Turbine Hall, 2003).

Some might argue that these examples of audience participation are precisely the opposite of the kind of worker exploitation detractors accused *You Me Bum Bum Train* of perpetrating. Indeed, it might be that in these instances, audience members are not *passively exploited*, but rather *actively exploit* opportunities to be expressive, to be empowered, to claim agency in the making of art and performance, to be 'spectator-performers'[2] and to be artists. Whatever one's position in these arguments, they indicate, first, that labour is circulating widely across makers and audiences in contemporary art and performance, and second, that this circulation of labour is important and demands scrutiny because it articulates and significantly affects social power relations.

In this part of the book, I explore labour trends in contemporary art and performance to ask what social power relations they create and thus how they may be politically enabling and/or problematic. I propose that longstanding rules and etiquettes that have limited audiences' active participation in art and performance are, in many contexts, loosening up, bringing about a kind of deregulation of art and performance's labour laws and pools so that, often, 'the artist is no longer the central agent in his or her own work, but operates through a range of individuals, communities, and surrogates' (Bishop and Sladen, 2008, p. 9). I consider how this labour deregulation in art and performance corresponds to the broader deregulation of markets – particularly labour markets – under neoliberal capitalism. I interrogate what the effects of this artistic deregulation are for social power relations, art, performance, individuals and groups. And I explore how understanding patterns of labour in contemporary art and performance can help us better understand and negotiate patterns of labour and their social power dynamics in culture more broadly (see Bishop, 2012; Jackson, 2011; Kattwinkel, 2003; Kester, 2004; Miessen and Basar, 2006).

In the next section, I describe in more detail the kind of art and performance that delegates labour and/or agency principally to its audiences but also to others. Then I explore, first, some of the potential social benefits of art and performance which make everyone an artist, and second, some of the potential social problems of this trend, particularly as these problems relate to shifts in contemporary labour patterns. Then I consider the relation of the participating audience member to what American futurologists Alvin and Heidi Toffler called the 'prosumer' – the consumer who also designs and produces what she consumes. Finally, I consider what this trend, which appears often to empower *individuals*, might do for groups, group dynamics and social good. Though I acknowledge that art and performance's delegation of labour – or agency – offers some important social benefits, I argue that in many instances it risks reproducing some of the most egregious conditions and effects of contemporary labour relations, though at its best, it draws self-reflexive critical attention to that risk.

Delegated art and performance

Art and performance that delegate activity cover a huge range of forms and examples but their delegation usually follows one of two routes: more frequently, they delegate to audiences who participate without remuneration; less often, they delegate to people – whether amateur or expert – who are specifically contracted to do something by the artist or performance company.[3] One could say that audience participation is always required to make successful art or performance. Indeed, Jacques Rancière argues that the apparent passivity of the audience member in conventionally organized theatre is precisely that, apparent, since the spectator is, in Rancière's terminology, 'emancipated', actively engaging with the production intellectually and critically (Rancière, 2009). I agree with Rancière that, ideally, this is true. But the art and performance I focus on here usually requires its audiences physically to act, often implicitly suggesting that this audience is more 'emancipated' than Rancière's, though I will be interrogating this suggestion. This kind of cultivation of physically active audience participation usually happens, in theatre, in immersive environments, one-to-one events and performances where audience members are deliberately outnumbered by performers, and in visual and sculptural art, through large-scale immersive or relational environments. In both theatre and visual/sculptural art, 'making' is also sometimes delegated to specifically commissioned others, both expert and amateur. In what follows, I outline these varieties of delegation – acknowledging that they do not exhaust the list of potential contexts for cultivating active audience participation – before moving on to explore their social effects.

Immersive theatre and art

Immersive theatre characteristically creates a through-designed environment which surrounds audience members and in which they are generally invited to move about. Theatre scholar Adam Alston (2012, p. 194) describes it succinctly as 'a promenade theatre form which allows audiences the benefit of free-roaming within hands-on and multi-sensory performance environments'. Realist theatre's usual fourth wall is not so much removed (as on a proscenium arch stage) as moved, such that it and the other 'three' walls of the theatrical fictional space encompass the audience along with the theatre performers. This kind of performance seldom if ever uses an auditorium that is separate from the stage space, so it is often produced not in purpose-built theatres but rather in large and usually flexible spaces such as railway arches, disused factories, vacant offices, and civic buildings such as schools and town halls.

In the United Kingdom, one of the greatest exponents and best-known makers of immersive theatre is the London-based Punchdrunk, formed in 2000. In their own words, Punchdrunk make 'immersive theatre in which roaming audiences experience epic storytelling inside sensory theatrical worlds'.[4] Their 2006/7 adaptation of Goethe's *Faust*, co-produced with the National Theatre in a six-month run, played to a total audience of almost 30,000 people in 119 performances in a five-storey, 150,000 square foot former archive building in the old London neighbourhood of Wapping (Punchdrunk, 2011, Archive page). Even before entering the building, the audience began to be immersed in the show's ambience by being disoriented: the venue was far from any of London's main theatre districts in a neighbourhood whose industrial past was at the time only partially gentrified; the building's adapted use was only minimally sign-posted; and getting from the gated entrance to the site on Wapping Lane to the building's actual entrance required circumnavigation of almost the whole of the building's perimeter (see Marini, 2013, ch. 2). Inside, audience members were ushered into a lively, crowded bar and given undecorated Venetian carnival masks to wear. In small groups they were then escorted in an elevator up to the top floor and released to explore the rest of the building's 40-odd rooms and environments. Set in 1950s United States, the spaces of this *Faust* were variously designed as a dance hall, a diner complete with booths and plastic mustard bottles, a domestic sitting room, a corn field with real stands of corn, a pine forest headily scented by real trees, a maze of filing cabinets, a cinema and a row of shops. Audience members could follow performers, go exploring the many atmospheric environments, chase a narrative and/or re-watch repeated scenes. Equally, they could move in ways apparently unmotivated by the show itself, for example, following another audience member, moving against audience and performer flows or even staying put in a single location. Every audience member's experience was uniquely composed by him or her, and though commentators often reported failing to gather a strong sense of the performance's overarching narrative, they also reported that the show produced a palpable sense of excitement, engagement and opportunity (see Clapp, 2006; Glusker, 2006; Lightig, 2007).[5] 'It's theater for the interactive age', observed reviewer Anne Glusker in *The New York Times*, '[b]ut instead of moving a cursor, you simply move yourself, choosing whatever character you want to follow, whatever sound intrigues you, whichever enticing corridor you are drawn to explore' (Glusker, 2006). In immersive theatre events such as this, each audience member chooses what show to compose for him or herself.

Visual, sculptural and aural art that immerses its audiences in similar ways is generally installation art that sometimes produces relational aesthetics. Installation art is not simply composed of an object or objects but produces an environment which, as in immersive theatre, surrounds and contextualizes the audience (see Bishop, 2005). For *Test Site* in London's Tate Modern Turbine Hall, for example, Carsten Höller installed five aluminium and Perspex spiralling slides ranging in height from four storeys to one. Turbine Hall visitors were invited to slide down the slides or simply to watch while others did so. Höller transformed the Turbine Hall at least partly into a playground (Höller, 2006). For his Turbine Hall commission, *The weather project,* Olafur Eliasson installed a mirrored ceiling, apparatuses that emitted mist and, high on the Hall's eastern wall, a large half-circle screen backed by monofrequency lights. This screen doubled in the ceiling mirror to form a 'sun' and largely limited colour perception in the Hall to a range between yellow and black. Eliasson's installation immersed Turbine Hall visitors in a slightly eerie indoor microclimate in which, again, they watched each another and played, making patterns on the floor to be reflected in the ceiling (see Harvie, 2009b). In Sehgal's *These Associations,* there were no material objects, simply human participants, both those hired by Sehgal to move around the Turbine Hall, play in it and speak to visitors, and those visitors who responded by interacting and 'associating' with Sehgal's designated delegates. Art critic and curator Nicolas Bourriaud has influentially described relational art as 'an art taking as its theoretical horizon the realm of human interactions and its social context, rather than the assertion of an independent and *private* symbolic space' (2002, p. 14, italics original). What is 'relational' about *Test Site, The weather project, These Associations* and other installations like them is that they cultivate social interaction rather than private contemplation, and that their important 'content' might be not so much objects (for example, slides, mirrors or lighting) as social interactions and relations.

One-to-one performance

One-to-one theatre events are similar to immersive theatre in that each audience member experiences a unique event, however similarly the performer repeats it for each audience member. Similarly, in many-to-one performances such as *You Me Bum Bum Train,* the individual audience member is treated as though she is the only audience member in a series of quickly sequenced mono-performances. In fact, each scene performed uniquely for her will swiftly be performed uniquely for the next audience member, and the next, and so on in a kind of serial mono-performance. Beyond creating a sense of a unique performance, however, performance produced for solo audiences can be seen to invite those solo audiences to co-create the performance in ways that go beyond usual expectations about audience energy or even the responsiveness typically required of immersive theatre, since performance for a solo audience member usually entails direct address and requires, or at least requests audience interaction. Thus, in performance for solo audiences, the audience member should actively be able to change the performance's outcome. In *You Me Bum Bum Train*, for example, different audience members will develop different pep talks for the football team and different host personae for the chat show. Similarly, each audience member will establish a different relationship in solo encounters with Ashery or Howells.

Art delegated to contracted workers

Though art which delegates labour and/or agency from the artist to others most commonly delegates to audiences, sometimes it delegates to experts or amateurs who are explicitly commissioned by the artist to produce the work. In visual and fine art in general, artists regularly contract work to other experts, for example to realize a work in a particular medium (one of Tracey Emin's writings in fluorescent lighting, for instance) or to create infrastructure for the artwork, such as its frame or lighting. But the *scale* of much immersive and relational art practice in large spaces like Tate Modern's Turbine Hall means that artists are currently creating works that require much more substantial contributions of expertise from workers from other disciplines, such as engineering, in order to realize the work's technical complexity.

Anish Kapoor's 2002 Turbine Hall installation *Marsyas*, for example, was a massive, red, horn-like sculpture with three apertures, one facing out at each end of the Hall, and one opening over the bridge that spans the Hall. The apertures were held open by giant rings made of a total of 40 tonnes of high-strength structural steel; the 'horn' was composed of an enormous single span of 3500 metres of red PVC membrane (De Salvo, 2002, p. 14). The piece entailed careful work managing its suspension, balance and tensions across the membrane and rings so that nothing would tear, buckle or bag, and it involved close collaboration with engineering designer Cecil Balmond and a team of his colleagues from architecture firm Arup. Doris Salcedo's *Shibboleth* (2007) was a 167-metre-long crack in the Turbine Hall's concrete floor that was pre-prepared and then built in. In his Foreword to the Tate Publishing monograph on *Shibboleth*, Tate's then-Director Vincente Todolí dedicates two paragraphs (2007, pp. 7–8, 8–9) to thanking Salcedo's 'team of architects and technicians' and those who planned and oversaw the process of installation; each paragraph is long to accommodate naming the many, many collaborators. Delegation to experts is also typical of work that is not so much technically complex (though specialist) as quantitatively enormous. For his 2010 Turbine Hall installation, *Sunflower Seeds*, Ai Weiwei employed approximately 1600 artisans in China's 'porcelain city' of Jingdezhen to produce over one million individually hand-painted ceramic sunflower seeds with which he covered approximately 1000 square metres of the eastern end of the Turbine Hall floor to a depth of 10 centimetres (Bingham, 2010, pp. 24, 101; see Hancox, 2013). Such scale is not confined only to Tate Modern. Antony Gormley's vast outdoor sculpture *The Angel of the North* (1998) in Gateshead, northeast England, for example, was made with 600 tonnes of concrete and 200 tonnes of steel. Furthermore, delegation is also typical of work that simply requires specialist skill if not on a monumental scale, as when Martin Creed commissioned runners to sprint at regular intervals through Tate Britain's Duveen Galleries for *Work No. 850* (2008).

It is not only large spaces such as the Turbine Hall that rely on the expert technical labour and support of engineers and builders. Roger Hiorns's *Seizure* (2008), commissioned by Artangel and the Jerwood Foundation and discussed in more detail later in Chapter 3, worked on what was comparatively a much smaller scale but again created an immersive environment reliant on specialist engineering. Hiorns's vision for this piece was to transform a small flat by encrusting all of its interior surfaces with a thick layer of bright blue copper sulphate crystals. To do so, he and his collaborators needed to turn the flat into a sealed tank into which they could pour – through a hole in the floor of the empty flat above – 75,000 litres of hot copper sulphate solution which then cooled and crystallized over about two and a half weeks. The collaborators then had to drain and capture the remaining solution for recycling while not, of course, damaging the resulting crystals (see Dillon, 2008; Harvie, 2011a; Searle, 2008; Wilkes, 2008).

For his well-known vitrine containing a shark floating in formaldehyde solution, *The Physical Impossibility of Death in the Mind of Someone Living* (1991), Damien Hirst purchased the original 14-metre-long shark from an Australian fisherman for £6000 (BBC News, 2004). Due to deterioration, the original shark was replaced in 2006 with another, also purchased from a fisherman working in Australia. It made its two-month voyage to the United Kingdom by sea freighter in a special 20-foot freezer equipped with backup power. To better preserve this shark, Hirst brought in experts such as Oliver Crimmen, a scientist and fish curator at London's Natural History Museum. Crimmen's procedure was complex. *The New York Times* reported, 'A shark's skin is armored with tiny teeth, so Mr. Crimmen and his team had to first drill small holes in the skin, filling them with temporary pins in preparation for the injection of the formaldehyde. Because a shark's skin is so rough, the tiny holes won't leave noticeable marks once the fish is properly preserved' (Vogel, 2006, p. 3). Sculptor-taxidermist Emily Mayer has supplied and repaired many animals for Hirst's artworks, providing several replacement severed cow heads for *A Thousand Years* (1990), an upright grizzly bear for *Last Night I Dreamt I Didn't Have a Head* (1997), sides of beef for *The Pursuit of Oblivion* (2004), as well as doing skeleton repairs and shark work (Milgrom, 2010, pp. 135, 197–8). Without the expertise of Crimmen, Mayer and others, Hirst would not be able to create, preserve or replace the concepts he imagines.

Alongside those examples where artists commission experts to complete the work, many artists are deliberately contracting amateurs to do so, drawing attention to the fact of the delegation given that it is not apparently 'necessary', as it might appear to be when work is delegated to 'experts', and also challenging ideas of expertise and the expert. Artist Phil Collins, for example, frequently delegates to others. In *free fotolab* (2004–), he developed others' unprocessed 35mm film for free in exchange for permission to select and display any of the resulting images. For a residency in Jerusalem, he created his famous two-channel video installation *they shoot horses* (2004), contracting nine teenagers to dance continuously to pop music in front of a video camera for eight hours over two consecutive days (see Bishop, 2006b). In each of these cases, the idea for the work is Collins's, but the work is, in a variety of ways, performed and executed by others. Collins acknowledges that his work relies on others' contributions, and may well be motivated by their desires; for example, their desire to have their 35mm film processed when funds are low and processing facilities are rare; or to dance in a video. But he also acknowledges his potential exploitation of their desire in order to leverage their participation in his work. In his own words, he is 'unevenly staging a terrain of shared desire' (Bishop and Collins, 2008, p. 30). Similarly and notoriously, Santiago Sierra hires workers – usually very disadvantaged workers, such as illegal immigrants – to execute his works such as *Workers Paid to Remain Inside Cardboard Boxes* (from 1999) and *160cm Line Tattooed on 4 People* (2000). As I will consider in more detail below, Sierra hires others to do particular tasks to draw attention to the social and economic inequalities that govern so many hierarchies of labour.

Everyone is an artist[6]

All of the examples cited above demonstrate a significant trend in which artists delegate their labour to others, most often audience members but sometimes also other experts. People who are not, nominally, 'the artist' make, or contribute to making, the art or performance. In this section, I explore the many ways that this art and performance's delegation – or, perhaps, its labour's deregulation – can have socially empowering effects by, for example, distributing agency to a greater number of people, celebrating the equal access of amateurs to art practice, also valuing expertise, potentially developing knowledge, cultivating social engagement and social awareness and drawing attention to exploitative trends in contemporary patterns of labour.

Most importantly, delegated performance offers audiences potentially expanded degrees of agency in making art and its meanings, enabling individual expressivity, extending to all participants the opportunity to be an artist and democratizing the role of artist. For example, as noted above, anyone who visits the Tate Modern Turbine Hall during one of its installations – such as Eliasson's *The weather project* or Sehgal's *These Associations* – can participate and collaborate in the artwork. Access to being an artist is opened to everyone, regardless of how excluded from art people might otherwise feel they are, whether due to restraints that are material (not having art's tools) or educational (not having art instruction) or because of the enormously powerful and pervasive constraints of cultural capital, which actively and passively collude to train many people to believe that certain areas of cultural practice are simply 'not for them'. Delegated art and performance thus celebrate amateurism, doing art for the pleasure of it, regardless of ability, and they celebrate the amateur. Participants are – usually implicitly – compelled to accept that it is not necessary to be expert in order to engage in art practice. Sometimes, they are more precisely entreated to recognize that they actually have sufficient expertise – for example, at talking to a stranger in *These Associations* or manipulating their own bodies as images in *The weather project* – and that expertise is not as rarefied or exclusive as at first it might appear. By treating everyone as an artist, delegated art offers exemplary equality of opportunity to all.

The act of delegating and including apparent non-artists as artists can also make visible by contrast the fact that some people are excluded not only from practising art, but also from many other important aspects of cultural engagement and potential cultural understanding. Collins's delegation to select amateurs, for example, renders more visible some of the many restrictions – especially material ones – which inhibit his recruits' engagement in art practice as well as broader aspects of culture. Without participation in *free fotolab*, Collins's collaborators might not otherwise be able to afford to process their film; he supports their practice through funding and by supplying the increasingly uncommon service of film processing. In *they shoot horses,* Collins's collaborators are noticeably constrained by curfews as they individually leave the dancing when necessary in order to complete their sometimes long commutes home in good time. *They shoot horses* highlights this limit to cultural engagement, it highlights the participants' limited energy which visibly wanes as the dance marathon progresses, and it highlights the participants' limited spaces, Collins's camera effectively capturing the dancers in a restricted frame against a short expanse of bright pink and red wall. Those three foregrounded limits resonate with other constraints on the participants, including fashion and gender, but also the multiple intersecting pressures of politics, economics, geography and religion. *They shoot horses* emphasizes the many constraints on cultural participation that inherently limit cross-cultural engagement. More cross-cultural interaction and possible understanding might be achievable were material conditions of engagement less prohibiting, as Collins makes temporarily possible and powerfully visible in *they shoot horses.*

As discussed above, some art – or aspects of it – is delegated not only to mass amateur audiences or to specific amateur recruits but to professional experts such as engineers. This practice can celebrate the apparent exclusivity of expertise, but it can also be socially progressive. As with mass delegation, it demonstrates how the practice of art is generally socially embedded and socially dependent, despite its frequent appearance as the pursuit of a single, genius artist. Furthermore, by demonstrating expertise this art and performance might inspire its audiences to learn and develop their skills and understanding, and by recontextualizing scientific expertise it might contribute to developing expert knowledge and practice.

Works created with expert collaboration such as those described above can fire interest not just in what they are, but also in *how* they have been made. Salcedo's *Shibboleth,* for example, was surrounded by speculation about, first, how she and collaborators had created the giant crack in the Turbine Hall floor that appeared to be a natural occurrence rather than a human creation and, second, how they had done so without jeopardizing the rest of the monumental building which rested on that cracked floor. In a collaborative effort with some builders and an architect, *Guardian* journalist Jon Henley speculated, 'how on earth did [the crack] get there?' and 'could it be dangerous?' (Henley, 2007; see Dorment, 2007; Jones, 2007; Searle *et al.* 2010). Likewise, article after article – including one in *Chemical and Engineering News* – recounts the tale of how structural and chemical engineering transformed an apparently banal little flat into the bejewelled Aladdin's cave of Hiorns's *Seizure* (Halford, 2009; see Dillon, 2008; Milliard, 2008; Searle, 2008; Wilkes, 2008; Williams, 2008).

Some observers and artists, such as Salcedo, warn that audiences might be so 'distracted' by material considerations such as how the work is made that they risk neglecting the art itself and its ideas. However, works such as these can stimulate people's interest in several aspects of the art, including how it is made as well as what it might mean and how it might feel. Knowing details of the ingenuity and collective labour that have created an artwork might give it a sense of achievability alongside, for example, its wondrousness – a combination that is not only inspiring but also enabling because it precisely demystifies artwork as not just about individual genius. Furthermore, the wonder and thrill that audiences often experience in 'doing' works such as these – riding down Töller's slides, standing dwarfed by and invited to speak into Kapoor's horn, tracing the length of Salcedo's cracked floor, entering Hiorns's cave – can inspire them to engage with ideas in science and engineering in ways that they otherwise might not. Such work might therefore stimulate interest in – and enable engagement in – science and engineering in audiences who come to it from this very different direction than the more usual educational or industrial routes.

Secondly, art and performance work that deploys such expertise gives scientists and engineers opportunities to experiment with and test materials and practices in contexts and conditions they might not encounter in their everyday work. Not only can they address different audiences, therefore, they might also make new discoveries. While working on Hirst's shark, for example, Crimmen commented that the size of the beast posed an unusual challenge and that the task made him pay attention to both the scientific aspects of his work and its aesthetics, an approach which might affect the audience reach of his work more broadly. 'As a fish curator', he said, 'I generally preserve things for science and then I don't have to pay attention to aesthetics. This is a novel angle for me' (Vogel, 2006). Work on Kapoor's *Marsyas* allowed the Advanced Geometry Unit at architecture firm Arup to experiment with methods for controlling tensions and for combining 'hydrostatic pressure and nonlinear surface tension' to give 'areas of synclastic and anticlastic curvature that yielded spectacular, if slightly unnerving biomorphic forms' (Simmonds, Self and Bosia, 2006, p. 86). In having the opportunity to practise their skills outside of their usual disciplinary and professional contexts, 'non-art' experts involved in this artwork are able to develop those skills, as well as to value and promote them in new and potentially more public contexts. As I explore in more detail below, this is especially welcome in a labour economy where skills often quickly become obsolete and where workers, therefore, often experience deskilling and a sense of personal devaluation and anxiety.

Delegated art practices can also cultivate participants' social engagement. Where much art simply invites its audiences to contemplate it and does not require people to interact, by contrast, art which delegates to its audiences often requires them to engage, negotiate and collaborate. Sometimes this interaction is extensive and verbal. In theatre company Uninvited Guests' interactive, immersive *Make Better Please* (first produced at the Bristol Old Vic, 2010), audiences were seated in groups at tables loaded with enormous teapots, cups, biscuits and the day's newspapers. They were asked individually to peruse the newspapers, identify items which made them angry or upset that they would present to the group at their table and then do so. Each table group then discussed the multiple selected stories to choose a single story which they presented to the entire audience and Uninvited Guests company team. The show required audience members not simply to discuss current news with strangers, but to share their own sense of what was important as well as to negotiate group agreement about stories' importance, a task many people might seldom do with strangers.

In other contexts, delegated art's interaction is non-verbal and apparently more modest, but even so it can compel audiences to reflect critically on social relations. By interacting apparently with the mirror of Eliasson's *The weather project*, for example, audiences found themselves actually interacting with other reflected audience members, often playfully waving to one another or making complementary shapes or rhythms of movement. Tate curator Jessica Morgan observes that 'the work became not only a meeting place, but a location for events and protests, picnics, yoga and photo opportunities' (Morgan, 2006, p. 11). The vertical separation provided by the ceiling mirror provoked people to interact with neighbours who might actually have been quite proximate horizontally. Such acts might have provoked participants to rethink the constraining effects of conventional etiquettes of interaction and to recognize the social value not only of respecting personal space as usual, but of interacting playfully. In visiting Hiorns's *Seizure*, audiences directly contributed to its production of space as cramped. By negotiating the literally overcrowded space of the crystallized flat, audiences may have been provoked to reflect, by extension, on the similarly overcrowded conditions of the social housing market (as explored in detail in Chapter 3 of this book).

The social interactions that delegated art provokes are admittedly generally quite modest; group negotiation practices of *Make Better Please* may aim to make things better, but they do not propose to save the world. Nevertheless, the social interactions this art facilitates compel its participants to practise negotiation with strangers, to play with others and to recalibrate their expectations about social interaction. To a degree, therefore, delegated art practices model shared participation, engagement, community and responsibility-taking, features which are perhaps particularly important if conventional political models of democracy such as parliamentary democracy are feeling worn, slow, disappointing, faulty, moribund or dysfunctional. I explore further aspects and effects of this art and performance practice's group engagement later in this chapter.

Delegated art practices can cultivate awareness about social interaction per se, but they can also potentially challenge social hierarchies by effectively levelling participants as all, simply, participants, or by inverting conventional social hierarchies. Audiences in this work are usually cast as performers simply because of their presence and not because of their expertise, profession or any other signification of status. In *Make Better Please*, for example, groups discussing news items generally would not know who their fellow discussants were; the opinions of students, journalists, shop workers and ecologists all merited attention. In *The weather project* and *Test Site*, children's comfort at playing in public meant that what they did led others' behaviour, inverting conventional social hierarchies where adults lead, instruct and discipline children.

Delegated art practices can also draw attention to exploitative labour trends and other ethical implications arising from delegation. Sierra's work highlights much more aggressively than Collins's, for example, how those who are most economically deprived are most constrained in the 'choices' they make about their work. The economic deprivation of the workers Sierra hires compels them to take on the often demeaning labour of his commissions, to stand in a line, to stay inside cardboard boxes in a gallery, to have a line tattooed on their backs. Participants in his work are not 'freed' to be artists – as many participants in immersive theatre might feel they are. However, these labourers' boldly visible constraint draws attention to the economic and social precariousness of their labour conditions, precariousness I explore in more detail below. The ceramists and painters of Ai's *Sunflower Seeds* are not profoundly demeaned as Sierra's workers often are; however, the sheer scale of *Sunflower Seeds* makes evident the repetitiveness of their labour. The examples of Sierra's and Ai's work draw attention to some of the social challenges of contemporary global labour markets, where global material inequalities allow those people with the most privilege to delegate the most demeaning and/or alienating labour well out of their sight.

The innovations and expansions of audience engagement, participation and labour in recent performance often offer audiences fun, stimulating experiences. They also offer these many social benefits: extending agency and authority to a greater number and range of potentially non-expert participants; cultivating social engagement and awareness; modelling practices of social collaboration; providing experts with opportunities to experiment in challenging new contexts; and drawing attention to exploitative trends in contemporary labour markets.

Everyone is an extra

The social engagement delegated performance offers can alternatively be seen as at best limited, possibly compromising and even malign. The agency and egalitarianism it proffers can be modest, superficially placating or problematically and spectacularly distracting, diverting attention from, for example, the simultaneous *material* disempowerment of millions of people by increasingly insecure global labour markets, as well as the Conservative-led coalition government's enormous cuts to public services, cuts preceded by years of erosion under New Labour. It can conscript audiences' participation in acts, situations and dynamics they might not otherwise support. Its endorsement of amateurism can risk de-professionalizing the artist and devaluing artistic expertise, skill, commitment, training and education in ways that resonate again with the Cameron government's move, initiated in 2010, to withdraw all state funding to higher education teaching in arts and humanities, including the fine arts. Finally, its delegation of labour to audiences who are usually unpaid and, indeed, often *paying* can exploit free labour in ways that replicate, extend and potentially naturalize exploitative trends in contemporary labour markets more broadly.

Audience pleasures of participation in this work are often more limited than the first blush of excited engagement might suggest. *What* the audience can actually do in delegated performance and art is often extremely limited. The artwork does offer 'hidden' spaces that audience members are able to discover – such as small, designed rooms in Punchdrunk's *Faust* and the chasm opened up by Salcedo's *Shibboleth*. But, there are still substantial 'backstage' areas where trespass is prohibited, and there are histories which remain concealed. Salcedo and Tate Modern, for example, refused to reveal more than basic details about *Shibboleth*'s construction process in order to concentrate audience's focus on the completed work (Salcedo, 2007). And though in theory individual audience members might be able to follow action as they choose, in practice it can often be difficult to follow one's desires to see or hear particular things or go to particular places simply because the mass of *other* audience members prevents it. In one-to-one performances it may be more possible to do as one wishes as an audience member, but these performances tend nevertheless to limit the audience's choices and actions, occurring often in small spaces such as single rooms and with the performer more directly leading his or her solo interlocutor. In art installations, acute intervention is often explicitly prohibited. For example, the edges of Salcedo's *Shibboleth* were literally patrolled by security guards and safety notices; audiences could peer into the chasm but by no means enter it. Even before considering these forms' labour relations, it is possible to see how they may offer more a spectre of participation than a substantial opportunity to interact and to determine the performance or art. In this sense, these participatory performance and art forms can be seen as part of what French theorist Guy Debord famously called the society of the spectacle, in which social relations are diminished as people increasingly engage through and with images and mediations rather than directly with each other, though the spectre of interaction may feel palpable (Debord, 1994 [1967]).

Similarly, this practice's apparent egalitarianism may be superficial and distracting. Though everyone is implicitly invited to participate, the invitation may nevertheless effectively be more available to those with existing substantial cultural capital than to those with little. Because this art practice shifts conventional rules of engagement, participants may remain the people with the most secure sense of their entitlement to go along with challenging conventional rules of art and performance. Furthermore, though this work appears to delegate to and empower its audiences, it may effectively preserve the elitism of the star artist or company whose (brand) name usually retains authorship of, for example, Kate Bond and Morgan Lloyd's *You Me Bum Bum Train*, the Punchdrunk show, the Shunt installation, or the Collins, Sierra, Sehgal, Kapoor or Salcedo artwork.

Not only can delegated art and performance practice conscript audiences and other makers to produce work for which they are not properly attributed authorship, it can conscript them as authors of work they do not *effectively* author or do not actually *want* to author. In many immersive performances, audiences are explicitly bossed around and instructed to do things. In *Faust* as in other Punchdrunk shows, audience members are required to wear masks, and to wait to be 'released' into the show. In Uninvited Guests' *The Good Neighbour* (Battersea Arts Centre, London, 2012), audiences were led in small groups around

Battersea and Clapham in South London, where they heard stories about various local sites' histories, for example about a long-dead, once-resident political campaigner; a fire that happened in the area's large department store over a century ago; and the riots of summer 2011. A handful of audience members were asked to carry large and cumbersome musical instruments embedded with speakers which played out soundtracks to accompany scenes; all audience members were asked to wear masks and hats, to sniff lavender, to follow particular performers, to march and to sing. In these ways, rather than being empowered by the performance, audiences were subservient to the company, dutifully performing as instructed, when instructed.

Admittedly, *The Good Neighbour* offered other opportunities for audiences to contribute with more autonomy; for example, when performers asked audience members where they were from, or where they were during the London riots of summer 2011. And even when delegated art and performance's power dynamics are uneven like this, this work sometimes constructively draws attention to such inequalities and to the complicated ways that people can find themselves inadvertently embedded in them. Sierra's work's tendency to push these inequalities as far as he dares does this. In *The Good Neighbour*, audience members' conscription into the show casts them multiply and often simultaneously as outside observers of the riots and – when masked as some of the rioters had been – as participants in them, breaking down simple 'us' and 'them' distinctions and hierarchies.

Despite these opportunities to contribute meaningfully and to reflect critically on problems that delegation produces, delegated art's potential to cast everyone in its audiences as infinitely replaceable supernumerary extras significantly undermines the social benefits of such work by exploiting its audiences. The picture of how participatory art and performance's social value may be compromised becomes more complex if the things audiences do in it are seen to entail a particular set of *labour* relations. In the next section, I explore in more detail how what might appear to be *participation* in such art and performance might be understood more accurately as delegated or outsourced labour (see Bishop, 2006b, and 2012, pp. 11–40; Jackson, 2011; Ridout, 2008).

Delegated and outsourced labour

Outsourcing work usually entails finding a less expensive labour pool to perform a task in less advantageous labour conditions; it therefore has an intrinsically hierarchical structure, where delegation might not (see Ridout, 2008). Within the United Kingdom, outsourced labour is often displaced from the metropolis of London to poorer, usually northern cities such as Belfast and Glasgow, or to workers with less cultural capital within the metropolis. Outsourcing's iconic example is the Indian call centre, where wealthy companies from the global north hire Indian workers to provide services such as computer support over the phone to northern clients while talking with British or North American accents. Workers in such contexts are usually expected to earn a wage which is significantly less than it would be for comparable work performed in the prosperous, first world metropolis (though wages are often comparatively good in the workers' local context). These workers are also expected to submit to alienating work conditions that many in the metropolitan global north would refuse; for example, they play down their real accents, languages, cultural contexts and selves; their work tasks are repetitive; those in the global south work at night to provide day-time service to clients half a world away; and they perform the social labour of reassuring and placating strangers who may be angry and frustrated. Outsourcing labour is advantageous in at least some ways for all its participants: for the company from the metropolitan global north because it reduces costs of labour and infrastructure such as office space; for the client because she receives the service she seeks; and even for the worker in the global south or non-metropolitan north because she has paid work. Nevertheless, it clearly exacerbates grossly uneven global labour relations and development, with the worker in the global south or peripheral north working in ways, in conditions and for wages which, in elite spheres of the metropolitan north, would not be widely accepted and might even be illegal.

Labour in delegated or outsourced performance in the global north rarely goes as far away as the global south, though it sometimes does; for example in Rimini Protokoll's performance *Call Cutta in a Box* (from 2008) and motiroti and The Builders Association's *Alladeen* (2002–5), which both explore labour and social relations between workers in India and comparatively privileged audiences/clients in Europe and North America, and which Ridout (2008) and Jackson (2011, pp. 163ff.) both discuss. In these works, audiences are provoked to be self-reflexive about the gross unevenness of global economies of labour and of global social hierarchies.

Audiences as flexible and precarious labourers

But it is more often the case in this performance that the worker to whom the labour is outsourced is present – he or she is *you*, the audience member. This relation draws more attention to another problematic condition of labour in what social and cultural theorist Richard Sennett has called 'the culture of the new capitalism' (in my terms, 'neoliberal capitalism'): its dependence on flexibility, or what Maurizio Lazzarato identifies as precariousness (1996), or what sociologist Ulrich Beck sees as fragility (1999). Beck remarked that '*fragile* work increases rapidly, that is, part-time, self-employed work, limited-term jobs and other forms for which we have barely found proper descriptions' (1999, p. 11; italics original). As numerous observers have noted, for many people, the job-for-life or the career – which Sennett (1998, p. 9) glosses as the 'lifelong channel for one's economic pursuits' – is a thing of the past. Job security has diminished. Labour conditions require workers more frequently to change both their work practices and their employers. Workers therefore have to adapt to new conditions of labour and new colleagues more frequently. Rapidly evolving technology means that workers need constantly to update their skills. And, when work fails, the welfare structures people might formerly have relied on to bridge them to their next employment are now also less secure or, as Sennett puts it, 'more short-term and more erratic' (2006, p. 25). '"Flexibility" is demanded everywhere', writes Beck,

> – or, in other words, an 'employer' should be able to fire 'employees' more easily. 'Flexibility' also means a redistribution of risks from state and economy to individuals. The jobs available become more and more short-term and 'renewable' – which is to say, 'terminable'. ... Consequently, the more work relations are 'deregulated' and 'flexibilized', the faster work society turns into a risk society that is not open to calculation by individuals or by politics .... So, the expression 'precarious freedoms' denotes a basic ambivalence between the cultural script of individual self-fulfilment and the new political economy of uncertainty and risk. All too swiftly, the 'elective', 'reflexive' or 'do-it-yourself' biography can become the breakdown biography.
>
> (1999, p. 12)

A defender of work conditions in this culture of the new capitalism might hail them as freeing, self-fulfilling and a welcome attack on the rigidities of bureaucracy. For Beck, Sennett and others, they are, on the contrary, fundamentally compromising. This idea of 'insecurity as the new freedom' is 'familiar neoliberal snake-oil, of course', observes social geographer Jamie Peck (2005, p. 759). Fundamentally compromised, too, are the workers whom this culture requires and cultivates, as Sennett explores in both his 1998 book *The Corrosion of Character: The*

Personal Consequences of Work in the New Capitalism and his 2006 book, *The Culture of the New Capitalism*. In the latter, Sennett writes:

> A self oriented to the short term, focused on potential ability, willing to abandon past experience is – to put a kindly face on the matter – an unusual sort of human being. Most people are not like this; they need a sustaining life narrative, they take pride in being good at something specific, and they value the experiences they've lived through. The cultural ideal required in new institutions thus damages many of the people who inhabit them.
>
> (2006, p. 5)

Increasingly compromised conditions of labour make for increasingly compromised labourers.

Given the ways conditions of labour emerging more broadly in society are detrimental to workers, that they should find resemblances – or, as Ridout (2008, pp. 128, 130) rightfully insists, straightforward manifestations – in the flexible labour of delegated performance should give us pause. I suggest they find such manifestations in at least three aspects: job insecurity, unfamiliarity with tasks and colleagues, and deskilling. At first, it might seem slightly ridiculous to refer to job security in relation to the audience's role – audiences do not, after all, generally expect to clock in at a performance or artwork every day. However, western audiences do generally expect to perform particular 'duties' – to be quiet, watch, listen, sit still and behave respectfully to their fellow audience members as well as the performers. Clearly, recent forms of participatory, one-to-one and relational art and performance require audiences to change what they do – sometimes to do as they have done before, but also or alternatively to move, to explore and to respond actively to performers' instructions. In this sense, audience's work *is* insecure, in that they do not know what they are going to be called upon to do. This partly explains the dread that many people feel about 'audience participation' which contracts audiences to do something that cannot be anticipated, as well as to perform it in front of strangers. And this reinforces the point that those with the most cultural capital may feel most able to be flexible in this brave new world of shifting audience rules.

A second aspect of flexible spectatorship also resembles the conditions of flexible labour: people are called on to work with co-workers and for audiences whom they do not know. Where past, more secure and long-term forms of labour allowed workers to get to know colleagues and clients and to develop working relations with them, emerging demands for flexible labour require people to work more frequently with strangers and to develop relationships quickly and therefore often superficially. Sennett cites financial guru George Soros's observation that '"transactions" have replaced "relationships" in people's dealings with one another' (Sennett, 2006, p. 25; Soros, 1998). Similarly, in non-participatory theatre and art, audiences have rarely had to work collaboratively with each other; however, in 'flexible' theatre and art, audiences are frequently called upon to collaborate and negotiate. This has its pleasures, happy surprises and potential social benefits; for example, people may find that they collaborate well with perfect strangers, and that the very idea of 'perfect strangers' is less secure than it may at first appear, as perhaps in the example of audience discussions and negotiations about daily news items in *Make Better Please* cited above. Given the rapid global flows of people and communication that are symptomatic of contemporary culture, the ability to collaborate effectively with strangers, and to build confidence in doing so, is indeed desirable. However, if working with strangers replaces working with colleagues, people lose the benefits that arise from knowing co-workers, their strengths, how to work with them most effectively and how they feel. In other words, we stand to lose the deeper social relationships that can be built over time and through collaboration; we stand to lose complex qualitative aspects of relationships as we infinitely expand our quantities of relationships.

Finally, the flexible labour of this emerging form of spectatorship potentially deskills its participants. Because this labour rarely 'knows' its participant/workers but recruits them all equally, it casts them to perform in usually quite basic ways, often literally as part of a crowd – for example, as patrons in *Faust*'s diner or students at its school hall dance, or as rioters in *The Good Neighbour*. These audiences become the epitome of the underemployed theatre worker. They become sword carriers, usually with no swords, though with masks in both examples, and with musical instruments in *The Good Neighbour*. They fill the scene, create the spectacle and help concentrate the focus on the key players. Whatever skills an audience member might actually have – for example, as a professional waitress, dancer or journalist – these are very unlikely to be either called on or effectively permitted in the immersive performance. Thus, like Sennett's worker in the institutions of the new capitalism, the audience member in emerging participatory theatre and art 'abandon[s] past experience' and relinquishes the opportunity to 'take pride in being good at something specific' (Sennett, 2006, p. 5). The audience member as worker in this flexible art and performance economy is rendered, in many ways, insecure, deskilled and alienated.

One might argue that at least when this art practice delegates to experts, as discussed above, it recognizes skill and preserves security. Nevertheless, it preserves inequalities. While labour that is insecure, deskilled and alienating is being experienced, then, by the larger group of audience members (the amateurs, the mass, the 'people' to whom this people-power work is supposed to have been delegated), the privilege of using skills in satisfying labour remains the prerogative of a comparatively very small group – an elite class – of experts. There is a significant gap between the privileges of the elite expert worker – who is comparatively well paid, enjoys the satisfaction of exercising skills and realizes the *benefits* of flexible labour by being able to contract into specialist jobs of his or her choice – and the exploitations of the great majority of flexible workers – whose work is insecure, deskilling and alienating. Furthermore, labour is distributed in a pyramid structure, with the vast majority of workers/audience members occupying disadvantaged flexible positions while only a comparatively extremely small number of expert collaborators enjoy the privileges and pleasures of highly skilled work.

A connected problem takes us back to some of the social and financial risks of outsourcing, where, the Indian call centre worker, for example, is required to 'pass' as American or British by modifying her accent and perhaps adopting a pseudonym. She erases her real identity for the perceived benefit of the employing company's work and the preservation of its brand identity as, amongst other things, recognizably American or British. A similar kind of 'passing' is often expected from experts who contribute to artists' work in order to preserve the sense that it is the artist's creation alone. Information about such experts is frequently suppressed, whether explicitly through contractual confidentiality agreements, implicitly through 'gentlemen's agreements' or, more insidiously perhaps, through the lack of interest in this aspect of artwork demonstrated by both audiences and the media in thrall to the celebrity status of particular artists. For example, Salcedo widely acknowledged her *Shibboleth* collaborators, but did not offer substantial detail on their contributions (Salcedo, 2007, pp. 10–11). 'At any given time', artist Damien Hirst reportedly 'employs more than forty artists and technicians to do his behind-the-scenes work', casting resin pills for his medicine cabinet works, painting his signature spot paintings and preparing the many animal bodies he uses (Milgrom, 2010, pp. 196–7). His taxidermist collaborator, Emily Mayer, has garnered some attention, but very little compared to his enormous renown (ibid.). This practice of outsourcing might more closely resemble that of the ghost writer because the particular aspects of brand identity it is most focused on preserving – or performatively creating – are a sense of the artist's autonomy, her status as principle – or genius – creator of her artwork and her celebrity. This labour trend in the contemporary economy of art and performance therefore potentially demonstrates three problems with that economy: it attempts to deny art as labour (and therefore to deny the potentially uneven labour dynamics that undergird art); it works to mystify how that labour is social or collaborative; and, in the society of the spectacle, it privileges celebrities as the most elite class, preserving and reinforcing class hierarchies.

Although the work modelled in this art and performance may bear all the hallmarks of the precariousness of work in the culture of the new capitalism, it may also provide the socially valuable service of furnishing audiences with contexts in which they can safely *rehearse* ways of working in and negotiating emerging conditions of work, such as the need to be able to respond quickly and flexibly to new tasks and new colleagues. And while security may be desirable at work, at leisure, audiences may very well welcome insecurity's exciting adventures, risks and surprises. In other words, leisure may also provide a context in which to embrace the potential thrills of precariousness. Furthermore, leisure may become a comparatively safe context in which to prepare to negotiate the unfolding challenges of work, what Ulrich Beck refers to as 'a *political economy* of uncertainty, the political economy of world risk society' (1999, p. 11, italics original). However, it is also possible to argue that this art and performance practice effectively naturalizes capitalism's desire for and reliance on workers' flexibility in what Sennett (2005, p. 3) refers to as the 'unstable, fragmentary social conditions' of the era. In helping audiences to rehearse their flexibility at work, these art and performance practices manage workers' expectations about using – or, rather, not using – their skills and enhance workers' flexibility with both tasks and co-workers in ways that the new capitalism precisely desires to ensure its own profitability.

The kind of worker insecurity audiences are invited to experience in these art and performance practices has long been part of the great majority of actors' experiences. Though actors may not usually be deskilled, they are usually subject to both alienation, performing notoriously repetitive labour, and job insecurity, often working for short contracts, moving from company to company, literally and repeatedly taking on new roles even if they continue to perform the same task (acting), working with new colleagues in each casting, and often temporarily being unemployed or underemployed because they take up insecure, unskilled jobs such as bar-tending to remain available for acting work. Fine artists, too, work in insecure conditions, likewise often taking unskilled work to support art practice. The insecure labour conditions that Sennett and others note are on the increase are the kinds of conditions that have long typified creative labour. Audiences' adoption of artists' precariousness, therefore, may tantalize with the spectre of the benefits of artists' creativity and autonomy while delivering the constraints of artists' insecurity and alienation that are already endemic in cultural labour.

The art and performance that conscripts audiences to co-make it offers the pleasures of action, self-determination and discovery; it appears quite straightforwardly to empower its audiences as co-makers. But its benefits are much more compromised than they at first appear. The engagements it offers are actually very limited, even illusionary. Its egalitarianism is compromised by its tendency to retain authorial status for the producing company or 'real' artist. It outsources work in ways that resonate with – if they do not precisely reproduce – global inequalities between labourers and both their clients and their employers. The engagement it offers participants bears all the hallmarks of the insecurities of labour in the culture of the new capitalism – it is insecure, deskilling and alienating. It reinforces class-based divisions of labour by mystifying art's labour and reinforcing a cultural economy that privileges celebrity. Thus, for all its potential benefits, delegated art and performance rehearse audiences for, and naturalize them to, these harmful conditions of labour.

Everyone is a prosumer

Audience members of delegated art and performance might be understood as what the American futurologists Alvin and Heidi Toffler named 'prosumers'. Prosumers are combined producers and consumers who do for themselves what would formerly have been done for them by others (more specifically, other workers) and who fulfil their own needs by producing what they want to consume, whether that be a commodity or a service. I consider the delegated audience as prosumer in order to expand my analysis of the benefits and detractions that the role of prosumer offers both the individual audience member and society more broadly.

Benefits to the individual of this innovation in labour distribution may include greater convenience, efficiency, self-sufficiency, self-articulation, and possibly fun. Instead of relying on someone else to manage things such as the prosumer's banking, mobile phone account or university course registration, she can do it herself at her own convenience and her own pace, for example online or at a bank machine/ATM. She can tailor her own running shoes, Second Life avatar, school exam revision programme or contribution to a Wiki site. She can create a customized register of podcasts to be downloaded daily to her computer, smart phone or mp3 player, or a customized grocery list for weekly delivery. Instead of attending a performance at a given time for a given duration, the theatre-going prosumer can download from the internet an audio walk such as Janet Cardiff's *The Missing Voice (Case Study B)* and perform it herself, whenever she likes and in her own time.[7] In a performance such as Punchdrunk's *Faust*, she can focus her version of the show on one character by attempting to pursue him throughout the performance; or she could make herself a show about the bar or the diner by remaining in one location. Whatever she actually chooses to do, she is being a prosumer in that she is making more choices about what she does and therefore what she experiences than she would at a conventional auditorium-based performance. With displayed fine art, it is generally the case that audiences can engage at their own pace and in their own time. The current increased potential for prosumerism in participatory art arises from the fact that it offers audiences many more opportunities to do something in relation to it, so they can determine their engagement and experience in far greater detail. For example, instead of simply observing the artworks, audiences can ride down Höller's slides, yell into Kapoor's *Marsyas* to explore its sonic potentials or run with or dodge the individual runners who, every 30 seconds, sprinted down the 86-metre length of Tate Britain's Duveen Galleries in Martin Creed's *Work No. 850* in 2008.

The prosumer may do labour formerly done for her by others; for example, she becomes her own bank teller, tutor, performance director, performer and/or artist. But for her trouble, she will expect – and, at least to some degree, receive – a product, service or event that is tailored to her specifications and desires. She is quite likely, therefore, to enjoy her experience of prosumerism; her work should not feel like work. More broadly, prosumerism might benefit society and the environment by reducing waste, as production schedules can reduce both stock and the labour of producing unwanted commodities or services by responding directly to demand instead of trying – and often failing – to predict it. As cultural geographer Nigel Thrift points out, prosumerism may also make production practices more ethical, as consumer demand stimulates ethical production. Thrift makes even bolder claims for prosumerism, arguing that its 'open innovation' can be seen as 'a means of challenging current property regimes by building new kinds of creative commons through a wider culture of knowledge' (2008, p. 54). He points out, 'some commentators argue that a democratization of innovation is occurring which enhances overall and not just corporate welfare' (ibid.).

But alongside these potential advantages, prosumerism has various drawbacks. Three drawbacks I focus on here relate to the uneven distribution of labour and pay, the penetration of work responsibilities into leisure time and several ways the prosumer is actually increasingly exploited rather than enabled by her prosumerism.

First, as the prosumer takes on certain tasks, often with the aid of developments in technology, these and other related tasks are at least partially lost to the very people who formerly performed them as paid workers. These latter people are often manual and/or service labourers, who are already comparatively less well remunerated than their managers. So prosumerism may apparently benefit the individual – as he gets to do more of what he wants in his own time – but its broader cultural effects may be disastrous, as it takes swathes of labourers out of paid employment, displaced by an army of unpaid prosuming volunteers, as we might see happening with *You Me Bum Bum Train*. Granted, a lot of the work that is assimilated by prosumers may be repetitive or may require little creativity or thought; it may thus be comparatively unsatisfying, even alienating work that is happily lost by those who previously performed it. On the other hand, some of this labour – for example, that of the tutor, the theatre director, the theatre technician, the artist, the designer and the actor – does require specialist skill, creativity and social engagement, all of which can be rewarding to perform. A second reward that is lost to workers, of course, is remuneration, as critics of *You Me Bum Bum Train* pointed out. Thirdly, workers lose their most important tool for protecting their labour. I recently received an email from an airline company regarding an impending strike by their customer service and sales staff. The airline advised me to check myself in online before venturing to the airport. Were I to undertake such labour, I would undermine the strikers' protest by, effectively, crossing their picket line, doing their work and effectively denying their right to *refuse* work. My adoption of the customer service staff's labour not only becomes an additional, possibly unwelcome task for me and a problematic dilution of my leisure time with labour; it also undermines one of the only legitimate ways that the workers can protest unfair labour conditions. Those who are already socially and economically disadvantaged, therefore, can become even more so as prosumerism withdraws some of their most satisfying labour, many of the ways they make a living and their means of protecting their livelihoods.

It may be difficult to see how this precise problem with prosumerism might seriously affect theatre and art practices which are already so often labours of love rather than labour which earns significant and/or steady remuneration. But here too, when a solo audience member downloads an audio walk, manual (technical) labourers will not be needed to run her show once someone has initially uploaded the artwork online, and administrators will not be required to book her tickets. On a larger scale, the rapid distribution – and apparent consolidation – of consumer opinion in Wiki review blogs at festivals such as the Edinburgh Fringe can quickly make or break shows. Thus, the prosuming Wiki contributor/theatregoer helps to determine (or produce) the festival market in ways that direct demand. Unfortunately, while some companies benefit enormously, others will feel like residual surplus 'stock', performing to small houses, effectively underemployed while nevertheless, of course, having laid out extensive initial investment in rehearsal time and space, design, venue hire, company fees and so on. In the prosuming theatre market, the prosumer may get what he wants, but to the detriment of a larger ecology of theatre and artwork and theatre and art labour.

Secondly, while there may be advantages for the prosumer to the ways the work of prosumerism is infused with leisure and fun, the inverse effect – that his or her leisure or simply non-work life may become infused with work – is likely less appealing and can be seriously damaging, making workers' 'entire life ... labor, an invisible and indivisible economy' (Lotringer, 2004, p. 12). In the scenario regarding the airline cited above, for example, if I check in myself, I draw the labour that is legitimately the airline's responsibility (and legitimately their expense) into my time, be it leisure time or otherwise. More insidiously, proliferating media of communication such as email, combined with what cultural studies theorist Melissa Gregg refers to as the mobile office's 'seduction of convenience' (2011, pp. 39ff.), result in people taking more and more labour out of regular work hours and regular spaces of work. Workers are constantly 'on call'; work is unstoppably dispersed, saturating all life; 'workaholism' is naturalized (de Peuter and Dyer-Witheford, 2006; Oakley, 2009a, p. 47); and the last vestiges of private, intimate life, relationships and emotions are, often unwittingly and gradually, sacrificed to work.

In theatre, problems produced by this kind of penetration of work into leisure – problems such as the erosion of genuine intimacy – is manifested in the ways that immersive theatre works to individualize everyone's experience, socially isolating them, as well as in its practices of deeply seducing audiences into apparently rich worlds, only to abandon them at the show's end. Not untypically, Nancy Groves (2011) concluded her review of *YMBBT* for *What's On Stage*: 'And then, just like that, you're plunged, blinking, back into reality'. Further evidence of these problems is notable in expressions of audience fatigue with having to make the work for oneself, whether one wants to or not, and especially when one finds the outcome of such work unsatisfying in ways that suggest theatre companies are neglecting their responsibilities to make good work. This attitude is implicit in *Guardian* culture columnist Charlotte Higgins's remarks at the end of a pretty disappointed review of an immersive theatre event: 'As we left the theatre, I found myself saying to my friend: "For god's sake, bring back the fourth wall. And seats"' (2009). Higgins longs not to be 'poked and prodded' by performers in an immersive theatre event that she apparently found superficial. Implicitly, she registers her objection to being co-opted to participate/work in a performance which, for her, is unsuccessful. Furthermore, she longs for a theatre which is less content simply to be immersive and which takes seriously its professional responsibility to do more affectively and intellectually than this piece did for her.

Thirdly, while the prosumer may believe himself to be empowered by his opportunities to produce what he wants to consume, there are several ways that this opportunity may be more exploitative than enabling. While he may feel that he is prosuming as he desires, *what* he can actually prosume may be severely restricted in ways that are obscure to him. For example, for the prosumer who tailors his own shoes online, simply having the opportunity to design his bespoke shoe encourages him to feel self-actualizing and naturalizes that feeling. But that self-actualization is limited by such considerations as the fact that he is likely to be offered only a very limited range of tailoring options, and the fact that at least some of his choices are apt to be prompted by the shoe company or its agents. Further to this point, contrary to my suggestion above that prosumerism might diminish waste by increasing efficiency, it might instead increase waste by stimulating unnecessary over-consumption. Capitalizing on the pleasure and sense of empowerment the prosumer often feels in his prosumption, companies and organizations he interacts with often ruthlessly attempt to convert this literally happy prosumerism outcome into yet more prosumerism by automatically generating a series of recommendations phrased along the lines of, 'If you liked this, you might also like this'. Many a prosumer is seduced into producing and consuming more, given the sense that such prompts have been provoked and actively produced by his taste. More precisely of course, what has been 'active' is not so much his taste as his consumption, patterns in which have accumulated to build a customer profile which the company he is interacting with now works to exploit to their benefit. The prosumer does not act originally let alone critically; he provides 'benign acclimation' (Warner, 2002, p. 50) to neoliberal consumer logics fed incessantly to him.

The naturalization of the prosumer's sense of empowerment is visible in immersive theatre in the expectations it has accrued about offering its individual audience member experiences which are both unique to him alone, and specially, qualitatively enhanced for him. The uniqueness of these experiences is predicated on the fact that he designs them through his particular practices of participation, including, for example, his selection of specific routes through them. In one-to-one performance, this sense of uniqueness is also a function of the perceived privacy of the performance encounter; it is easier to preserve the idea that one's experience is singular when engagement is direct and if one does not observe others having the same experience. Sometimes, this experience may be unique and meaningful. However, it may also offer, again, a spectre of uniqueness that reinforces the prosumer's *sense* of her authorial power while actually offering little such power.

There are real potential social advantages to be had in the prosumer trend, especially its invitation to the audience member to take more creative initiative in making her own experience of an art- or theatre-work. However, the prosumer experience also risks eroding paid, distributed labour; saturating all time with work time; eroding private life; and reducing the quality of our experiences of art as, distracted by the spectres of distributed authorship and experience over content, neither prosuming audience member nor immersive theatre company, for example, takes sufficient responsibility for the quality of performance outcomes.

Everyone is all: collective labour

Thus far, I have focused primarily on how *the individual* benefits or not through the labour relations that are modelled in these forms of performance and art practice. A focus on the individual is important because this practice seems to guarantee the individual agency, self-articulation, self-realization, flexibility, pleasure, autonomy and independence; an offering which is attractive and yet, as I have shown above, often compromised. But this apparent promise of individual independence is also problematic for its implicit denigration of *dependence* on others. Here, I explore in more detail than I have above how these art and performance practices stage groups' and people's social interdependence.

Why is it important to consider how this work stages groups? Contemporary neoliberal cultures venerate independence, celebrating individuals who are entrepreneurial self-starters (as I explore in more detail in the book's next chapter), and 'treating those who are dependent on the state with the suspicion that they are social parasites, rather than truly helpless' (Sennett, 1998, p. 139). In his 2012 autumn mini-budget statement, UK Chancellor George Osborne implied that those dependent on state support were lazy, work-shy 'shirkers', witnessed by their neighbours going off to work as 'still asleep, living a life on benefits' (Osborne, 2012), rather than genuinely in need of help in an economy that is in recession and that increasingly privileges the already privileged.

Such neoliberal attitudes are both deficient and damaging, personally and socially, as Richard Sennett observes in *The Corrosion of Character*, forcefully subtitled, *The Personal Consequences of Work in the New Capitalism*. 'A more positive view of dependence', he argues, 'would first of all challenge the commonplace opposition of dependence and independence' (Sennett, 1998. p. 140), and it would recognize that people are necessarily interdependent. With reference to the work of psychologist John Bowlby, he notes that even people who are apparently most soundly self-reliant know that they must trust, rely and depend on others when their own abilities or resources are inadequate (ibid., p. 140; Bowlby, 1973, p. 359). Sennett's project across much of his work is to make the case that people are socially interdependent; that neoliberal structures of work damage people by, for example, exploiting, alienating and isolating workers; and that it is necessary to reclaim, repair and/or invent work structures that restore constructive, humane social relations. As I hope is clear, I share Sennett's commitment to understanding sound sociality not as based on the celebration of the individual but as interdependent, collaborative and mutually supportive. However, I also share his and others' recognition that not all groups produce positive social relations; groups can be hierarchical, only superficially collaborative, exclusive and corrupt. So it is important to consider how the art and performance practices I am exploring in this chapter constitute, not only individuals, but also groups and social relations. How, I ask, might this constitution mitigate against the celebration of individualism as well as limits to individual agency, and how might it model sound interdependent group relations, genuine collaboration and mutual support.

Although much of the performance and art work I am exploring in this part of the book apparently delegates to individuals, it is almost always experienced in groups and therefore invites consideration of how it constitutes group relations. Here, I first outline the ways this work produces groups and then I explore the qualities of the social relations it stages. I acknowledge that these relations risk being problematically superficial and temporary. However, I suggest that they sometimes redress those problems by being qualitatively powerful, especially by cultivating shared feelings, and by self-reflexively drawing attention to their places in broader social networks. They thus offer, as a kind of public art, what art and public policy theorist Randy Martin identifies in a slightly different context as 'a medium for people to gather together to reflect on the very idea of being together' (2006, p. 4). Group modelling in these art practices offers participants opportunities to explore the possibilities as well as the risks of the 'networked society' and at least to begin to model relations of shared, more equitable responsibility and care.

Formally, much of this work is specifically experienced by and in groups as audiences, rather than solely as individuals. This makes it different from many of the forms of prosumerism discussed above, where the perceived quality of the individual's prosuming experience rests precisely on the ways it works with and for his or her autonomous independence. Much delegated performance and artwork specifically addresses and engages its audiences as groups, allowing them to act individually in certain ways, but usually alongside other audience members, and therefore often in concert or collaboration with them. Sometimes, audiences in this work are explicitly formed into groups; for example, when cohorts of audience members are gradually released into the space of Punchdrunk's *Faust* (though they are not required to stay together), or when groups of audience members are seated at tables together in discussion groups in *Make Better Please* and later in that show, when everyone is asked to pay attention to the same things at the same time.[8] Sometimes, the formation of groups happens more organically, as when audiences gather at particular points and places in immersive theatre. In large-scale installation art contexts such as the Tate Modern Turbine Hall, the individual audience member can determine what he or she does to a certain extent; for example, she chooses whether to ride down one of Höller's slides, to lie down on the floor to gaze on Eliasson's mirrored ceiling or to speak into Kapoor's vaulting, stretched-skin *Marsyas*. But the audience member's experience of her individual act is almost necessarily influenced by other audience members participating in the artwork at the same time.[9] Work in the Turbine Hall and other similar sites of large-scale installation art is almost necessarily relational, relying on and engaging with the ways that audiences interact with one another, whether that engagement is about simply observing each other or more active interaction. Even 'only' watching others can be interactive in that what they do can trigger one's own feelings and actions. The mere sight of someone else embarking with excitement on Höller's five-storey slide might fill an onlooker with trepidation; seeing someone else spell out a letter with her body on the floor of the Turbine Hall to have it reflected in Eliasson's far-away mirrored ceiling might inspire an onlooker to spell out a response.

Even art and performance works which are experienced apparently much more autonomously – including apparently alone – often incorporate interaction with others. For example, Blast Theory's performance *Rider Spoke* (first presented in London at the Barbican in 2007) invited individual audience members to mount a bicycle fitted with a mini-computer and to travel off on self-selected routes, electronically gathering stories 'deposited' previously by Blast Theory and other riders as well as recording one's own, which future riders would then be alerted to when they traversed those stories' recording locations (see Harvie, 2009a). The piece was experienced individually insofar as riders were encouraged to cycle alone and to make their own paths and associated stories; but it was experienced as a group, or perhaps a network, in that individuals heard each others' stories, could respond to them and knew that the stories they were creating would be there for future audience members. Formally, as well as politically, therefore, it is fitting to consider this work's production of, and opportunities for, groups; to see it as what Shannon Jackson (2011) resonantly refers to, literally and metaphorically, as 'social works'.

It is politically important to do so, as discussed above and as Jackson reminds us, because it might model social relations of mutual support as well as what curator and critic Maria Lind identifies as an 'intrinsic critique of individualism and profit-seeking' (2007, p. 28). So, what are these relations? One might argue that, as these forms of practice hold out the apparent promise of granting individual agency and only partially fulfil that promise, the group connections they appear to offer might problematically be – by definition – temporary, and therefore likely also superficial or, as art historian Stephen Wright puts it, 'frivolous' (Lind, 2007, p. 21; Wright, 2004). Audiences are not invited to form lasting relationships with fellow visitors to the Turbine Hall, a Punchdrunk show, Uninvited Guests' *Make Better Please* or Blast Theory's *Rider Spoke*. If audiences are interdependent in these contexts, that interdependence is modest at best, relying on shared negotiation of space, some discussion or some storytelling. One could say this social modelling is modest, and at worst superficial and distracting, seeming to offer social bonds which are, in fact, thin.

However, one could also argue that these practices model social relations which are relevant to contemporary lived experiences, offering contexts to explore and understand those experiences. These works might help audiences to explore their place in a networked society, where people tend to know a little about a lot of people through, for example, social networking sites, and multiple blogs instead of one's daily newspaper and favourite columnist. Admittedly, this art practice's engagement in networked culture might seem to acquiesce regrettably – or indefensibly – to the idea that the deeply connected social culture which Sennett longs for in some – old – models of labour is no more, and gone with it is the sense of responsibility to others integral to that culture. Alternatively, this engagement in networked culture need not deny the coexistence of those models of sociality and mutual responsibility, at the same time as it facilitates creative engagement with both networked culture's potentials – for meaningful if brief encounters and for wide connectivity and mutual responsibility across degrees of otherness – and its limitations and frustrations, such as its superficiality and its posturing as the sole, obligatory way to engage in culture.

Likewise, many of the practices I have referred to in this part of the book draw self-reflexively on the networks of labour that enable them – the dancers in Collins's *they shoot horses*, the workers in Sierra's works, but also the discussants that audiences are turned into in *Make Better Please* and the storytelling riders audiences become in *Rider Spoke*. Social interconnectedness in this work provides not only the work's content but, manifestly, its possibility. This work might not provide powerfully connected groups, but it does often provide reminders of the vast, pervasive networks of mutual support in and by which we live. And, in the cases cited just above at least, it highlights people's mutual responsibility to each other, even where it portrays that responsibility as betrayed.

Richard Sennett refers to 'we' as 'the dangerous pronoun', acknowledging that the 'usage "we" has become an act of self-protection' in contexts where 'the desire for community is defensive, often expressed as rejection of immigrants or other outsiders' (1998, pp. 136–8). But he argues that the pronoun can be, should be and is invoked to seek a 'shared fate', which works together to achieve common purposes, for example, to challenge and resist the oppressive labour conditions of the new capitalism and the potential social anaemia of societies so broadly networked and work-saturated that they cannot sustain deep relationships. The kinds of art and performance practices discussed in this part of the book provide opportunities to explore and practice the 'we' even where 'we' may be attenuated across vast networks, and to practise collaboration, interdependence and a 'social imaginary', however modest (Warner, 2002, p. 12).

Conclusion

In some privileged global contexts, work and culture are changing in ways that seem to offer individuals more. At work, patterns of increased flexibility and outsourcing suggest the worker can be more self-directing and self-actualized, have more autonomy and more voice and choose to do only the work she prefers, to a schedule she designs in a work-life balance she determines. In art and culture, patterns of increased audience engagement and participation propose the audience member can likewise be more self-directing and self-actualized, have more autonomy and be the artist-maker who creates the artwork and/or performance to her specifications and designs. As this chapter has explored, however, these changes to the engagement of workers and audiences are neither straightforwardly nor entirely beneficial. Work's increased flexibility can alternatively be seen to disadvantage most workers, jeopardizing their authority over their work in a market crowded with competitors, relying on the exploitation of many to fulfil the job satisfactions of a few and producing a way of working and living that feels less carefree and flexible and more precarious, insecure and work-dominated. Similarly, in art and performance, the audience to whom responsibility to make the artwork has been delegated can find that her opportunities to create or intervene are limited; that social hierarchies are not only preserved but, insidiously, naturalized; that she is conscripted to participate in ways she does not want to; that the quality of the artwork produced is negatively affected by the dispersal of responsibility for the work and the deskilling that dispersal can inadvertently produce; that her leisure time becomes increasingly saturated by labour; and that the labour provided by her and by others is exploited.

However, the delegation of responsibility to audiences can also have other constructive effects. First, it can powerfully bring to audiences' attention precisely these problems with contemporary labour dynamics cited above by enacting them, highlighting them and embedding audiences in their antagonisms, as does the work of Phil Collins and Santiago Sierra. Further, it can help audiences to recognize their social responsibility for such labour dynamics and for social dynamics more broadly by, again, embedding them in those dynamics. As Nicholas

Ridout argues, the fact that performance is a service economy – and not simply a reflection of it – 'enables it to enact some kind of critique of its procedures' (2008, p. 128). In this context, delegated art and performance can help audiences not only to identify and critique problematic social relations but also begin to resist them, and to seek to form better social relations by participating in models not so much of delegation but of shared responsibility and mutual dependence, however provisional those models might be.

2
The 'Artrepreneur': Artists and Entrepreneurialism

Introduction: the entrepreneurial arist

This chapter asks what it means, now, to be an artist. It asks partly because the question of what it means to be an artist is relevant to so many people, given the participatory trends in art and performance which the last chapter explored and which increasingly encourage everyone to be artists. But this chapter asks not just who artists are, but what artists are now because current social, economic and political contexts, in England in particular but also more widely in the United Kingdom, are radically reconfiguring what an artist is expected to be and, in so doing, putting the value of being an artist at serious ideological risk.

Political, economic and social mandates to foster creative economies are increasingly casting art practice as economic practice and the artist as entrepreneur. Funding regimes in particular regularly exhort artists to model creative entrepreneurialism, marked by independence and the ability to take initiative, take risks, self-start, think laterally, problem-solve, innovate ideas and practices, be productive, effect impact and realize or at least stimulate financial profits. This emphasis on artists as creative entrepreneurs – or 'artrepreneurs' or 'culturepreneurs'[1] as some would have it – is not damaging insofar as it accurately describes, indeed celebrates, many artistic qualities which are socially valuable and highly desirable, not least because they are expedient, helping artists to survive and sometimes thrive even while formerly semi-stable sources of public support for arts practices erode. I will return to the potential benefits of 'artrepeneurialism' below.

But the bulk of this chapter focuses on the potentially detrimental effects of hegemonic expectations imposed on artists to model entrepreneurialism in ways that both indulge and inherently celebrate neoliberal capitalism. I argue that because the 'artrepreneur' works privately for her own advantage, she models neoliberalism, the contemporary form of economic practice that privileges the 'liberty' of individuals to trade as they please and, in so doing, promotes private enterprise within apparently 'free' or 'open' markets over publicly regulated economies.

I argue further that artists' implicit requirement to model entrepreneurialism and to prioritize its values potentially damages artists, art and culture in three crucial ways. One, it insists that art prioritizes self-interest and individualism. Two, it requires art to acquiesce to creative destruction as an apparently inevitable by-product of innovation (I elaborate on what 'creative destruction' means later in the chapter). And three, it obliges art relentlessly to pursue productivity, permanent growth and profit. Crudely articulated, such insalubrious capitalist characteristics might often (though certainly not always) struggle to thrive within art's domain; but dressed up *as art*, exploiting the artist's attractive characteristics as whitewashing disguise, they pass, bringing their invidious effects along with them.

However, this chapter is not wholly alarmist and cautionary. It does argue that artists are under pressure to capitulate to neoliberal capitalist risks of selfish individualism, destruction as an apparently necessary consequence of innovation and growth for growth's sake. However, it also argues that artists are both highlighting and challenging such risks. Overall, the chapter explores how contemporary artists resist being wholly appropriated as tools of neoliberal capitalist skills training and ideological modelling, and instead continue to develop their work in ways that are both aesthetically and socially valuable, even if emerging conditions require they cultivate new ways of doing so.

Admittedly, the 'problem' of 'the absorption of the artist into the Culture Industry' has been what creative industries analyst Justin O'Connor identifies as 'a key index of cultural catastrophe' at least since the eighteenth century, when an understanding of the artist as 'radically free creative genius' became central 'to the western art tradition' (O'Connor, 2010, p. 25), not to mention to culture more broadly. What sets this problem apart in the early twenty-first century is the particular way that the artist's 'absorption' is taking place – as entrepreneur – and the multiplicity and strength of the powers that are driving it. This chapter begins by developing an understanding of what characterizes an entrepreneur and by detailing manifold ways that artists are being produced as, compelled to be and interpellated as entrepreneurs – through creative industries' aspirations, cultural policy discourses and funding regimes. It considers some of the potential benefits of entrepreneurialism for art and for artists. It then focuses on the problems – to do with individualism, creative destruction and profit-driven productivity – that entrepreneurialism produces for artists and art practice. And it considers some of the critical responses and challenges to those problems that artists have devised, for example by forming horizontal networks of support that challenge individualism, pursuing the putative logic of creative destruction to its conclusions, and exploring the value of craftsmanship despite neoliberal cultural pressures that emphasize growth, productivity and profit.

This chapter's concentration on how artists are being conscripted as entrepreneurs offers a focused way into a broader question regarding how artists, arts and culture are currently being instrumentalized as economically important. Coming in many forms, such instrumentalization includes artists' employment within non-arts industries as communication coaches and creativity experts (see Atavar, 2012; Stevenson, 2012).[2] It includes artists' apparently willing engagement with – or cultivation of – exorbitant art prices; consider the example of Damien Hirst, one of the original 'Young British Artists' of the late-1980s to late-1990s and apparently the richest contemporary artist in the world in 2009, when *The Sunday Times* 'Rich List' valued him at £235 million (Gleadell, 2012). Art's economic instrumentalization has, however, perhaps most wholly transpired through its recognition – or mobilization, depending on how you look at it – as a crucial part of the cultural industries. At least since New Labour's 1997 election, UK governments have heralded the cultural industries as economic miracles, sent to save the United Kingdom from post-industrial ruin. They have been credited with providing over 7 per cent of UK employment in 2001 and average incomes 37 per cent higher than in the UK economy as a whole in 2006 (Higgs, Cunningham and Bakhshi, 2008, pp. 5, 6, 55). Some claim they provide twice the European average contribution to GDP at 6–7 per cent of UK GDP (Burrows and Ussher, 2011, p. 12; European Commission, 2010, p. 183). As captains of the cultural industries dubiously like to boast, this is as much as is contributed by the financial industries.[3] All of these – and many more – are ways that art practices are currently particularly embroiled with economics that prioritize productivity, growth and profit. I do not mean to argue that instead of making money, art should, either solely or directly, be doing the work of social democracy – addressing sources and effects of social inequality and seeking collective good. But I do mean to argue that it is important to reflect critically on art's apparently ever-expanding relationship with – or imbrications in – neoliberal economies, with their emphasis on individual self-interest, and to explore how art might better support social democracy's commitments to collective good.

Where considerations of art's relationship to commercial culture often look at objects of exchange – what audiences attend and shoppers buy – I am focusing on subjects – who is making art, what kind of artists those artists are compelled to be and what practices they are expected to perform. This is not because I think what is made is irrelevant to understanding how power and value circulate; I do not think that, as I hope my examination below of examples of art practices illustrates. Rather, my focus reflects my concern with the ways neoliberal capitalism infiltrates and reconfigures *structures, practices* and *subjectivities*, not just objects, in ways that potentially extend its effects while simultaneously, dangerously, naturalizing them. This chapter argues that the pressures of neoliberal capitalism as manifested in increasing demands made on artists to act as entrepreneurs are indeed destructive, multiple and insidious, but also that art practices are demonstrating inspiring ways of highlighting those pressures, and of challenging them (see Sholette, 2011).

How is the artist entrepreneurial? Basic connections between the artist and the entrepreneur are not difficult to find. Derived from the French word *entreprendre*, to undertake, an entrepreneur is someone who sets up a business and takes on financial risk in the hope of profit (Stevenson, 2010). Economists highlight the necessity for the entrepreneur to be risk-taking, while sociologists tend to 'define the entrepreneur as a creative innovator in the business sphere', differentiated from the conventional business-person, 'who conforms more often to established procedures and objectives' (Scott and Marshall, 2009). Entrepreneurs and artists can generally be seen to share special capacities for risk-taking and innovation, or what economist Jason Potts calls 'the "human capital" of creativity, novelty generation, new interpretations and meanings' and 'the creative skills and abilities that enable humans to continually change and adapt' (Potts, 2011, p. 3). Those who promote the growth of entrepreneurial creative industries are often, not surprisingly, especially keen to make connections between entrepreneurs and artists: for example, a 2007 publication by the employment think-tank the Work Foundation enthuses that 'The creative impulse everywhere has certain characteristics in common, whether in an entrepreneur or a performing artist: a certain level of expertise, the willingness to take the risks and the motivation derived from the pleasure of doing the job' (Work Foundation, 2007, p. 69).

But why is the artist under pressure to behave increasingly entrepreneurially? This pressure comes from at least three key, connected sources. First, in the face of declining or simply disappearing traditional industries in manufacturing and mining, post-Fordist, so-called 'developed' economies have been anxiously seeking ways to diversify and expand industries with capacity for growth; a notoriously important sector in such economic growth strategies has been the creative industries, which associates of UK public policy think-tank Demos, Helen Burrows and Kitty Ussher (2011, back cover), call 'the UK's "Cinderella sector"', presumably for its belated recognition as hard-working and heroic, not to mention – in at least some respects – glamorous. Second, in this context, artists have been pressed to grow their industries and be more business-like in the process. In concluding *Creative Nation: Advancing Britain's Creative Industries*, published by the Smith Institute, 'an independent think tank ... set up to undertake research and education in issues that flow from the changing relationship between social values and economic imperatives' (Koester, 2006, p. 3), editor Cathy Koester argues that 'Britain should marry the commercial drive of the US with the artistic innovation of the European art-house scene in order to avoid the excesses of both' (ibid., p. 114). Third, such post-industrial economies simultaneously seek more entrepreneurs; as *A Dictionary of Finance and Banking* notes, '[i]n modern capitalist economies the initiative of entrepreneurs is regarded as an important element in creating a society's wealth; governments are therefore encouraged to establish conditions in which they will thrive' (Law and Smullen, 2008). Post-industrial capitalist economies bent on permanent growth want both more creative industries and more entrepreneurial innovation and risk-taking; the perfect hybrid of these requirements is entrepreneurial creative industry practitioners, or, entrepreneurial artists. An *Art Monthly* commentator observes, 'Indeed, in the era of info-capital and the rise of the creative industries the artist has become the model worker. Innovation, flexibility, creativity – these are valued above all' (Millar, 2012).

These various pressures on artists to behave entrepreneurially are manifested both indirectly and directly. Indirectly, they are expressed through the contraction of formerly available public structures of support such as government arts funding and arts agencies, a contraction which compels artists to build such support independently, a topic I address in detail in Chapter 4. Directly, they are manifested through creative industries' management discourses and civic-, national- and international-level policy discourses and funding regimes that appear to be multiplying exponentially. I offer below some examples of these directly manifested pressures in order to show their growing pervasiveness, naturalization and aggressiveness across UK cultural economies since the late 1980s, and to identify some of the ideologies they prioritize and seek to propagate.

Creative industries management and policy discourses

Justin O'Connor outlines how, from as early as the late-1980s in some post-industrial settings, '[c]ultural workers were no longer to be characterised as creatives crushed by the wheels of a corporate sector whose values they resisted as best they could; it was precisely these people who were in possession of the means to operate most effectively' in the emerging 'knowledge economy' (O'Connor, 2010, p. 37). The most important of creative workers' 'means to operate most successfully' (read: to realize profit) was their creativity, coupled with their capacity for enterprise, qualities which were both catalyst and reactant in an economy experiencing 'culturalization' as it abandoned old organizational structures, and sought models for change and growth precisely in cultural practice. From the beginnings of its governments in 1997, New Labour fiercely pursued this model of creative economy. Reflecting back on New Labour's relationship with the arts over its first decade in government, then-Prime Minister Tony Blair gave an important speech at Tate Modern on 6 March, 2007.

> Years ago, before coming to government, I said that we would make the arts and culture part of our 'core script' .... I didn't say it because I thought we, as a government, were of great importance to you, the arts, but rather because you, the arts, were going to be of fundamental importance to the country.
>
> A country like Britain today survives and prospers by the talent and ability of its people. Human capital is key. The more it is developed, the better we are. Modern goods and services require high-value added input. Some of it comes from technology or financial capital – both instantly transferable. Much of it comes from people – their ability to innovate, to think anew, to be creative. Such people are broad-minded: they thrive on curiosity about the next idea; they welcome the challenge of an open world. Such breadth of mind is enormously enhanced by interaction with art and culture.
>
> ... A nation that cares about art will not just be a better nation. In the early 21st Century it will be a more successful one.
>
> (Blair, 2007; see Holden, 2007, p. 30)

Labour's advocacy of the creative industries throughout their terms of government from 1997 to 2010 is exemplified in the creative industries infrastructures they built: they published numerous creative industries mapping documents (see DCMS, 1998, 2001; Harvie, 2003, 2005, ch. 2; Smith, 1998), they formed the Creative Economy Programme (launched in November 2005 and followed by a major policy document in 2008), they encouraged higher education to develop entrepreneurs for the creative industries (DCMS, 2006), and more (see DCMS, 2008). It is also evident in their establishment in 1998 of NESTA, the National Endowment for Science, Technology and the Arts, set up 'to stimulate a more receptive climate for innovation and creativity in the United Kingdom' (Glinkowski, 2007, p. 33). New Labour advocated mercilessly for the creative industries, explicitly recognizing, in the words of their first and long-standing Culture Minister Chris Smith, '[t]he importance of the entrepreneur' in the context of the growing cultural industries, as 'highlighted in the Government's [1998] Competitiveness White Paper' and in its position of 'high priority on the agenda of the Creative Industries Task Force' (Smith, 2000, p. 7).

Evidence of this cultural shift under New Labour to demanding that artists act in increasingly entrepreneurial ways is almost everywhere, so a few examples will have to suffice. *Theatre Assessment 2009*, conducted and published by Arts Council England (ACE), examined the health of the theatre industry over the bulk of the first decade of the twenty-first century. In what feels like a comparatively rare instance of recognition by a state-associated apparatus of some of the perils of arts' increasing entrepreneurialism, the *Assessment* reports that a number of people in the industry whom it consulted 'expressed worries about the proliferation of unpaid internships... often for work which previously would have been remunerated, and were dependent on the intern having some sort of family or other support' (ACE, 2009a, p. 51). In the period under the *Assessment*'s review, in a sample of 74 organizations that were then receiving regular Arts Council funding, the number of volunteer workers who managed 'entrepreneurially' to support their free labour doubled to almost 1400 (ibid., p. 65, fig. 15).

It is not only unpaid internships which proliferate in the arts under New Labour but, to an even greater degree, self-employment and freelancing. Writing in 2007, Ralph Brown notes that while only 13 per cent of the UK's total labour force are self-employed, '[i]n the creative sector 34 per cent of individuals work on a self-employed basis' (Brown, 2007, p. 127). Freelancing and self-employment are, he claims, 'the most frequent types of employment in the creative sector, and there are particularly large concentrations of small enterprises and sole traders in music and the performing arts, film, TV and radio. Estimates have suggested that less than 50 per cent of employment in the arts sector involves a primary occupation – people doing one type of work' (ibid., p. 127; Summerton, 2001, pp. 8–9).

Labour governments' advocacy of the creative industries was picked up by the Conservative-led coalition government elected in spring 2010, which signalled its understanding of culture as embedded in industry by, amongst other things, creating a ministerial portfolio which actually captures both: Culture, Communications and Creative Industries, held by Conservative MP Ed Vaizey since 2010. Conservative Prime Minister David Cameron expressed his will to continue to put support 'behind those industries where Britain enjoys competitive advantage' in a speech to the Confederation of British Industry (CBI) in October 2010, claiming, 'We have great industrial strengths across our country, underpinned by world-beating companies ... [including] creative industries in London, Manchester and Glasgow' (Burrows and Ussher, 2011, p. 11; Cameron, 2010). His government's advocacy of artistic entrepreneurialism has filtered directly into policy produced by Arts Council England (ACE). In December 2010, ACE published a booklet commissioned by the then Secretary of State for Culture, Media and Sport (DCMS), Conservative Jeremy Hunt, *Endowments in the Arts*, a would-be handbook for arts organizations on seeking and securing private funding. In 2011, ACE, the Heritage Lottery Fund and the DCMS followed up that handbook with real money, launching the £100m Catalyst Scheme which aims 'to boost private giving to the cultural sector and build long-term resilience, sustainability and innovation' through schemes designed to develop endowments and other forms of private funding (ACE, 2011a), provided arts organizations can master the necessary entrepreneurial 'culture of asking' which *Endowments in the Arts* suggests 'is arguably a more critical factor for success than the culture of giving' (ACE, 2010b, p. 21).[4] (I address this emphasis on entrepreneurialism in arts funding cultures in more detail in Chapter 4 of this book.)

Trends in policy and culture not only to support the creative industries but to insist they are seen and practised precisely *as* industries reach a kind of zenith in the policy document published by ACE in July 2011. I examine *Supporting Growth in the Arts Economy* in some detail below because of both the ideas it advocates and the force with which it does so. It reads as a two-headed command to artists to be more business-like, and to ACE to support artists in being so (Fleming and Erskine, 2011). In his section of the Foreword to the document, ACE Chief Executive Alan Davey sets up what he sees as the economic necessity for this instruction.

> It is commonly acknowledged that the arts are the bedrock of the creative economy, making a significant contribution to the nation's

> prosperity and its international reputation. Yet, as we look to make the arts more sustainable we are also interested in how the sector can operate more effectively in a commercial environment, by learning from creative businesses and making better use of finance.
>
> ... [I]t is essential for the Arts Council to develop our thinking around how we can build mutually beneficial links between the arts sector and the creative economy.
>
> (Davey, 2011, pp. 1–2)

In his own brief section of the Foreword, Vaizey implicitly mandates the arts to merge more fully with the creative industries. He admires the UK's 'most innovative arts organisations in the world, which continually look beyond their own sector, and work with other industries and technologies to help develop both their art and their audiences'. And he states (or possibly instructs), 'I firmly believe that the lines will continue to blur between what we consider the arts ecology and the creative economy' (Vaizey, 2011).

Supporting Growth authors Tom Fleming and Andrew Erskine argue that the arts simply need to become more business-like: 'The Arts Council recognises that ... business models for arts organisations need to change' (Fleming and Erskine, 2011, p. 6). They elaborate on the – economic – importance of this commitment to change:

> To develop a sustainable and resilient arts sector that delivers multiple types of value to the nation requires constant innovation, a willingness to adapt organisational and business models, and an openness to change – the relationship between producer and consumer, investor and investee, artform-specific and interdisciplinary [*sic*], and the balance between intrinsic and instrumental [*sic*]. ... Organisations that are able to exploit the productive tensions between any of the above will be the most successful.
>
> One such productive tension can be seen in the relationship between a notional 'arts ecology' (driven by intrinsic arts and cultural activities; expressive of a social relationship between producers and audiences; strongly linked to public investment and not-for-profit activities), and a 'creative economy' (driven as much by commercial as artistic and cultural factors; expressive of an economic and social transaction between producers and markets; operating in a mixed economy of different types of private investment, alongside public investment).
>
> (2011, pp. 6–7)

Having 'notionally' set up a binary opposition between an 'arts ecology' and a 'creative economy', they acknowledge first what the 'arts ecology' contributes to the 'creative economy', though they rename 'individual artists' as 'micro-creative businesses' in the process:

> This paper ... asserts that the range of core development activities and outcomes delivered from arts organisations is critical to the growth and sustainability of the creative economy. It also reasserts that individual artists are themselves micro-creative businesses and the organisations they support and are supported by are providers of talent, ideas, content and markets for the wider creative economy.
>
> (Fleming and Erskine, 2011, p. 7)

Having nodded to the value of the 'arts ecology', they proceed to lecture artists/'micro-creative businesses' on the necessity of becoming more business-like, or more fully signed up to the creative economy. They demonstrate how 'arts organisations and practitioners are realigning the way they work and the way they think about their work, to embed approaches and adopt business models that deliver a dual outcome of artistic and economic value' (ibid., p. 7). They simply refute naysayers who might argue that conscripting the arts into the service of creative economies risks damaging arts' intrinsic worth (let alone other non-financial values). Indeed, by their reckoning, art practised entrepreneurially miraculously produces better art effects: 'by working more entrepreneurially, flexibly and openly across the overall ecology (thus relieving some of the "creative economy imperative"), art will not only get better, but it will be enjoyed by more people, on their own terms, and in deeper and more interactive ways' (ibid., p. 7). Their introduction concludes by simply mandating artists to be more business-like. They write,

> it is not enough to focus on the arts ecology and enjoy its positive influence on the creative economy. To ensure sustainability, resilience and growth across the arts requires an approach that invests in the interface between the arts ecology and creative economy: supporting arts organisations to develop new business models that encourage different value chains to flourish; enabling talent to progress and knowledge to flow between organisations and businesses; and brokering different types of partnership and co-investment.
>
> (Fleming and Erskine, 2011, pp. 7–8)

As becomes increasingly clear over the arc of their introduction, though Fleming and Erskine are keen to credit the value that arts practices contribute to creative industries, they are principally concerned to drag recalcitrant artists more fully into the fold of the profitable, entrepreneurial creative industries. In their view, 'too few [arts organisations] "cross-over" to establish a coherent commercial offer; they struggle to articulate their value to investors; and the organisational narrative can be too dependent on a relatively narrow source of public investment' (ibid., p. 24). Thankfully, the 'creative economy' is at hand to model a remedy for this failing 'arts ecology': 'Sustainable and resilient organisations have deep and collaborative relationships with funders and keenly maximise the yield of their [intellectual property] and services. They embed an entrepreneurial culture across all activities, pursue new business models to drive innovation and, as a result, they innovate with their audiences' (ibid., p. 24). Because the apparently silly arts ecology 'rarely [puts innovation] at the heart of operational and strategic thinking' and adheres 'to old business models', it foolishly 'stifles growth overall, stymies talent development, and reduces potential for collaboration' (ibid., p. 24). Once again, the creative economies come riding to the rescue, demonstrating 'an embrace with openness – in how art is developed, presented and made into something commercial' as well as 'commitment to "sweating" assets and ideas more entrepreneurially' (ibid., p. 24).

Fleming and Erskine may claim to focus on 'maximising the capacity of the arts to reach and enthral audiences', but it is very difficult not to see this as being in service to 'maximising [...] the agility of the arts and collaborators in creative businesses to nurture markets, revenue and investment as a direct outcome of audience development' in order to make 'markets grow' and 'the creative economy enter ... a new period of competitiveness' (ibid., pp. 32–3). They advocate continued public investment in 'growing the relationship between the arts and creative economy' but rhetorically assume, 'Clearly prioritisation will be required on programmes, organisations and initiatives that will deliver the highest ROI [return on investment]' (ibid., p. 81).

Supporting Growth aggressively and explicitly advises arts practitioners to behave in more business-like ways and it tries to make the economic case for the opportunities it feels can be realized by following this advice. What the document is less explicit about are the things that its advice puts in jeopardy. One such thing is the arts themselves: though the business-focused approach to the arts advocated by Fleming and Erskine need not necessarily obliterate artistic effects, it will certainly de-prioritize and potentially endanger them. A second thing jeopardized – through an emphasis on competitiveness – is collaborative sociality. And a third thing is, simply, humanity: a commitment to exploiting – or 'sweating' – assets may, after all, include exploiting human assets.

Supporting Growth was specifically endorsed by ACE's Chief Executive and the Conservative Minister for Culture, Communications and Creative Industries, Ed Vaizey. Indeed, for Vaizey and others the culture change Fleming and Erskine advocate had already been achieved. A 2008 conference on 'The Art of Giving' held at Tate Modern included a discussion on 'Locating the Artist in Public Funding'. Conference organizer Paul Glinkowski summarized some of the attitudes expressed there, including those of Munira Mirza, appointed in May 2008 as Director of Arts, Culture and the Creative Industries Policy to the Conservative Mayor of London, Boris Johnson. Glinkowski wrote that Mirza commented,

> in her experience artists were more entrepreneurial and better at developing strategies for economic survival than the discussion to date had given them credit for. 'There is a tendency to talk about artists as victims of the funding system and to imagine that they are reliant on state funding', she said, 'but lots of young artists are very good at hustling and very good at negotiating and navigating different schemes.'
>
> (Glinkowski, 2008, n.p.)

Vaizey, at that time Shadow Minister for Culture,

> agreed with Mirza that today's artists were generally more economically and commercially astute than those of previous generations. 'A legacy of Thatcherism', he said, 'is the entrepreneurial artist; an artist who is very aware of their brand, of their selling power. There will, I think, from now on be an aspect of the artist's persona that is "the artist as salesman".'
>
> (Glinkowski, 2008, n.p.)

In a closing plenary discussion, art theorist Martin Quinn asked whether 'the old style of self-subsidising artist [was] turning into a more professional fund-generating artist: the culturepreneur' (ibid.). No doubt Conservative Party member Vaizey and Conservative Party affiliate Mirza would have answered, yes.

The New Labour government worked aggressively to institutionalize major public sector infrastructure designed to promote the Creative

Industries and their intrinsic linking of creativity and entrepreneurialism. New Labour's efforts seem to have worked: Conservative politicians such as Vaizey now take these links for granted; and ACE's 2011 policy document, *Supporting Growth in the Arts Economy*, simply insists on artists' entrepreneurialism. Since the late 1990s at least, government and ACE policy obliging artists to become entrepreneurial has been pervasive, increasingly naturalized and – I hope I have shown here, through reference to its history, extent and insistent discourses – uncompromising.

Entrepreneurialism's benefits for the arts

I expand below on some of the ideological and cultural risks of mandating artists to become more and more entrepreneurial. But first I explore briefly some of the possible cultural, social and, indeed, financial benefits, for artists and audiences, of encouraging artists not only to practise customary artistic traits – taking risks and innovating – but also increasingly to foster such business-related skills as raising, managing and diversifying sources of finance; cultivating institutional and/or personal development; enhancing the arts sector more broadly, including its networks for sharing resources and expertise; managing market change; and nurturing new audiences and markets.

One very important potential beneficiary of such a shift in emphasis, because they stand to gain more of what they want, is audiences. No longer do arts organizations simply follow long-established practices of trying to predict what audiences want by polling them by telephone or following the local history of their selections. Routinely now, arts organizations and independent artists exploit emerging, multiplying and increasingly accessible means of mapping audience preferences available through the internet, where contact databases as well as preference histories are easily shared on such social networks as Facebook. Furthermore, as Fleming and Erskine note, the kind of '[s]ustainable and resilient organisations' that they admire actively 'innovate with their audiences' (Fleming and Erskine, 2011, p. 24). Artists and arts organizations no longer simply predict audience preferences or invite audiences to say what they want; they offer audiences opportunities actively to shape their artistic experiences. As explored in the previous chapter, audiences are increasingly invited to exercise people-power, influencing artistic offerings through interaction in immersive theatre, one-to-one performance and relational installations. As that chapter explored, however, such business-conscious care to respond to and cultivate audiences can have its own risks for audiences – potentially offering agency that is more apparent than real and exploiting audience labour. And it can also have risks for artists, who may reasonably be less interested in 'satisfying' audiences than in challenging and changing audiences' expectations.

Nevertheless, there is much to be gained – or at least protected – for artists in becoming more entrepreneurial, including enhanced self-sufficiency and independence. Many artists simply cross-subsidize their art practice with other jobs, and many find ways of using these jobs not just as income earners but as sources of other resources, such as rehearsal/workshop space, computers, software, printers, photocopiers, cameras, stationary supplies, contact lists and more. The entrepreneurial artist can also retain artistic control instead of ceding it to others such as producers or even members of the public. 'The phrase "public art" turns my stomach', says British artist Grayson Perry, whose work I examine in more detail later in this chapter. 'For me art is a very private thing. As an artist my job description is Who am I? What do I want to do?' (in Glinkowski, 2008, n.p.). Artists need to be self-reliant not only as financial producers and marketers but also in other, artistic, capacities.

Artists' entrepreneurialism can lead them to develop multiple artistically complementary talents and modes of expression in, for example, film-making, editing, visual and audio design, scenography, prop-making, creative consultancy, blogging and creating other interactive online environments as well as, for example, teaching (performance, art, literacy and more), curating, teaching and practising body work (such as pilates and yoga), counselling and working in the catering industry, in arts administration and as an extra in film and television. Indeed, material pressure on artists to diversify their skills has not only encouraged artists to become more extensively skilled; I surmise that it has fostered more cross-arts practice in general. A very small sample of artists whose 'day-jobs' have constructively influenced their art practices might include, for example, through catering, Jenny Hunt and Holly Darton with their *Hunt & Darton Cafe* (2012); through teaching, Lois Weaver, Brian Lobel, Minty Donald, curious (Leslie Hill and Helen Paris) and many more; and through Shunt Collective co-founder and performer David Rosenberg's work as an anaesthesiologist, the piece he and other Shunt members co-created with Sound & Fury, *Ether Frolics* (2005) (see Garner Jr, 2008, p. 312).

Perhaps most importantly, the artist who develops her business skills simply helps to make her livelihood and her art more sustainable and resilient. This is especially important – indeed, necessary – as external forms of support shrink. Such external, shrinking forms include networks and institutions such as the UK Film Council, closed down by Cameron's government in 2011; Glasgow-based organization New Moves International and its live art festival, New Territories, closed due to 'financial irregularities' in 2011 (see Dibdin, 2011; Miller, 2011); and the National Review of Live Art (NRLA), held in Nottingham, London and then for many years in Glasgow, until its last occasion in 2010 (see Holtom, 2010; NRLA, 2012). The value of such creative hubs is evidenced in the excellent work that some remaining organizations continue to do. For example, the Live Art Development Agency (LADA), led by Lois Keidan and based in east London, provides a library, communications networks, training and mentoring opportunities, funding sources, commissions, expert staffing, an online shop and more to help generations of artists grow and develop their work (Live Art Development Agency, 2012).

A second shrinking form of support is, of course, public funding for the arts. I explore this topic in more detail in Chapter 4, but suffice here to say that in the face of cuts in public funding, artists' and arts organizations' adoption of a profit motive is by no means intrinsically bad. It can mean basic commercial viability instead of bankruptcy and company 'death' (as the language of business calls it) (see Burrows and Ussher, 2011). It can mean that it is not only people with private sources of funding (such as wealthy families) who can continue to make art. And it can furnish conditions for making particularly risky and challenging arts projects, with little to no guaranteed market, provided artists are prepared and able to cross-subsidize them from the proceeds of other commercially successful projects. In many respects, therefore, increasingly entrepreneurial artists are to be welcomed and celebrated.

Entrepreneurialism's risks for the arts

But that is not the whole story; the cultivation of artist as entrepreneur is also to be considered with caution. Geographer Joe Painter acknowledges that for some, the entrepreneur signifies 'excitement, innovation and wealth creation' alongside the qualities of independence and survival that I have focused on above. However, for others, 'the entrepreneur symbolises greed, oppression and exploitation' (Painter, 1998, p. 259). The relationship specifically of artists to entrepreneurialism has likewise been – perhaps particularly – vexed, as has the broader 'relationship between culture and economy, between art and capitalism', which social theorist David Harvey describes as 'always [having] been problematic'. 'Ever since the early nineteenth century', he observes,

> artists have had to submit to the vagaries of an art market, but their position within that market system (as artisans? as cultural producers working to the command of hegemonic class interest? as rebels seeking new insights? as an avant-garde of social revolution? a mere bohemian fringe?) has never been as securely anchored as the ranks of professionals (academics, jurists, doctors and the like) who make up the bulk of what Marx referred to as the 'ideological classes' of capitalist society.
>
> (Harvey, 1988, pp. x–xi)

For Harvey, the artist's role in the market potentially ranges from the beneficent artisan on one end of a politically inflected spectrum through to the duped lackey at the other end, passing through calibrations marking the radical rebel, the politicized avant-garde and the toothlessly benign bohemian fringe. The art market produces vagaries not only in evaluating styles and trends in artistic practice, therefore, but also in defining what artists are, and in crediting them with great political effect or as political puppets to be dismissed as irrelevant or worse.

The main question I pursue in the rest of this chapter has to do with where on Harvey's spectrum artists are in the age of the 'artrepreneur'. What, I ask, are the political, cultural and social risks of cultivating entrepreneurial artists? For me, the risks are profound and many and I will focus on three which I think are the most urgent, to do with sociality, people and the value of art. The first of these risks is that individual self-interest is emphasized in ways that damage social relations and principles of social equality. This is a risk in any political economy that prioritizes the rights of the individual, so it is a risk in any neoliberal economy. I suggest it becomes an especially acute social problem when artists are conscripted to its priorities. One might ask why artists should be relied on to hold the fort of sociality and equality, probably to their own financial cost, while (some) corporate bankers, for example, waltz off getting individually rich. I for one want to preserve principles of sociality and equality; I believe many artists do too; and I would like to see artists' efforts transform – or at least challenge – dominant political economy. The second risk of cultivating entrepreneurial artists is that it becomes increasingly accepted that destruction is necessary in capitalist processes of creative destruction to produce growth. Important economic analysts such as Karl Marx and Joseph Schumpeter have seen destruction as intrinsic to capitalism (see Marx and Engels, 1998; Schumpeter, 1994). I want to explore how this form of destruction is a particularly acute risk within the arts which demonstrate vividly that it is not just outdated technologies that are at risk of 'creative' destruction and replacement, but workers, livelihoods – in so many words, people. The third and final risk of requiring artists to become more entrepreneurial that I look at here is that it asks them to focus on productivity. To use the business term, the 'opportunity cost' of this focus is that many other possible *cultural* values of art practices are sorely neglected and underdeveloped, especially, I argue, principles of sociality and egalitarianism. Overall, accepting that artists should be entrepreneurial, that they must marketize to survive, fundamentally reifies neoliberal values as legitimate and legitimately ubiquitous. As part of a broader spectrum of activities within neoliberal governmentality, this acceptance contributes to a process which 'resignifies democracy as ubiquitous entrepreneurialism' (Brown, 2005, p. 50). What the rise and entrenchment of the entrepreneurial artist potentially portends, then, is the devaluation of sociality, people, art and democracy.

In response to this set of acute problems, however, I also explore a second question: what is the political value of the artist in an age of entrepreneurialism? My argument is that artists have not only resisted many of the cultural risks of entrepreneurialism; like canaries in a cultural mine shaft, they have posed direct challenges to the neoliberal marketization of culture and to the devaluation of sociality, people, art and democracy.

I explore these two linked questions – regarding the risks and potential values of cultivating entrepreneurial artists – in three parts which consider the three distinct risks of entrepreneurial, neoliberal marketized culture that I have identified above. The first part explores this culture's valorization of self-interested individualism and its threats to concepts of collective good and practices of social engagement and responsibility-taking. It then considers artistic responses which, first, explore how practices of individualism might support the historic underdog rather than the hegemonic master class and thereby destabilize neoliberal capitalism and, second, demonstrate the survival and, indeed, flourishing of networks of support that give the lie to the appearance of social atomization. The second part looks at neoliberal capitalist culture's structural reliance on creative destruction as apparently not only unavoidable but necessary, and it explores creative responses that draw attention to that relationship, denaturalize it and challenge it. The third part examines how neoliberal capitalist culture's emphasis on productivity and profit can come at the cost of other important values. And it explores one creative rejoinder to this emphasis: craftsmanship.

Entrepreneurialism's risks for the arts: Part I Individualism

Neoliberal capitalism's valorization of the individual is core to its meaning since it proposes that 'human well-being can best be advanced by the maximization of entrepreneurial freedoms within an institutional framework characterized by private property rights, individual liberty, unencumbered markets, and free trade' (Harvey, 2007, p. 22). For many, the inherent problems in this emphasis on individualism are chiefly to do with the ways it neglects or damages the social, as grounded in ideas of social equality and social responsibility. Sociologist Zygmunt Bauman observes that '[t]he individual tends to be lukewarm, sceptical or wary of "common good", "good society" or "just society" ... the other side of individualization seems to be the corrosion and slow disintegration of citizenship' (Bauman, 2002, pp. xvii–xviii). For political theorist Wendy Brown, likewise, neoliberal capitalism's emphasis on the individual means it is very damagingly not public-minded, to understate her point.

> The model neoliberal citizen is one who strategizes for her- or himself among various social, political, and economic options, not one who strives with others to alter or organize these options. A fully realized neoliberal citizenry would be the opposite of public-minded; indeed, it would barely exist as a public. The body politic ceases to be a body but is rather a group of individual entrepreneurs and consumers... which is, of course, exactly how voters are addressed in most American campaign discourse.
>
> (Brown, 2005, p. 43, ellipsis original)

Brown's 'model neoliberal citizen' works only in self-interest and not in *social* interest for things such as universal healthcare and education, support for those who are unemployed and, simply, less poverty.

The 'model neoliberal subjectivity' Brown identifies in the United States exists also in the United Kingdom and elsewhere. In his 2007 book, London-based psychologist Oliver James argued that neoliberal capitalist cultures are increasingly suffering from 'affluenza', the book's eponymous title and a neologism that captures both the epidemic proportions and the damagingly disease-like effects of these cultures' obsession with accruing wealth. His 2008 follow-up book, *The Selfish Capitalist*, argued that the current dominant form of capitalism – which 'approximates most closely to Neo-liberalism' (James, 2008, p. 121) – is not only self-oriented but fundamentally selfish. He specifically uses the phrase 'Selfish Capitalist' in order to emphasize how this is a 'Look After Number One, bugger everyone else, way of organising things; selfish, in fact' (ibid., p. 123). James explores how, contrary to understandings cultivated by the kinds of government discourses cited above, even the *economic* effects of this selfish capitalism are, in fact, deleterious, arguing that it has seen working conditions worsen, as more people labour longer hours, and average wages decline. Quebec-based artist and cultural analyst Marc James Léger corroborates James's claims, noting that neoliberalism has 'result[ed] in less economic growth in all regions of the global economy and greater concentration of surplus capital in the hands of the few' (Léger, 2011, p. 9; see Harvey, 2005). Harvey notes that neoliberalism has concentrated – and continues to concentrate – wealth with the wealthy in ways that associate it with 'attempts to restore or reconstruct upper-class power' (Harvey, 2007, p. 28). In summary, selfish and/or neoliberal capitalism inherently intensifies inequality and so is culturally divisive and destructive.

This point is key. The individualism of neoliberal capitalism is 'bad' not because it rewards some, but because it contributes enormously to the deprivations of many. Its susceptibility to exacerbate social inequality is intrinsic to its founding principles in the Washington Consensus, described by James as 'a list of eleven key policy commitments largely devised by American and British political economists to facilitate globalisation after 1975'. These commitments are:

> the liberalisation of international financial markets; the same in domestic financial markets; trade liberalisations (especially in developing nations); labour market 'flexibility'; security of private property, financial and physical assets; weak rights over human assets (particularly skills); reduced public sector spending, for example via privatisations and making business less regulated by the state; shifting the tax burden from rich to poor and from capital assets to workers, with subsidies increasingly for capital rather than workers; independent central banks; reduced welfare provisions, such as sickness and unemployment benefits; and privatisation (to charitable or voluntary organisations) and liberalisation of social policy.
>
> (James, 2008, pp. 121–2)

The demographic groups who most benefit within the terms of these 'commitments' are those with property, financial assets and physical assets, as these things are increasingly secured and decreasingly taxed.

Those who most suffer are those whose main asset is their labour (for example, manual and industrial labourers but also workers in the 'knowledge economy', including artists), those without capital assets such as property or finance and those who are poor. While already-wealthy individuals get richer, the poor get poorer.

The internal logic of this heinous conclusion becomes only clearer in light of Harvey's point that increased inequality is not so much an unfortunate by-product of neoliberalism as it is one of its *requirements* as a necessary stimulus for its own growth. Within the expanding neoliberalism of the 1980s on, Harvey (2007, p. 34) argues, 'Increased social inequality was necessary to encourage entrepreneurial risk and innovation.' As the influential post-Marxist analyst Maurizio Lazzarato reflects, 'Only inequality has the capacity to create a dynamics that stimulates the desires, instincts and brains of individuals and incites them to compete with one another' (Lazzarato in Léger, 2011, p. 9). For neoliberalism to thrive, competition must be cultivated, so social inequality must be too. Damage to social equality is not only an effect of neoliberal capitalism, it is an enabling condition of neoliberal capitalism.

Neoliberalism's propensity to extend inequality is acutely visible in contemporary performance practices' increasing reliance on – or demands for – volunteer labour, as noted above. Individuals' ability to volunteer their labour depends on their capacity otherwise to support themselves, whether through other paid work, personal wealth or the support of family and friends. Especially in difficult economic times, access to volunteer labour can therefore tend to be the privilege of the middle and upper classes; the future careers that depend on this early stage volunteering likewise, therefore, tend to remain the privilege of the same classes. In other words, as cultural policy analyst Kate Oakley puts it, 'unpaid work' is 'an entry criterion to the cultural labour market' (2009a, p. 12). This inequality extends not only to class, but also ethnicity. Oakley (ibid., p. 10) has noted, for example, 'Only 9 per cent of those working in [the cultural and creative] sectors in London are from an ethnic minority background, compared to 30 per cent of the labour force in general in London.' This inequality can partially be attributed to varying attitudes towards cultural labour in different ethnic groups, but it is almost certainly also a symptom of economic exclusion from the cultural sector's volunteer labour markets.

Responding to individualism's problems

However much contemporary neoliberal culture might encourage artists to behave entrepreneurially, and however much this might enlist them in spreading that culture's coveted, indeed requisite and also damaging individualism, artists are challenging some of the socially deleterious aspects of the current dominant political economy's individualism in at least two important respects. First, like latter-day Robin Hoods, they are redistributing resources in ways that challenge existing hierarchies. And second, they are resisting social atomization by retaining and expanding strong social networks of support that potentially reconfigure – rather than surrender – understandings of social connectedness and its political power.

If one of the risks of individualism is that it exacerbates inequality by extending deprivation, one constructive response to dismantling this problem is not to attempt to obliterate it, nor simply to aim to *prevent* the accumulation of wealth and opportunity at the top – both outcomes which may be beyond the grasp of art alone in any case – but to nurture the greater distribution of wealth and opportunity to those who are deprived by enfranchising *them* with individuality. Such a move not only benefits the deprived, it also challenges the dominance of the elite and of an elitist neoliberal social system. It is in this spirit that the role of the 'enterprising self' promoted by Margaret Thatcher's Conservative government and subsequent governments has been adopted by many people who 'did not necessarily share her values', as Justin O'Connor gently puts it. 'The "enterprising self"', he suggests, 'chimed not just with small corner shops in Grantham', two of which Thatcher's father had owned while she was growing up. It chimed also 'with many who had been marked by the counter-culture's rejection of the "organisation man" .... Against this they asserted a do-it-yourself, work-for-yourself attitude that represented a powerful feeling of liberation' (O'Connor, 2010, pp. 38–9).

Indeed, as O'Connor points out, the urge to independence came not only from Thatcher's Conservative corner, but also from a variety of non-conservative, radical political directions, including punk and rave cultures interested in 'taking back ... control of cultural production in the face of corporate control'.

> The proliferation of freelancers and micro-businesses in the cultural industries across the 1980s and 1990s ... [t]he ideas of breaking the 9–5, doing it for oneself, charting your own life course, of looking to express yourself, cannot be put down simply to the 'enterprise culture' *per se* .... What [Raymond] Williams had identified at the end of *Culture* (1981) – where technologies of reproduction seemed ever more accessible to the everyday person – happened at the same time

> as the 'punk ethos' precisely stressed the 'do it yourself' impulse. .... Its later manifestation in 'rave culture' also used technologies in this way .... In different ways they were about contesting established culture and making the technologies of reproduction work for you.
>
> (O'Connor, 2010, pp. 42–3)

In this historical context, particular 'technologies of reproduction' which artists made work for them included the 'enterprise allowance scheme' (or EAS), launched nationally by Thatcher's government in 1983 to nurture 'the development of an enterprise culture' (Gray and Stanworth, 1986, p. 5). Writing in 1986, business analysts Colin Gray and John Stanworth explain:

> the EAS represents an open invitation to Britain's unemployed to create their own jobs. ... [T]he EAS offers some unemployed a one year opportunity to establish their own business. For applicants, over the age of 18, who can demonstrate that they have a valid business proposal, access to £1,000 to invest in that proposed business and who have been unemployed for 13 weeks (dropped to 8 weeks in April 1986), the government undertakes to provide, in lieu of employment or supplementary benefits, £40 a week for one year, an annual sum of just over two thousand pounds.
>
> (1986, p. 5)

To put these details in context, what was worth £40 in 1983, by 2010 would have had the value of £105 in terms of its purchasing power for an average household, or up to £190 in terms of its comparative influence (see Measuring Worth, 2012a).

The EAS was very successful; by 1986, 'almost 200,000 previously unemployed people had entered the scheme' (New Deal of the Mind, 2009, p. 5; 2010). Though not fully appreciated at the time, it was later recognized how beneficial the scheme was for the UK's *creative* industries in particular. The Creative Society (the new name for New Deal of the Mind, since 2012), an organization which advocates for creative workers and specifically for the reintroduction of an EAS scheme, notes in a 2009 report for ACE:

> The academic research cannot be conclusive on the impact of the scheme on overall unemployment. However, several high-profile 'alumni' of the scheme provide anecdotal evidence that EAS allowed creative people to develop fruitful independent careers. These

> include Alan McGee, the founder of Creation Records, the founders of the heavy-metal record label Earache, Julian Dunkerton of the Superdry fashion label and Turner Prize nominated installation artists, the Wilson Sisters [Jane and Louise Wilson].
>
> (New Deal of the Mind, 2009, p. 5)

Other 'alumni' include artist Jeremy Deller (discussed in more detail below) and Shân Maclennan, who used her EAS funding to found a gallery in Edinburgh and later became the Creative Director of Learning and Participation at one of the largest cultural organizations in the United Kingdom, the Southbank Centre (see Gunnell, 2011; New Deal of the Mind, 2009, p. 12; Southbank Centre, 2011, p. 21). In Gray and Stanworth's qualitative assessment of the EAS, they interview 29 participants, at least seven of whom, or almost a quarter, started businesses in the cultural industries.[5] Sir David Trippier was one of the scheme's architects as Small Firms and Enterprise Minister from 1985, and he has commented: 'Initially, we didn't realise that there would be positive effects beyond economic growth. But EAS firms were so diverse. There were so many different types of small businesses. There were cultural and arts-related firms springing up everywhere. I remember going to Newcastle to visit some EAS shop units, and all the units were occupied by people in the cultural and design industries' (New Deal of the Mind, 2009, p. 12). French economist Françoise Benhamou has calculated that, between 1985 and 1989, there were 35,177 cultural sector participants in the EAS (Benhamou, 2000; Gunnell and Bright, n.d., p. 18). '"Thatcher's children"', O'Connor concludes (2010, p. 43), 'were those forced to become entrepreneurs because there were no other options. Or rather, there were other options and they chose a cultural one.' He implies that entrepreneurialism was compulsory but that some shrewdly chose to exploit it to pursue cultural work. Enterprising independence was not, in other words, 'owned' by Conservatism; indeed, its genealogy in punk and rave cultures and its legacy in the art practices of, for example, Deller are embedded in various political cultures in ways that destabilize elitist neoliberal capitalist culture's claim on it. Furthermore, when adopted by those with few other available resources – such as many artists and other cultural workers – its benefits accrue not, as usual, to the elite.

British cultural sociologist Angela McRobbie seems to concur that it is possible for the artist-producer to resist and even challenge neo-liberalized individualism, but she emphasizes that this possibility is likely more challenging to realize in the twenty-first century than it was in the 1980s.[6] She distinguishes between two recent phases of artist-as-producer. In the first, from about 1985–95, artists were supported by the dole (that is, unemployment allowance, or possibly by the enterprise allowance) and successfully maintained independence from corporatization. In the second phase, artists are more likely to be culturally disadvantaged by their recruitment as entrepreneurs, becoming 'de-specialized cultural entrepreneurs' in a context which 'has the effect of interrupting careers and imposing multi-skilling on creative individuals' (McRobbie, 2011, p. 84). Furthermore, in this second phase, society too is likely to be disadvantaged by artists' entrepreneurialization: because '[t]he members of the new creative class of workers are a Metropolitan elite, highly educated and with sufficient cultural capital to take risks', and because they are 'able to be individualistic by virtue of their assets', McRobbie argues that they are both 'in effect complicit with an economy characterized by ever-increasing divides between wealth and poverty' and 'well placed as agents of the new anti-egalitarian meritocracy' (ibid., p. 89).

In many respects, I agree with McRobbie's warnings that artists' entrepreneurialization since the mid-1990s is more at risk of reproducing neoliberal individualism and anti-egalitarian meritocracy than it was in the earlier era. One reason I agree is that the Conservative-led coalition government has reintroduced the EAS since 2011, but in a form that is much less supportive, and which therefore relies much more on individuals' (privileged) ability to self-support than its 1980s predecessor. This so-called New Enterprise Allowance (NEA) offers only about 60 per cent of the total allowance its predecessor offered (£1274 compared to £2080 in the 1980s) in a period of support lasting only six months instead of a year.[7] Given inflation, claimants are effectively asked to create new businesses while living on less than a half to less than a quarter of what they were allowed in the 1980s; and they are expected to make a success of their businesses in half the time.

However, while I agree with aspects of the warnings about artists' entrepreneurialization that McRobbie draws attention to, I want to make two claims for the ways art and performance are nevertheless preserving cultural value and/or resisting social damage. First, I would argue that the de-specialization that this entrepreneurialization seems to have demanded of artists does not necessarily or always mean that they are deskilled and therefore diminished as artists. On the contrary, as I suggested above, it can sometimes mean that artists become increasingly multi-skilled and that art forms productively cross-fertilize. I fully agree with McRobbie's point that the loss of adequate *structures* of support such as the dole or a *sufficient* enterprise allowance can have the culturally eroding effect of making it economically necessary that, in her example, '[a]rchitects double up as online editors' (McRobbie, 2011, p. 84), effectively seeking non-creative work to cross-subsidize creative work and losing time for art in ways that inherently damage art through neglect. However, it is also the case that such interdisciplinary experiences can allow artists to learn new skills and practices which they can then deploy in their art, potentially enriching it. To follow up McRobbie's specific example of cultural workers developing online skills, it is possible to see how expertise – or at least fluency – in new media has contributed to art and performance projects that aim to address broader audiences by, for example, Brian Lobel (*Purge*, 2011), Oreet Ashery and Larissa Sansour (*Falafel Road*, 2010), Blast Theory and more (see Ashery and Sansour 2010; Lobel, 2011). It is also possible to see how paid work as, for example, a university teacher and facilitator of cultural discussion has contributed to Lois Weaver's Long Table forum and Tammy Whynot performance persona; how Bobby Baker's extensive work as a photography stylist, especially of food, can be tracked into the visual culture of such performance work as *Table Occasions* (1997); and how Polly Morgan's training in taxidermy allows her to create her artwork (see Baker, 1997; Morgan, 2012). In other words, the entrepreneurialization of artists and the diversification of their labour has sometimes resulted in a diversification of arts practices that has been beneficial both creatively – diversifying creative discourses and practices – and socially – reaching and engaging broader audiences.

Second, McRobbie herself is keen to avow in the second-wave entrepreneurialized artist a political potential grounded in an understanding that the artist never works wholly alone, never becomes solely individualized, never entirely forsakes the social. 'The individual might be or might perceive himself or herself to be alone or "singular"', she observes, 'but reflexivity requires engagement with texts, images, musics and communicative networks' (McRobbie, 2009, p. 90). She admits that such discursive and social connectedness can be cynically exploitative, that for 'a "creative" in a big ad agency', for example, it can mean '"ransacking" film noir for the right look'. But she contends that it is by no means always exploitative. Indeed, though she insists that she is not 'posit[ing] art and culture as essentially critical or human beings as essentially cooperative', nevertheless, she concludes, 'creative work becomes a site for re-socialization, since it is better done with or for others' (ibid., p. 91).

Is it possible to see in contemporary art and performance practices the kind of networking that McRobbie suggests and that retains and/or revives sociality? Chapter 1 of this book considered how we might see artists 'networking' in new ways with audiences, inviting them to participate and contribute, and it also examined how such relations might enhance social relations but also compromise them. Here, I consider patterns of artists networking with each other and the potential social and cultural costs and advantages of these patterns.

We can see this kind of artist-led network in the initial group shows of those who would later come to be known as the Young British Artists (YBAs) in the 'Cool Britannia' era of early New Labour. Most famously, fine art students and graduates from Goldsmiths College, led by Damien Hirst, organized and assertively promoted shows of their work in a trilogy of summer exhibitions titled *Freeze* in the old Port of London Authority building in Surrey Docks in the summer of 1988 (Muir, 2009, pp. 18–24). *Freeze* was 'Year Zero in the YBA calendar', according to YBA fellow-travelling journalist and curator Gregor Muir, and its exhibiting artists included some of the YBA's future luminaries such as Hirst, Mat Collinshaw, Anya Gallaccio, Gary Hume, Michael Landy and Sarah Lucas (ibid., p. 24). Some of the same artists, including Hirst and Landy (whose work I discuss in more detail below), followed up *Freeze* with another influential trilogy of exhibitions, two of which were group shows, at Bermondsey's Building One in 1990 (ibid., pp. 31–3). These artists' collective work promoted not just individuals but a collective identity, or brand, which enhanced the value of their work. Advantageously, the YBAs largely maintained control over their work instead of ceding it to larger galleries or agents. Problematically, in their example, individualism is not trumped by this collective engagement; if anything, it is ultimately enhanced, as various infamous individuals (Damien Hirst most prominently) realized most long-term benefit from the group's brand identity and, following the group shows, there remained no permanent resources for *collective* good – such as a shared gallery, let alone anything like, for example, a pension scheme.

Another example of group networked artists who perhaps offer more hope of social value in their collaboration is those affiliations of artists who come together for festivals or even simply nights of performance, such as at London's Duckie, one-to-one performance festivals such as at the Battersea Arts Centre (BAC) in London, Cruising for Art, Stoke Newington International Airport and at festivals such as Glasgow's now-defunct National Review of Live Art, Edinburgh's Fringe Festival, Spill Festival of Performance, Brighton Festival, Glastonbury, Bestival and Latitude.

These models of networked collaboration retain several social weaknesses. Patterns of connection are usually informal, temporary and insecure and, as the YBA example shows, individualism is hardly quashed; indeed, the temporary collective may simply give it immediate contexts for competition and the reassertion of individualism – for example, in helping to establish Hirst as the quintessential YBA. On the other hand, these models also offer some social advantages. First, artists explore – if not established *structures* of support – then perhaps networks or flows of support, to borrow vocabulary from the very influential work of Manuell Castells on the network society (2010). A particularly socially positive feature of these networks is that they are often horizontally connected, amongst equals and near-equals (here, emerging artists), rather than vertically connected, with dominating organizations or individuals mandating the behaviour of the artists and the terms of their work. Second, artists may learn effective techniques for working in, negotiating, surviving and understanding the challenging conditions for making art within a cultural context dominated by neoliberal capitalism, however contingent those techniques may be. This learning is especially valuable if, as sociologist Ulrich Beck argues, individualization is a non-negotiable condition of culture in the late twentieth century and early twenty-first (see Beck, 1999; Beck and Beck-Gernsheim, 2002). Finally, artists' entrepreneurial formation of networks might help model ways that entrepreneurial practices can be both socially and process-based, not simply or primarily individually- and product-based (Brown, 2007, p. 137). This is a point I will come back to in much more detail in this chapter's concluding discussion on craftsmanship.

Entrepreneurialism's risks for the arts: Part II Creative destruction

A second key problem with artists' embrace of entrepreneurialism, cultural industrialization and neoliberal capitalism is the complicity of neoliberal capitalism with creative destruction. Creative destruction describes how capitalist economic creativity, innovation or development rarely seems simply to add on to existing economic activity which remains undisturbed. Rather, innovation seems necessarily to destroy the existing economic context – or at least significant parts of it – making it obsolescent. There are many vivid cultural examples of creative destruction, such as the evolution of sound recording, which has seen a string of technologies – from the record album to the 8-track, cassette, CD and mp3 – created and then quickly rendered redundant by new innovations. In theatre, developments in lighting have usurped previous technologies, eradicated smoky interiors, minimized fire risks, finessed ways of focusing audience attention and sought methods of saving energy in the context of high energy prices and climate change. Evolving technologies and modes of acting, similarly, have rendered the melodramatic silent-film actor redundant with the triumph of talkies. The concept of creative destruction is attributed to Karl Marx (though he did not give it this particular name), and is subsequently addressed in detail by Austrian-American economist Joseph Schumpeter. Many champions of capitalism have taken it up as a principally positive force. Prominent critics influenced by Marxism – such as David Harvey and Marshall Berman – have identified it as both socially damaging, but also (along lines introduced by Schumpeter) potentially leading to the destruction of capitalism itself (see Berman, 1983; Harvey, 2011).

For its largely capitalist supporters, capitalism's creative destruction laudably exorcises 'dead wood' – practices, organizations, companies, technologies and workers which are outmoded, inefficient and stagnant. It is attributed with producing prosperity, progress, efficiency and – capitalism's holy grail – greater profit. It rewards competitiveness and dynamism. Destruction is simply the necessary (and normalized) cost of doing business. As the example of theatre lighting cited above suggests, creative destruction can certainly have social and cultural benefits alongside economic ones. Indeed, it is often attributed with heaving whole populations out of penury and into prosperity, for example with the mass decline in the nineteenth century of Western agrarian societies and the rise of industrialization, and with the increased global distribution of labour facilitated by late twentieth- and early twenty-first-century technologies of communication and transport.

For its critics, however, the huge costs of capitalism's creative destruction often outweigh its benefits. It relies on a concept of built-in obsolescence that produces enormous waste. It means the particular values of one apparently outmoded technology are devalued and lost to the relentless march of progress; for example, the record album's ambient crackle and its considered structural organization across A and B sides give way to the clean – or anodyne – sound of the mp3 and the audience-organized structure of the playlist. Creative destruction's contribution to the mobility of capital means that while select populations of workers can get wealthy quickly with a new invention, other populations can become as quickly impoverished; it thus contributes to inequality, to instability and to putting people increasingly at the mercy of globally mobile capital. For Harvey, its emphasis on continuous innovation 'exacerbates instability, insecurity, and in the end, becomes the prime force pushing capitalism into paroxysms of crisis'

(1995, p. 105). The costs of creative destruction, of these paroxysms of crisis, are especially acute as human costs. The 2008 collapse (or creative destruction) of the subprime mortgage market in the United States, for example, made thousands homeless; a 2007 forecast considered it 'likely that as many as two million families [would] be evicted from their homes' (BBC News, 2007). The delicate phrase 'downsizing' names a company's apparently efficient slimming rather than the individual worker's potentially catastrophic job loss. Ideally, processes of creative destruction offer workers who are laid-off from one company new, better employment in emerging, more prosperous businesses. Practically, such an outcome usually requires retraining which may be unavailable or unrealistic, it presumes that equal or greater numbers of jobs will be created when rules of efficiency suggests otherwise, it imagines that emerging jobs will be geographically accessible and not remote let alone offshore, and it does not account for the time lapse between jobs when the unemployed and those dependent on them may experience real hardship. Of course, the human cost of creative destruction can also be injury and even death when workers suffer the collateral damage of exposure to environments that are stressful and unsafe, whether due to neglect or clear and present danger.

How do the arts and creative industries in particular fare in the face of creative destruction? In many ways, they benefited from the phase of creative destruction that saw the decline of traditional industries and the rise of the knowledge economy and of all kinds of government support for that economy alongside it. But though some parts of these industries are particularly adaptable to waves of creative destruction because they have little infrastructure (a feature which can also render them unstable), other parts have proven extremely vulnerable to creative destruction's assaults, including that of the economic recession which began in 2007. In ACE's 2011 publication *Supporting Growth in the Arts Economy*, Fleming and Erskine (2011, p. 77) acknowledge that the UK creative industries 'have been badly affected by the recession' and that they continue to be under threat from at least three factors which Fleming and Erskine draw from the Work Foundation's 2010 publication, *A Creative Block*: recession-induced funding cuts; 'the global trends towards convergence and digitalisation'; and 'concrete actions from other governments to maximise the recovery-boosting economic potential of their own creative industries' (Reid, Albert and Hopkins, 2010, n.p., in Fleming and Erskine, 2011, p. 77). In such competitive circumstances, the creative industries' recovery may be possible but not swift; indeed, Fleming and Erskine are forced to admit that 'some scenarios see job numbers in the creative industries only returning to their pre-recession numbers by 2020' (Fleming and Erskine, 2011, p. 77).[8]

Art's response to creative destruction: Michael Landy

Artists are being conscripted to neoliberal entrepreneurialism; creative destruction is intrinsic to neoliberalism; and the social and cultural threats posed by creative destruction are many and profound. How do art and performance practices respond to those threats in ways that challenge them? Focusing on the work of Michael Landy, I demonstrate how artists are using the particular affective force of the live performative and relational event to highlight for audiences the particularly human costs of creative destruction.

As explored in Chapter 1, many contemporary artists and performance makers are experimenting with both who they employ and how they employ people in their work, often delegating or outsourcing labour from the maker himself, herself or themselves to other hired artists or to paying audiences. One of the effects of this trend may be to draw audiences' attention to the distribution of labour in ways that specifically highlight the artist's redundancy and the delegated performer's exploitation, be she or he a paying audience member or another 'puppet' of the artist. One contemporary British artist who has long explored issues around human redundancy and obsolescence in current economies of both labour and consumerism is Michael Landy. Here I explore some of the ways his work draws audiences' attention to the particularly human costs of creative destruction through its themes and especially, through the ways it affectively engages audiences.

Michael Landy's work has consistently explored economies of exchange, specifically the human costs of markets which treat people as disposable, and he regularly makes installations which invite his audiences to enter the economies he depicts. In *Market*, first shown in 1990 in London, he filled his exhibition space (Bermondsey's Building One, a former Peak Freen's then Nabisco biscuit factory) with the physical apparatus of a street fruit and vegetable market – brown metal stepped scaffoldings laid with vivid green artificial turf and neighboured by mini-towers of stacked brown plastic pallet boxes – but he left the space empty of produce, salespeople and shoppers (Slyce, 2004, p. 51). His steel, plastic, skeletal and deserted *Market* eerily, but also somewhat comically, suggested the aftermath of a destructive force that had removed the stuff of life and all life itself. In 1995's *Scrapheap Services* he very explicitly showed the destructive and traumatic effects of worker lay-off – being thrown on the 'scrapheap'. Unemployed, on the dole and under pressure from Social Security officials to find whatever kind of work he could – however unsuitable – despite the historical context of 'corporate down-sizing, mass redundancy, and privatization of state-owned industries', Landy 'showed entrepreneurial initiative by inventing a bogus company to employ himself' (Nesbitt, 2004, p. 19). Appearing in a red cleaner's suit bearing a logo of human figures piled in a heap, he wearily swept up, binned and dumped into a machine named 'the Vulture' hundreds of cut-outs bearing the same human shape as in the logo and cut from rubbish such as empty cigarette packets and tin cans. Since Landy himself had the same human, boiler-suited profile as the cut-out logo, it was clear that the service he delivered could or eventually would equally consign him to the scrapheap. And it was clear from the worn-down attitude of his performance that his depiction of this economy was by no means triumphal, but rather forlornly resigned.

Landy's most famous work to date is likely his 2001 *Break Down*.[9] For this piece, he catalogued all of his over 7000 belongings, from socks to kitchenware, artworks by himself and others, passport, stereo and Saab car. He then occupied a temporarily unused department store on London's central shopping thoroughfare, Oxford Street. Here, he posted on the walls the catalogued lists of his belongings and he installed what looked like an assembly line. In practice, it turned out to be a disassembly line, where Landy and 18 hired operatives worked over two weeks systematically breaking down all of his possessions except the boiler suit that he stood up in.

Break Down focused thematically on the creative destruction that is at the heart of neoliberal capitalism by accelerating and highlighting the final stage of consumerism – destructive disposal – that is comparatively concealed, after consumerism's more alluring stages of spectacular marketing, potentially exciting and often conspicuous consumption and use. This acceleration also drew attention to the ways that currently dominant economies which depend on consumer spending compel consumers to move objects quickly towards obsolescence. Landy further amplified the work's focus on consumerism by situating it both geographically and architecturally in meccas of shopping, and by offering brief descriptors for objects that told their retail history; for example, item number 'E797 Sony KV16WT1 black plastic widescreen portable colour television, 1600 screen, purchased at Curry's, Old Kent Road', and item number 'K1725 Medium size clear glass dinner plate, purchased at Woolworth's, Whitstable' (Landy, 2001b, n.p.). He suggested that consumer culture saturates people's lives by treating all of the objects on his assembly line equivalently – including Ikea cups, a

SAAB car, a stereo, gifts from loved ones and artworks.[10] Thematically, Landy offered a powerful critique of consumerism's structural reliance on built-in obsolescence/destruction and the enormous wastefulness that it produces but aims to conceal.

This thematic emphasis on the destructive element of capitalism's creativity and growth was vastly enhanced through *Break Down*'s affective force. Its processes were presented almost entirely with clinical detachment: the printed inventory was typeset, offered virtually no commentary and classified objects by their function rather than their lived history of use; the objects themselves travelled around the disassembly line in clear plastic bags, perhaps like legal evidence bags, within standard yellow plastic trays; and workers were made anonymous and functionary by their matching blue boiler-suit uniforms, offered no narrative on the items and simply went about destroying them systematically. The apparent objectivity of these processes highlighted by contrast the subjectivity at stake, while the title *Break Down* referred both to the work's material processes and to a psychological trauma which, the work suggested, might provoke or be provoked by such a process of 'stocktaking' and which Landy invoked by noting that he was making the piece at the same mid-life age at which his own father had suffered an industrial accident that ended his ability to work.[11] The processes' objectivity was also explicitly contrasted by a small programme which visitors to *Break Down* received and which included a few hand-drawn illustrations by Landy of some of his belongings as well as some short handwritten commentaries on the objects. Here was evidence of the human cost of Landy's project, in particular in the story about the last item to be destroyed, inventory number C714, a sheepskin coat – sculpted to a body like a glove – handed down to Landy and painstakingly purchased on instalments by his mother for his father, just before his father suffered his life-changing industrial accident. Here were poignantly visible the effects of creative destruction at its most vicious and voracious in the consignment to the 'scrap heap' of the worker chronically disabled by an industrial accident and left evermore unable to work.

Many might consider *Break Down*'s engagement with consumerism and its complicity with creative destruction daftly futile, given that Landy had immediately to follow it with a frenzied re-entry into consumer culture, buying new clothes, new keys to his girlfriend's flat and so on. But I would argue that the piece potentially suggested the foolishness not of his behaviour, but of consumer culture itself and of the creative destruction it relies on, both of which he modelled merely in condensed acceleration.

Landy's next major installation, in 2004 in Tate Britain's Duveen Galleries, offered an extended consideration of his father John Landy's life after the accident in which a tunnel roof collapsed on him, breaking his back (see Nesbitt, 2004, pp. 13–14). In *Semi-Detached* Michael Landy installed full-scale replicas of the front and back elevations of his parents' Essex home, complete with pebble-dashing, UPCV windows and satellite dish (Landy, 2004). On the blank, black insides of these two walls, Landy projected a series of carefully observed films about his father's daily life within the relatively confined limits of the house. As Tate curator Judith Nesbitt observes, *Semi-Detached* draws attention to the ways that identity is constituted not so much by what we have – as in *Break Down* – as by what we can or cannot do (Nesbitt, 2004, p. 13). Despite his many injury-related disabilities, John's environment is full of tools, materials and manuals for repairing things, and much of his own time is spent on his own self-care. The work witnesses the damage wrought on John Landy by his injury, but also the perseverance, resilience and ingenuity that he performs daily in its wake. It is a work that acknowledges the damaging potential of creative destruction but also testifies to creative survival – both in John's represented activities and environments, and in Michael's representational environments, films and drawings.

Landy is of course not the only contemporary British artist whose work engages with destruction.[12] To name just a few others, Jeremy Deller (whose work I discuss in more detail below) has toured and exhibited the wreck of a car destroyed by bombing in Iraq, *It Is What It Is* (2009). Rachel Whiteread produces apparently pristine sculptures which are casts of absent structures including boxes, staircases, single rooms such as the library of her *Holocaust Memorial* (2000) in Vienna's Judenplatz (see Schneider, 2002; Young, 2004), and famously a destroyed East London terrace house in 1993's *House* (see Lingwood, 1995; Mullins, 2004; Townsend, 2004). Cornelia Parker makes installations that appear to capture exploding objects in suspended animation, most famously in her exploded garden shed, its fragments suspended around a single domestic 200 watt light bulb, *Cold Dark Matter: An Exploded View* (1991; see Parker, 1991). Parker also submits things to slower 'destruction', drawing the metal of a single bullet in to a long wire in *Bullet Drawings* (2007); elegantly suspending silver-plated objects such as a ladle, platters and candelabra after they have been crushed in a 250-ton industrial press in *Endless Column III* (2006) (Parker, 2007); and making ink blots with ferric oxide retrieved from dissolved pornographic videos seized by HM Customs and Excise in *Pornographic Drawings* (1997) (Parker, 2000, 2001).

The work of all these artists explores the human contexts and costs of destruction – the changing of urban neighbourhoods in Whiteread's *House*; the crushing oppressions of hierarchical cultures of (silver) service in Parker's *Endless Column III;* and the devastations of war in Deller's *It Is What It Is*, Whiteread's *Holocaust Memorial* and Parker's *Bullet Drawings*. Parker's exploded shed in *Cold Dark Matter* invokes not only a eureka moment – where an idea has exploded forth after many hours of work in that vernacular laboratory, the potting shed – but also the long, enduring shadows cast by its lingering trail of devastation. Though all of these artists invoke the human costs of destruction, what makes Landy's work stand out from the others' in relation to the 'artrepreneur' is its explicit focus on the human costs exacted by the shifting labour economies of creative destruction – costs to people's ability to labour with dignity, to labour at all, to be independent and not to be consumed by the enforced obsolescence mandated by creative destruction. His work offers a resonant challenge to neoliberal capitalism's apparent acceptance that destruction – including human destruction – is an unavoidable cost of growth. Entrepreneurial neoliberal capitalist culture may appear to necessitate creative destruction; artists such as Landy draw acute, detailed attention to its manifold, exacting and painful human costs.

Entrepreneurialism's risks for the arts: Part III Productivity and profitability

A third and final set of problems raised by the entrepreneurialization of the artist has to do with neoliberal capitalism's relentless deployment of labour as instrumental to the cultivation of productivity, wealth and profit. This deployment can jeopardize other features of labour which might be considered valuable in different ways, or instrumental in achieving other things besides products, wealth and profit. Here, I explore how craftsmanship can offer an alternative approach to understanding artistic labour as comparatively *in*efficient and bearing specifically *social* value. By 'craft', I generally mean made with not basic but expert skills (though I will review this in what follows). And following Richard Sennett in his book *The Craftsman*, I mean by 'craftsmanship', 'the skill of making things well', 'the desire to do a job well for its own sake' and 'quality-driven work' (Sennett, 2009, pp. 8, 9 and 24).[13] I consider craftsmanship in contemporary art and performance practices to explore how it might help value art, labour and quality not for their financial profit, but rather for their own sakes, and, in so doing, how it might offer a model of production marked not by individual self-interest but by social interdependence and egalitarianism. Contemporary British art's engagement with craft and craftsmanship makes the case for championing the arts' intrinsic value over their (financially) instrumental value; it also makes the case for recognizing and honouring our social interdependence.

First, how does the entrepreneurialization of the artist insist on profit and productivity? Though the consecutive UK governments and ACE policy documents I quoted earlier in this chapter often emphasize that their exhortations to artists to become entrepreneurial are motivated by commitments as much to developing good art as to stimulating financial economies, it is very difficult not to see their chief priorities as financial profit-making. To reiterate a point I articulate above, the authors of the 2011 ACE publication *Supporting Growth in the Arts Economy*, Fleming and Erskine claim to be interested in 'maximising the capacity of the arts to reach and enthral audiences', but their focus is clearly on 'maximising ... the agility of the arts and collaborators in creative businesses to nurture markets, revenue and investment as a direct outcome of audience development' in order to make 'markets grow' and 'the creative economy enter ... a new period of competitiveness' (2011, p. 24). Their emphasis is on markets not audiences, and so on material profits not immaterial effects such as the pleasure an audience might feel, the ideas it might explore or the relationships it might develop.

What is wrong with entrepreneurialism's emphasis on the arts being business-minded and profit-driven? There is nothing intrinsically wrong with wealth creation; indeed, some wealth is necessary to secure the basics of life, such as food, shelter and care and more money can enhance quality of life. However, as I hope I have demonstrated above, there is often a lot *socially* wrong with a system of profit-driven wealth creation such as neoliberal capitalism because it tends to cultivate social relations that are given to gross inequality, whether because it distributes poverty and wealth unevenly, it apportions cost and profit unfairly, it fosters individualistic selfishness, it accepts (uneven) creative destruction as inevitable and necessary, or for many other reasons. For example, as Sennett outlines in *The Craftsman*, neoliberal capitalism has a propensity to celebrate competition and the hoarding of ideas in ways that actually stifle innovation and invention (Sennett, 2009, p. 33); to prefer Fordist models of efficiency that require acute specialization and lead to 'dissociated labour' (ibid., pp. 36, 46ff.) which alienates and isolates workers; to cultivate understandings of the 'head' and the 'hand', creative labour and manual labour, as separate in ways that damage both; and to emphasize productivity at the expense of other values (ibid.).

Craftmanship inefficiency, collaboration and egalitarianism

To resist these many problems posed by efforts to drive artists into profit-driven entrepreneurialism, I advocate here for ways artists might be both seen as and encouraged to become, instead, craftspeople. I appreciate that many people – particularly many artists and left-leaning cultural analysts of the arts such as me – would *obviously* advocate for a model of the artist predicated on the craftsperson rather than – or at least more than – the entrepreneur. What I aim to do here is elaborate on *why* such a model is preferable for reasons perhaps both obvious – to do with challenging the profit motive with apparent inefficiency – and less obvious – to do with modelling social interdependence and egalitarianism. To examine the deep history and many analyses of craftsmanship that Sennett offers in his monograph is beyond the scope of this section. But I will address some of his analyses of craftsmanship here to explore what they offer to a preferred understanding of the artist as more craftsperson than entrepreneur.[14]

Perhaps obviously, craftsmanship offers the positive values of quality workmanship, concern with quality over quantity, self-respect and satisfaction for the worker and a healthy integration of thinking and making, where good ideas are worked out and refined in their material realization. All of these qualities point to craftsmanship's demands as time-consuming and, often, difficult. It relies on the trained practice that leads to dependable skill rather than unreliable 'sudden inspiration' (Sennett, 2009, p. 37). '[P]rogress is not linear', Sennett notes. 'Skill builds by moving irregularly, and sometimes by taking detours' (ibid., p. 238). Craftsmanship is therefore equipped to work with difficulties, resistance and ambiguity, to find solutions and, in so doing, to develop (ibid., pp. 214ff.). It prioritizes not efficiency and productivity but, simply, quality, thereby immediately challenging entrepreneurialism's drive to profit.

Sennett's detailed examination of the rewards and challenges of craftsmanship in *The Craftsman* does not directly focus on the ways it can challenge a profit-driven instrumentalist approach to labour, however, this might be one of the strongest cumulative effects of what I believe Sennett argues craftsmanship does do, which is ideally to model equitable social relations. A direct challenge to the instrumentalism of craft does certainly form part of his project: in a discussion about *The Craftsman* at the 2008 London Literature Festival with, among others, Grayson Perry, whose work I examine in more detail below, Sennett claims he was interested 'in how people become skilled in something, and how they become committed to their skills. Doing something well because you want to get it done well, rather than for money, prestige or reputation' (Sennett et al., 2008, p. 53). As another important analyst of craft Glenn Adamson (2007, p. 3) emphasizes, craft is perhaps more usefully conceived not 'as a fixed set of things' – which might be marketed – but 'as a process'.

There are three other perhaps less obvious qualities that craftsmanship presents that I want to credit many current influential UK artists with displaying and advocate for here. First, 'material consciousness': in this phrase Sennett notes the craftsperson's curiosity about materials, be they the resources for making tools, pots, buildings or websites or, indeed, the skills for raising children.[15] He writes, 'This is the craftsman's proper conscious domain; all his or her efforts to do good quality work depend on curiosity about the material at hand' (2009, p. 120). As the example of raising children indicates, the phrase 'material consciousness' can imply care about, and self-reflexivity on, not simply material *objects* but also material *relations* of production, including the material and social networks between people that the craftsperson engages in; for example, between master and apprentice, and one craftsperson and her fellow craftspeople, suppliers, distributors and consumers. Related to this point and second, Sennett invokes craft's reliance on cooperation (ibid., p. 32), as demonstrated in the need for collaboration between different craftspeople, and the responsibility of the craftsperson to train and nurture apprentices in order to ensure the continuity of the craft (p. 68). Combined, these two points about material consciousness and collaboration indicate craft's reliance on and support of social relations of mutual responsibility.

Third, Sennett indicates that sound understandings of craftsmanship recognize people's basically equal potential. He writes:

> Our Enlightenment ancestors believed that Nature furnished humanity at large with the intelligence to do good work; they saw the human being as a capable animal; demands for greater equality depended on this conviction. Modern society tends to emphasise differences in ability; the 'skills economy' constantly seeks to separate smart from stupid. Our Enlightenment forebears had it right, at least as concerns craftsmanship. We share in common and in roughly equal measure the raw abilities that allow us to become good craftsmen; it is the motivation and aspiration for quality that takes people along different paths in their lives. Social conditions shape these motivations.
>
> (2009, p. 241)

'[N]early anyone', Sennett concludes, 'can become a good craftsman' (p. 268). Though the appellation 'craftsperson' might at first, therefore, suggest exclusivity, elitism and hierarchy – an esteemed title earned only by a privileged few with the resources to commit to long-term learning – Sennett emphasizes that, conceptually, craftsmanship is egalitarian. Neoliberal policy makers would no doubt like to persuade everyone that entrepreneurialism is egalitarian too; but though everyone might hypothetically be capable of becoming an entrepreneur, entrepreneurialism's *effects* in a neoliberal capitalist sphere are decisively anti-egalitarian. Sennett admits that although craftsmanship may be conceptually egalitarian, this egalitarianism is difficult to realize, given people's variable access to financial, cultural and social capital.

I consider below how there might be a continuum of craftsmanship from the highly skilled to the amateur and 'folk' that might help retain some of the values and liberations Sennett's model of craftsmanship offers, while simultaneously opening it up to more people with less access to various forms of capital. This is not a route of enquiry that Sennett particularly explores in *The Craftsman*, but it is one he shows sympathy with. In the discussion at the 2008 London Literary Festival, he had this to say about amateurism:

> The other side of amateurism is that it's collective in the sense that you're not withdrawing from other people to do it. Amateur music-making has this social bond, for example. And it's disinterested, it's not put to an economic end, and you're doing it for its own sake. In the 17th century the word 'amateur' meant the same as 'virtuoso', someone was interested in things and how they work. In the 19th century, they gradually split apart, so that the virtuoso became someone with unreachable power and the amateur someone insufficient, rather than someone doing something simply to see how it works. In this sense the craft of the amateur is something I would like to recover.
>
> (Sennett et al., 2008, p. 55)

I argue here that recognizing the craftsmanship of some current art practices challenges both the profit-driven instrumentalism of 'artrepreneurial' thinking and its fundamental unfairness by modelling art practice as in some basic respects socially collaborative and egalitarian. The pressures of neoliberal capitalism as manifested in increasing demands made on artists to act as entrepreneurs are indeed multiple, insidious and potentially destructive; nevertheless, art practices specifically engaged with craft are demonstrating inspiring ways of challenging those pressures.

I now look briefly at four examples of work by contemporary UK artists Ackroyd and Harvey, Steve McQueen, Grayson Perry and Jeremy Deller. I have selected this work because it actively engages qualities of craftsmanship in ways that highlight, variously, its inefficiency, social engagement, social reflexivity and potential egalitarianism.

Ackroyd and Harvey

Heather Ackroyd and Dan Harvey are likely best-known for the poetics of space they create by growing grass on unexpected surfaces and sites such as in picture frames, on the entire interior of a deconsecrated church in Dilston Grove in South London in 2003, and up two exterior walls of the National Theatre's Lyttelton fly tower in 2007 (see Ackroyd and Harvey, 2012). Their work is subtle: change happens gradually, the grass's life is limited and basic structures are unaltered. But it is also spectacular: they replace hard, lifeless often dull-coloured surfaces with soft, living, vibrant green ones. I see craftsmanship in their art because of the care they display for doing it well and the 'material consciousness' it requires in the meticulous preparation of surfaces, soils, seeds, irrigation and light. *FlyTower* covered 760 square meters with two tons of carefully prepared clay and approximately 1,875,000,000 seeds of three types of grass (Butler, 2007). I see craftsmanship in the work's inefficiency: it is labour-intensive to produce (*FlyTower* employed 22 assistants [Butler, 2007]); it is ephemeral, indeed, auto-destructive (*FlyTower* existed for only about five weeks); it cannot be efficiently produced and sold; and it challenges the very instrumentalism of grass in that it resists use for walking or lying on, let alone grazing (see *FlyTower*, 2007). It is also distinctly collaborative, in Ackroyd and Harvey's collaboration with each other, in their work with 22 assistants on *FlyTower* and in their cooperation with site managers and many different kinds of specialists, for example, in scaffold-construction, irrigation and botany.[16] Finally, it invokes egalitarianism both in that it is public in the case of *FlyTower*, and in its use, exploration and proliferation of that very pedestrian of materials, grass. *FlyTower may* possibly evoke the manicured lawns of stately homes and manors that Thorstein Veblen drily ridicules in *The Theory of the Leisure Class*.[17] I suggest it more precisely evokes an idea of common lands, in that, after being set to flourish, it is not continuously tended and managed to perfection, but rather left to the hazards of the weather.

Steve McQueen

Steve McQueen is likely best known for his films. He makes films for art contexts, such as *Caribs' Leap/Western Deep* (2002)[18] and *Giardini*, produced for the fifty-third Venice Biennale in 2009 (see McQueen, 2009). And he makes films for commercial cinematic release, for example *Hunger* (2008) on Irish hunger-striker Bobby Sands, and *Shame* (2011), which focused on its central character's apparent sex addiction. In both contexts, McQueen is a craftsman of film, demonstrating extraordinary care and lack of conventionalism in his shots' composition – their framing, perspective, duration, contextualization and juxtaposition. He might also be seen as a craftsman of his spectator's gaze, often forcing attention on, and consideration of, things that may be uncomfortable to witness, such as bodies labouring in punishing conditions in African gold mines in *Western Deep*, bodies starving to death in *Hunger*, and intense close-ups on Kerry Mulligan's singing face and Michael Fassbender's character desperately or despairingly engaged in sex in *Shame*.

The project I want to consider here, *Queen and Country*, also forces this kind of attention, though not through film. In response to a commission by the Imperial War Museum to 'create a work in response to the war in Iraq', McQueen developed the idea 'that British servicemen and women killed in Iraq be commemorated on official postage stamps' (McQueen, 2010, n.p.).[19] Receiving further support from the Manchester International Festival but not, crucially, the Ministry of Defence or the UK's postal service, Royal Mail, McQueen nevertheless wrote 'independently to the families [of servicemen and women killed in Iraq] to ask for their collaboration and inviting them to choose an image for the project'. He commissioned facsimile pages of stamps, each page made up of 168 stamps bearing the face of a single serviceman or woman, and he displayed them in commissioned oak cases in 2007 in Manchester. In the same year, The Art Fund gave £60,000 to the Imperial War Museum to acquire the work and also launched an online petition 'for the stamps to be issued by Royal Mail'. The stamps and cases have subsequently been displayed in London, Liverpool, Edinburgh, Middlesbrough, Wolverhampton and Colchester. By 2010, 160 service personnel were represented in the project and in the same year McQueen launched a book of *Queen and Country*, with each right-hand page showing one stamp of one individual and the facing page showing, across four lines, his or her rank and name, regiment, date of death and age. The book opens with a poem by Derek Walcott (originally from Saint Lucia), 'Requiem' (January 2010), which invokes the 'stamp' both as currency for postage and as the stamp of a soldier's boot that makes up part of the ritualized performance of the war memorial service.

Postage stamps might more conventionally be understood as design rather than craft since they are mechanically mass produced.[20] But

McQueen's *Queen and Country* both evokes and enacts craft in specific ways. It evokes the craftsmanship of philately, of developing expert knowledge on stamps and of forming, caring for and cherishing a collection. It evokes craftsmanship in the bespoke display cases McQueen commissioned. By identifying each service-person's role in the Iraq War – including, for example, Lance Bombardier Llwelyn Carl Evans, Royal Regiment of Artillery; Flight Lieutenant Sarah Mulvihill, Royal Air Force; Sapper Robert Thomson, Corps of Royal Engineers; and Gunner Samuela Vanua, Royal Regiment of Artillery – it suggests the craftsmanship of those roles. By paying singular attention to each individual service-person, it invokes each one's uniqueness, while still linking them all together as a 'mass', as part of a social group – indeed, as the 'country' invoked in the work's title, and in service to a country. In myriad ways, the project also modelled social interdependence. It did so in the explicit linkages across the service-people's units, for example, the eight members of the Royal Marines and the Royal Regiment of Artillery who died on 21 March, 2003, and with whom the book opens; in the evocation of country; in the role stamps play enabling communication by post across space between people; in the project's reliance on the collaboration of the service-people's families; and in The Art Fund's online petition to secure Royal Mail's agreement to print and release the stamps (see Art Fund, 2012).[21] The project modelled egalitarianism by suggesting various challenges to conventionally hierarchical relationships, especially between the queen and 'her' subjects: in the title, which rhetorically equated queen and countrymen/women as well as, perhaps, Queen and McQueen; in displacing from the centre of the stamps the queen's face, making way for the faces of the service personnel; in the invocation of the ultimate sacrifice made by the service-people for 'queen and country'; and in the stamps' literal, insistent and repetitive valuing and making-visible of the service-people, despite their deaths and absence. *Queen and Country*'s invocation of stamps as mass produced and mass distributed suggested the masses whose lives are affected by the Iraq War in particular, but by many wars in general. Its invocation of craft suggested both an ethic of care in the composition of the project and in the handling of its 'materials' – literally, the stamps, cases and photographs, but effectively, the lives and deaths of the service personnel and the feelings of their families. It highlighted the human networks across and around the war and its dead. And it challenged hierarchies of citizenship.

Grayson Perry

Grayson Perry is likely best known as a ceramicist and transvestite, but his oeuvre covers many more modes of making, including sketching, collages, etchings, a range of textiles (screen prints, machine embroideries, costumes, tapestries), other sculptural objects such as shrines, and other performative acts such as taking his talismanic teddy bear Alan Measles on a pilgrimage across Bavaria on a specially commissioned Kenilworth AM1 motorcycle in *Ten Days of Alan* in 2007 (see BBC Radio 4, 2010; Klein, 2009).[22] Perry's 2011–12 exhibition at the British Museum (BM) in London, *The Tomb of the Unknown Craftsman*, displayed his own recent works amongst 'objects made by unknown men and women throughout history from the British Museum's collection' (BM, 2011). It demonstrated Perry's enormous 'material consciousness' towards the histories of craft by, for example, including his own fetish objects and flags alongside resonant comparative examples from different times and places and doing so with social consciousness. 'I always try to balance my love of intricate historic detail (the hobbit) with social comment on my own time (the punk)', he writes, identifying *The Tomb of the Unknown Craftsman* as 'the culmination of a love affair with the artefacts of the past' (Perry, 2011, pp. 13 and 14). His work displays consciousness about the many properties of his materials, including the complexities of ceramics' built form and surface design (his ceramics are often loaded with overlapping colours, textures, bits of text and surface illustrations both found and made).

His work celebrates collaboration by showing connections across histories of craft and it champions egalitarianism by radically widening understanding of craft, including who can make it, what forms it can take and what subjects it can address. *The Tomb of the Unknown Craftsman* challenged exclusive ideas of who can make craft by including Perry's own work alongside that of numerous unknown craftspeople. 'One of the main themes of the exhibition', he wrote, 'is the idea of finding oneself in the collections of the BM ... seeing oneself, one's personal concerns as a human being, reflected back in the objects made long ago by fellow men and women with similar, equally human, concerns' (Perry, 2011, p. 11). He describes *The Tomb of the Unknown Craftsman* as 'a memorial to makers and builders, all those countless un-named skilled individuals who have made the beautiful man-made wonders of history', and he identifies the Unknown Craftsman as 'all craftsmen and women' (ibid., p. 20). The exhibition also opened up understanding of what craft can be by provocatively including what is conventionally understood as craft – such as ceramics – alongside the unexpected – such as acts of pilgrimage, including popular cultural pilgrimages. And it greatly expanded understanding of what makes suitable subject material for craft. It included such personal talismans as several totemic versions of Alan Measles, including *Tomb Guardian*

(2011), a large ceramic and highly decorated bear endowed with a smiling horned phallus (ibid., p. 160). It referred to sites of popular cultural pilgrimage such as Graceland, Glastonbury and Auschwitz in a large tapestry titled *Map of Truths and Beliefs* (ibid., p. 121). And it made pop cultural references to, for example, Twitter and mobile phones (see *You Are Here*, glazed ceramic, 2011, in ibid., pp. 28–9), and, with irony, to what is usually the meta-level discourse around museums rather than its subjects in, for example, *The Rosetta Vase* (2011) and its depiction of 'The Artist' as motivated by, amongst other things, 'curiosity' and 'personal beliefs' alongside 'career enhancement', 'celebrity' and 'vanity' (ibid., pp. 95–8). A 2008 exhibition of works from the Arts Council Collection which Perry curated, *Unpopular Culture*, similarly promoted the unconventional. Some of the material Perry selected he described as bearing 'an attractive humility and elegance, qualities that today might be described as not being media friendly, but which I wish to celebrate' (Perry, 2008a, p. 10), while commentator Blake Morrison described 'the art [Perry] values' as 'introverted, unglamorous and more interested in exploring byways and backwaters than in parading itself on the global stage' (Morrison, 2008, p. 16). Elsewhere Perry has indicated the guerrilla or stealth tactics that he uses to smuggle what might be socially challenging ideas into his audiences' purview by starting with familiar, even classical forms. 'Pots suit the scale of my ideas', he says, 'there is no bombastic confrontation, one is charmed into picking up my ideas from a pot. For me the shape has to be classical[,] invisible: then you've got a base that people can understand' (Perry, 2002, p. 14).

As I noted earlier in this chapter, Perry is on record claiming that art 'is a very private thing', an individual pursuit (in Glinkowski, 2008, n.p.). What *The Tomb of the Unknown Craftsman* and *Unpopular Culture* demonstrate, however, is that although Perry is committed to exploring personal questions such as 'Who am I? What do I want to do?' (ibid.), he recognizes these questions as the *shared* terrain of artists and craftspeople across different times and places. He tracks lineages across histories of craft, showing their interdependence. And he presents craft's makers, materials and subjects as radically open and egalitarian. In the 2008 London Literature Festival discussion with Richard Sennett that I referred to above, Perry claimed, 'Much of what I love is not the work of the big names, but the unknown craftsman – what you would almost call folk art' (Sennett et al., 2008, p. 54). Without romanticizing folk culture, Perry portrays art as radically open, as mass, folk culture. His is a broadly encompassing meritocracy, not what Sennett identifies in the same discussion as New Labour's version of meritocracy which rewarded only a few (ibid., p. 55).

Jeremy Deller

Jeremy Deller works across what is possibly an even greater array of art practices: he makes films, stages events, creates encounters, produces music, makes posters and transports objects. In the United Kingdom, he is likely best known for *The Battle of Orgreave*, a 2001 restaging of a confrontation between miners and police in the miners' strikes of 1984, which he describes as 'a thousand-person crime re-enactment' (Deller, 2012a, p. 98). Despite its formal variety, one quality that is consistent across Deller's work is its political engagement. This is sometimes recognizable on an explicitly political register, as in *The Battle of Orgreave*, and in *It Is What It Is* (2009), where he toured a bombed-out car from Baghdad across the United States to 'bring home' the realities of the conflict in Iraq to audiences in the United States and to provoke discussion about the war and its consequences (see Deller, 2012b). Oftentimes, however, his work is politically engaged on a more social register. For example, in *Our Hobby is Depeche Mode* (2006; see 2012a, pp. 120–5), he invited global fans of Depeche Mode to express their responses to the band on film and by submitting artworks to him for exhibition. The resulting popularly sourced 'archive' vividly demonstrates the passion of the fans' expression, their generosity in sharing it and the global social and emotional networks their fandom created, including across the Iron Curtain in the 1980s. Part of what his work therefore indicates is how forms of social expression that may appear to many to be non-political or even apolitical in their apparently customary, unthinking responses to pervasive forms of popular culture actually have important social and political effects, for example in facilitating what are *diverse* rather than standardized interpretive responses, as well as a sense of community for people such as teenagers who have legitimate reasons to feel socially disenfranchised.

Deller's work is emphatically populist, both for this engagement with 'popular' feeling and in that 'his' work is often largely not 'by' him but by many others: 800 re-enactors and 200 former miners participated in *The Battle of Orgreave*; he has commissioned brass bands to play acid house music (*Acid Brass*, 1997 [2012a, pp. 66–8]) and steel bands to play music by Joy Division (*Steel Harmony*, 2009 [ibid., pp. 174–5); for the 2009 Manchester International Festival he organized a procession of the city's people which he described as 'a bit like a procession you would see on *The Simpsons*' (ibid., p. 166); and his 2012 retrospective at London's Hayward Gallery was called *Joy in People* (22 February–13 May, 2012). There are several ways his work engages with craft, but I want to suggest here that he treats *collaboration* as craft. His collaborations are consistently time-consuming: *Procession*'s collaboration with hundreds of people took over a year (ibid., p. 170); *The Battle of Orgreave* took two years to develop (ibid., p. 98). They demonstrate 'material consciousness' about other people's carefully executed work – fans' drawings of and for Depeche Mode, Ed Hall's banners for processions, and musicians' committed engagement with music, even where that music is not what would conventionally be understood as their own. And his collaborations are egalitarian: *Time Out* journalist Ossian Ward has identified his works' persistent 'championing of the achievements of others' (Ward, n.d.). As in Perry's work, there is in Deller's an invocation of folk culture – important cultural expression shared across many people. This folk culture is not, importantly, folksy, old-fashioned or particularly nostalgic. Rather, it is vividly and actively engaged with current popular culture. Though the resources to develop craftsmanship may not be available to all, Deller nevertheless recognizes the value – emotional, political and social – of amateur expression, and he shares, if not precisely the means of *production*, at least the means of distribution and exhibition with a broad range of collaborators.

What is crafted across these artists' work is not so much commodities that will result in individual financial profit – though admittedly there will be some of that. What is crafted more consistently and carefully are practices of collaboration and models of egalitarianism that refuse both neoliberal self-interest and the social atomization intrinsic to being or becoming individual artists as what Fleming and Erskine call entrepreneurial 'micro-businesses'. Art and craft in the work of these artists and others of their generations is often individual and singular – recognizably the work and expression of an individual. Yet the understanding of the individual it promulgates is not that of liberal or neoliberal self-interest. The artwork preserves and values the autonomous expression of the individual – McQueen's individual service-people, Perry's fellow craftspeople and Deller's Depeche Mode fans – but not to the detriment or denunciation of the social. These artists demonstrate craft's 'mass production', not in the sense of mass quantities of identical, commercial mass-produced products as loathed by Adorno (1991), and loved by capitalism's champions of efficient economies of scale, but as in many *different* things produced with care by many. They model craftsmanship that extends from the highly skilled – but potentially elitist – forms celebrated by Sennett to the popular or folk cultural forms that are more achievable for the many who do not have the means to train. McQueen, Perry and Deller also share the means of display, even where it is not always possible to share the means of production. Whatever the pervasiveness and aggressiveness of government discourses that equate art and entrepreneurialism and advocate for artists to work with greater (financial) self-interest, artists are still responding with objects, narratives and activities that constellate craft, collaboration and equality in ways that continue to testify to art's precisely *social* value.

Conclusion

This chapter has explored what is at stake in being an artist in an era which has witnessed the rise of the cultural and creative industries, when artists are exhorted to behave as entrepreneurs and are celebrated for doing so by such powerful figures as New Labour pioneer Tony Blair and Conservative culture minister Ed Vaizey. It has focused on a selection of problems with artists' 'entrepreneurialization', especially its apparently tacit endorsement of individualism, creative destruction and self-interested profit-making, all problems which risk accentuating the uneven – and unfair – distribution of wealth, opportunity and even survival in contemporary culture. It acknowledges that the pressures of 'entrepreneurialization' are pervasive and strong, but also that artists are nevertheless resisting and challenging these pressures in at least three important ways. First, practically, they are forming networks of affiliation and mutual support that challenge both individualism and hierarchies of power. Second, they are testing the apparently beneficial effects of creative destruction by pushing them to their limits in practices that examine the destructions of war, gentrification and especially labour. Third, they are challenging emphases on profit and self-interest by connecting art practices to craftsmanship, with its affiliations to inherent quality, inefficiency and – most importantly – social interdependence and principles of egalitarianism. If this chapter was concerned with ways that neoliberal capitalism infiltrates and reconfigures structures, practices and subjectivities, not just objects, in ways that potentially extend its effects while simultaneously, dangerously, naturalizing them, it has also worked to demonstrate and argue that neoliberalism does not command all structures, practices and subjectivities in contemporary art practice. In the face of the aggressive emphasis on individual interests represented by neoliberalism and the UK governments' neoliberal policies at least since the 1980s, art, theatre and performance are maintaining and advocating for models of collectivism, social collaboration and forms of egalitarianism, however complex and, sometimes, compromised those models and forms may be.

3
Space: Exclusion and Engagement

Introduction

Space is socially contested. The ways people and organizations occupy and use space affects crucial social relations of privilege and power, such as who has the right to be where, when; what space is public, what private; who gets to live where; how mixed or segregated groups of people are; and what behaviours are encouraged, permitted, prevented or punished in particular places at particular times.[1] In the second decade of the twenty-first century in the United Kingdom – as in many places elsewhere – space is particularly acutely contested. State and corporate policing of would-be 'public' space through CCTV and public order legislation endures and risks becoming increasingly normalized. Nevertheless, protests in public space likewise persist in campaigns against such hegemonic acts of authority as state-mandated increases in Higher Education fees, major corporate tax-dodging, cuts to public services in the name of austerity, the uneven distribution of wealth and perceived police corruption; protests against this last point escalated in summer 2011 into riots across London and other UK cities. At the same time, such protests face aggressive spatial acts of policing such as kettling, eviction, arrest and imprisonment. Meanwhile, some of the most important spatial features of daily life – homes and housing – are becoming, for many, increasingly insecure in the face of insufficient planning, provision, quantity, quality, affordability, stability and accessibility, leading to ghettoized distribution. Housing prices continue to rise in apparently inverse proportion to available housing stock. Perhaps most insidiously, distribution patterns of wealth and health – and poverty and illness – remain spatially predictable.

Coinciding with these stresses on spatial social relations, contemporary art and performance practices are themselves actively engaging with space. Some of these engagements are explicitly political, as in performative public protests by such groups as Occupy, UK Uncut, Liberate Tate and the Counter Olympics Network; in public protests against issues such as HE fees increases (especially in November 2010), the detention of Russian punk band Pussy Riot (2012) and UK engagement in the war in Iraq (especially in February 2003); and in protests in publicly funded galleries and in audio journeys in the work of Platform, Liberate Tate and Art Not Oil. Some of the actively spatially engaged artistic practices are less explicitly political, but nevertheless often politically engaged. These include pop-up venues not located within conventional art contexts, and art produced and practised in social housing. They include artwork/performances that travel, such as Lone Twin's *The Boat Project* (2011 continuing), Alex Hartley's towable *Nowhereisland* and mobile embassy (2012) and Andrew Kötting and Iain Sinclair's journey in a swan-shaped pedalo and resulting film, *Swandown* (2012). They include big, encompassing installations commissioned annually in Tate Modern's Turbine Hall since 2000 by Doris Salcedo (*Shibboleth*, 2007–8), Dominique Gonzalez-Foerster (*TH.2058*, 2008–9), Ai Weiwei (*Sunflower Seeds*, 2010–11), Tino Sehgal (2012) and others. And they include immersive theatre environments by the likes of Punchdrunk, Shunt and Grid Iron. Furthermore, spatial reorientations that encourage participation in art are recognizable more broadly in UK government policy, introduced by Labour in 2001 but preserved by the Conservative-led government from 2010, mandating free entry to England's national museums, including those which formerly both were free (such as the Tates and the National Gallery) and charged (such as the Victoria and Albert and the Imperial War Museum). However, spatial exclusions exist simultaneously in the very same venues – and many other cultural organizations besides – given these venues' coinciding if not coincidental campaigns to expand income generation through proliferating private cafés, restaurants, bars and shops.

However explicit their politics, these art and performance practices test boundaries between public space and private space. They often make visible the unremarked private control of space by apparently provoking that control to assert itself. They explicitly critique the privatization of space and its collusions in preserving inequalities of wealth and opportunity. They provoke questions about social equality, social mobility and society itself. However, they are not all – or all consistently – oppositional. Sometimes they may cultivate an appetite for the claiming of private space, as in the 'unique' exploratory adventures proffered by Punchdrunk. And they may contribute to social ghettoization, for example, by privileging an already comparatively privileged so-called 'creative class' and facilitating processes of gentrification.

This chapter asks how current patterns of organizing and distributing space affect social relations, what social relations we want and how we might achieve them through art practices that make critical spatial and social interventions. Focusing on cities and London in particular, it explores how multiple contemporary conditions increasingly threaten to provoke gentrification's most damaging effects by segregating and ghettoizing comparatively advantaged and disadvantaged populations. These conditions are partly 'external' to art practices, and include such things as economic conditions and government ideologies and policies. However, they are also artistic and culture-led, including creative cities' policies and pop-up art practices. The chapter explores a range of these conditions and their potentially detrimental social effects. It then looks at spatially engaged art practices that respond to their own implication in processes of gentrification, reflect explicitly on the complex meanings of home and model modes of social engagement and collaboration that challenge forces of social segregation which may otherwise appear so pervasive, embedded and strong.

This chapter explores how contemporary art and performance are engaging in spatial relations in ways that both risk corroborating and challenge social relationships of oppression and exclusion. It explores their problematic potential to jeopardize social equality, segregate, ghettoize, exclude and, at worst, contribute to 'social cleansing'. And it explores their social benefits in protecting equality, drawing attention to ways space is being problematically redistributed and reclaiming space for less advantaged communities and for social collaboration and integration. It asks how contemporary art and performance can help us understand recalibrations in contemporary spatial relations and resulting social relations, and how they can contribute to improving the equality of those relations.

The chapter investigates a series of significant spatial trends in contemporary art and performance, across cultural policy and art practice. These trends often initially appear socially and culturally beneficial but tend to distribute benefit unevenly. The first section explores how a focus of recent urban cultural and development policy to foster 'creative cities' in order to attract a 'creative class' is potentially engineering urban populations in problematic and uneven ways. The policy approach claims socially beneficial objectives – to foster cities' economic competitiveness in the face of declining industrialization and to promote creative cities as socially tolerant. Nevertheless, its routine privileging of the 'creative class' risks exacerbating class distinctions.

The second section looks at a spatial trend in contemporary art and performance practices: pop-ups. Proliferating pop-up art venues operate only temporarily and in locations that are not normally galleries or exhibition/performance spaces. They have much to recommend them: in times of recession, they turn unused and sometimes neglected properties into active artistic spaces, often at affordable rates for artists; they can de-ghettoize art itself, potentially drawing new audiences by migrating art beyond districts that are comparatively over-endowed, such as London's Southbank; they can be site responsive; and they can model micro-utopian possibilities for cultural change. However, they also pose several potential problems. They risk spreading the marketization of space; operating as 'plop art', effectively parachuted in by an outside organization to a community with which neither the art nor the outside organization has much genuine interaction; camouflaging the broader lack of infrastructural support for art in the context of funding cutbacks; and contributing to changing perceptions of neighbourhoods, leading to gentrification and economically necessitating residents' gradual out-migration. Though I acknowledge that it is probably almost never artists' ambition to contribute to gentrification's negative social effects of exclusion and ghettoization, I look in some detail at how the social housing policies and practices of David Cameron's government are providing a perfect storm of conducive conditions highly likely to exacerbate this risk of gentrification.

Following on from the previous section's concern with housing inequality – and art practices' potential if unintentional collusion with it – the third section looks at a range of recent art practices that explicitly engage with, and often happen in, homes. Examining work by Marcus Coates, Michael Landy and Andy Hewitt and Mel Jordan among others, this section explores tactics artists are using to compel audiences critically to reflect on housing inequality and such social consequences of gentrification as social fragmentation and ghettoization.

One of the major problems of gentrification is increased social fragmentation as some are included and some excluded from zones of space, resource and opportunity. The final section of this chapter looks at art practices which aim to foster social cohesion through spatial practices that are, themselves, dispersed. The practices examined here were all commissioned for the London Cultural Olympiad coinciding with the lead-up to and event of the 2012 London Olympics and are mobile and dispersed, often taking the form of journeys. In different ways and to different degrees, each demonstrates an experiment in social collaboration and its potential to enhance social cohesion.

Space is literally the terrain on and in which contests over social equality and inequality are being worked out. Contemporary art and performance participates in and pushes these contests in ways both cautionary and constructive, exploiting available spatial resources in straightened economic times, demonstrating the pressures on housing in an age of neoliberal market ascendance, and – not uncritically – exploring practices of social collaboration as models of social cohesion.

Creative cities

My concern in this section and the next, on pop-ups, is with the social power relations that the city – London in particular – produces for its inhabitants through its spatial cultural practices. As in many other cities, in London there are enormous discrepancies between the very advantaged and the very disadvantaged. This polarity was starkly visible in the summer of 2011 in globally distributed images of the riots (and responses) that took place in parts of London – particularly comparatively poor parts, such as Tottenham and Hackney in North London and Brixton, Peckham and Clapham in South London – and spread to other English cities such as Birmingham and Manchester. This polarity was figured by the juxtaposition of rioters who were apparently poor and certainly culturally disenfranchised with politicians who were comparatively very wealthy (frequently multimillionaire), culturally powerful and practically unanimous in their vociferous condemnation of the rioters. Debate continues about the degree to which the rioting and looting were the result of, on one hand, structural constraints such as poor educational and work opportunities and, on the other, individual agency enacted by those whom Prime Minister Cameron characterized as 'sick and irresponsible' (in Shipman, 2011). The riots provide a highly visible, 'flash-point' example of London's gross social discrepancies in advantage and disadvantage, but extensive evidence shows that such discrepancies – in wealth, but also health, life expectancy, educational attainment and employment, as well as many other aspects of life – are pervasive.

London's population of approximately 7.5 million is marked by extremes of wealth and poverty, and this disparity is greater in Inner London than in any other region in England: '19% of the population of Inner London are in the top tenth for income nationwide, measured after housing costs. 16% are in the bottom tenth of income' (London's Poverty Profile [LPP], 2011a). Furthermore, there is a greater concentration of the highest incomes in London than anywhere else in England: 'In Inner

London ... 20% of people have 60% of the income' (ibid.). If we take into account housing costs – and we must, since housing is both necessary and, in London, comparatively expensive – poverty in London is at 28 per cent, compared to 22 per cent in the rest of England (LPP, 2011b). 'London has the highest rates of poverty and inequality of any region in the country', and the scale of the problem has 'in some respects been "getting worse" over the past decade' (Mulholland, 2009).[2] Health inequality is also painfully extreme in London. In its wealthiest ward, in Kensington and Chelsea in West London, male life expectancy as assessed in 2010 was 88 years. Mere miles away in Tottenham Green, north-east London, one of the city's poorest wards and where the riots of summer 2011 began, male life expectancy was 17 years shorter at 71 years. As *Guardian* journalist Randeep Ramesh observes, this is 'a period less than that found in Ecuador, China and Belize, countries all poorer with no national health systems' (Ramesh, 2010a; see Marmot Review Team, 2010, p. 2).

Influential geographers Ash Amin, Doreen Massey and Nigel Thrift (2000) argue that we need *Cities for the Many Not the Few*. This is one of the biggest and most important challenges of our times: where over half the world's population now lives in cities, where they offer enormous opportunity but also contain extraordinary poverty and disadvantage, we need to work on identifying what practices, including cultural practices, can not only produce urban prosperity and happiness, but also most fairly *distribute* that prosperity and happiness to the many, not just a privileged few. This problem of how cultural practices produce greater prosperity but also often, simultaneously, greater inequality is my focus in these two sections on creative cities and pop-ups.

This section looks at recent urban cultural theory on so-called 'creative cities' and their 'creative class' that has influenced cultural and development policy in the United States in particular, but also the United Kingdom and other countries. I argue that although shifts in urban policy-making in favour of the creative class have certainly had some social benefits, those benefits have been enjoyed largely by the middle classes, and the effects of further entrenching neoliberal capitalism and extending gentrification have been largely disadvantageous for London's enormous population of poor. The next section looks at recent pop-up performance and art events in London. I argue that though these practices too have several potential social benefits, they are dangerously placed to leverage gentrification that displaces underprivileged Londoners. This is a particular risk, I propose, because of a perfect storm of state-led and state-instituted conditions that are emerging from the

Conservative-led coalition government formed in spring 2010 and that threaten the future of London's affordable social housing and the welfare of its tenants.

In looking at both of these first two spatial trends in contemporary culture – for creative cities and pop-up cultural venues – I am concerned with which classes of people have what kinds of mobility and whether that mobility is desired or economically necessitated. The mobility I am concerned with is chiefly spatial – it is about who lives where, why and how people's access to resources and expectations about healthcare and longevity are improved or worsened by living in particular urban locations. The Conservative-led coalition government claims that 'improving social mobility [is] its principal social policy goal', stating, 'We will work across government to make life chances more equal so that what counts is how hard you work and the skills and talents you possess, not the school you went to or the jobs your parents did' (Cabinet Office, 2011). Social mobility is usually about movement up the ranks of class, and the government's insinuation is that that movement is – or should be – unaffected by such indicators of physical location as what 'school you went to' or therefore, for the vast majority of people, where you grew up. However, the difference I posed in the previous sentence between what is and what should be is the heart of the problem. A neoliberal entrepreneurial attitude would argue that will and application are sufficient enabling conditions to achieve social mobility; other approaches would argue that mobility depends on material conditions such as access to education, as well as socially enabling cultural capital. As the neighbourhood-specific statistics on longevity cited above indicate, social opportunity, including social mobility, is at least very often affected by people's physical location. And I argue that trends such as creative cities and pop-ups – supported by both UK and London Conservative-led governments – can actually undermine the kind of mobility the UK government claims it is committed to rather than supporting it, especially when that mobility is further restricted by other concurrent aspects of government policy to do with, amongst other things, urban planning and the allocation of housing benefits.

I am concerned here with how creative cities policy and pop-up arts practices relate to gentrification, with its twin effects of regeneration and social displacement, and how they risk contributing to urban social inequality. Both trends hold the promise of enhanced urban liveability and prosperity – but for whom and in what measure? While advocates of the creative city argue that it is precisely such cities' liveability that produces their prosperity, I explore here the inverse equation – that

London's cultural strategies designed for prosperity adversely affect livability for its most vulnerable citizens.

Creative cities and the creative class

The term 'creative class' has been popularized by the American academic Richard Florida in his influential 2002 book *The Rise of the Creative Class and How It's Transforming Work, Leisure, Community and Everyday Life* (see Florida, 2002, 2005, 2008).[3] Florida argues that workers distinguished by their creative talent are now driving post-industrial knowledge-based or 'creative' economies. The choices people in this creative class make increasingly influence not only work but, as his title claims, leisure, community, everyday life and, indeed, cities and regions. The chief way they influence cities is by inverting a long-standing pattern of movement between workers and cities. In earlier eras, people would follow jobs and companies – moving, for example, to Detroit for its automotive industry, or to London for its print industry. In the current economy, Florida argues, jobs and companies follow people since people are choosing to live in cities that appeal to them not so much for the work opportunities on offer as for other aspects of 'lifestyle choice' that they satisfy, such as particularly amenable neighbourhoods and a social climate that is, as Florida puts it, tolerant. In order for cities to be prosperous and to become successful creative cities in this creative economy, Florida argues that they need to concentrate on attracting and retaining not major companies or organizations, but this creative class of workers; in turn, the work will be drawn by this class of talented workers, alongside a provision of technology and a climate of tolerance. Florida's creative class are creative thinkers, not just creative artists or producers. They work not only in the cultural industries but across the economy and, according to Florida, anyone can potentially be a member of this class. That said, one of their chief characteristics is physical mobility, their openness to moving from city to city and their access to resources that enable such movement; so clearly not everyone can be a member of this class. The creative class's mobility is also why Florida encourages cities to aim to attract them in a trend which is producing inter-urban competition on a global scale (Peck, 2007, p. 1).[4] Florida's propositions have met some resistance. Opposition on the right has aimed primarily at his sympathy to gay and lesbian populations which he sees as fundamentally symptomatic of tolerant environments. Opposition on the left I detail below.

Despite some resistance, Florida's propositions have been widely taken up, particularly by American cities and regions, from which he draws his research and which he ranks with reference to what he sees as their attractiveness to the creative class. *The Rise of the Creative Class*'s rankings of US cities according to various criteria (creative workers, a 'gay' index, immigration and more) gave its 'winners' complimentary 'statistical civic boosterism' (O'Connor and Kong, 2009a, p. 3) in global competition for the creative class and effectively invited its 'losers' to contact Florida to seek instruction on improvement. Florida's 2005 book, *Cities and the Creative Class*, included 'Rankings of Top 50 Metropolitan Areas', all in the United States, according to such indices as technology provision, a 'gay index', a 'bohemian index' and a 'talent index'.[5] However, Florida's theories have also been influential beyond the United States. The website for his company, *Creative Class* (Florida, 2011), lists among its clients Dublin, Cape Town, Brisbane, and places in New Zealand and Canada (where he has been based in the Rotman School of Management at the University of Toronto since 2007). His ambitions are clearly global. His 2008 book, *Who's Your City? How the Creative Economy Is Making Where to Live the Most Important Decision of Your Life*, is pitched explicitly at a global market and name-drops London, England, at least 43 times.

Most of Florida's research draws on American examples and he principally addresses an American context. However, his ideas are very relevant to the United Kingdom and London for several reasons. There is extensive evidence that by the late twentieth century, the UK's economy had become predominantly the kind of knowledge-based model that is potentially Florida's creative city. The ratio of the value of intangible assets to raw materials in the United Kingdom almost completely inverted from 20:80 in the 1950s to 70:30 in the 1990s (Cooke and De Laurentis 2008, in Clifton, 2008, p. 64). Quantitative analysis from the first decade of the twenty-first century on the distribution of the creative class in England and Wales shows the largest concentrations generally, and not surprisingly, in London (Clifton, 2008). An emphasis on stimulating and supporting the cultural and creative industries has been an explicit and high-profile part of UK government policy since 1997's election of Tony Blair's New Labour government, as discussed in more detail in Chapter 2. In 1995, several years before the 2002 publication of Florida's *Rise of the Creative Class*, UK-based researchers Charles Landry and Franco Bianchini published *The Creative City*. Like Florida, they emphasize the importance to the success of the creative city of both creative workers and a conducive environment sympathetic to – or tolerant of – the contributions of immigrants and intercultural hybridity.[6]

Evidence of take-up of thinking along Florida's lines in UK government policy can be seen in the joint project *Living Places* (2011) started in 2003 by the Departments of Culture, Media and Sport and for Communities and Local Government. This programme aimed to support those local authorities where population growth was predicted by helping them make their districts more amenable places to live. Offering guidance on cultural infrastructure, it argued that 'better cultural planning brings jobs, confidence [and] *investment*' (Fleming and Erskine, 2011, p. 42, emphasis added). This strategic approach is directly reflected in, for example, Glasgow's Creative Clyde (2012), a creative business hub founded in 2011 as an outcome of collaborative partnerships between Scottish Enterprise, Scottish Development International, Clyde Waterfront, Glasgow City Council, Creative Scotland (which replaced the Scottish Arts Council and Scottish Screen in 2010), BBC Scotland, the performance and conference venue SECC, the University of Glasgow and some private enterprises. A launch article published both on Creative Clyde's website and in a glossy Scottish industry promotional book, introduced by Scottish First Minister Alex Salmond and entitled *World Class Scotland: A Place for Business*, made clear that Creative Clyde's explicit purpose was to develop Scotland's creative industries and attract inward migration of creative businesses. The article highlighted, amongst other things, Glasgow's creative industries' 'skilled workforce' and its 'attractive location', boasting, 'The partners behind Creative Clyde are determined to create the perfect environment for creative companies to locate and grow' (Creative Clyde, 2011; Scotland World Class, 2011, p. 47).

A creative cities strategic approach is also reflected in the 2011 *London Plan* or *Spatial Development Strategy for Greater London*. Conservative Mayor Boris Johnson (2011, p. 5) claims here that his 'vision for London embraces two objectives. London must retain and build upon its world city status as one of three business centres of global reach. It *must be somewhere people and businesses want to locate*' and 'London must also be *among the best cities in the world to live*' (emphasis added). As far as I know, Richard Florida has not explicitly been asked to advise London or Glasgow on improving their 'creativity indices' in order to attract more creative-class workers. Nevertheless, governments in London, Scotland and elsewhere in the United Kingdom are certainly buying into many of the ambitions, strategies and ensuing ideologies that Florida promotes. Assessing the relevance of Florida's creative-class theories in the United Kingdom, cultural policy theorist Kate Oakley claims that 'Richard Florida's notion of a "creative class" and the role that mobile knowledge workers can play in the economic development of cities and regions have been highly influential in UK policy circles' (2009b, p. 121).[7]

Creative cities for whom?

It is fair to say that London is a creative city with a creative class along lines mapped out by Florida. Florida claims that such creative cities will prosper. But do they? And how is that prosperity distributed among their citizens, especially in a city such as London whose citizens demonstrate gross discrepancies in standards of quality of living such as wealth and health? Here, I consider some of the potential *social* – not just economic – outcomes of the creative city to ask who benefits and on what terms. I argue that while creative city policy and practice produce some important social benefits, their social risks are enormous.

On the positive side, the kind of city Florida advocates is broadly sympathetic to creative and cultural workers, marking an advantageous shift for culture workers compared to earlier eras, which placed more value on other kinds of labour and industry such as manufacturing. Florida's creative city also specifically valorizes social tolerance of diverse sexualities and ethnicities. What Florida outlines has a feel-good factor, encouraging cities to be both good (socially tolerant) but also fun in order to attract the best workers and to be most prosperous. It is a seductive proposal.

However, as geographer Jamie Peck, artist Martha Rosler and others have eloquently and energetically detailed, there are many reasons to be wary of Florida's model.[8] Although at first, Florida's arguments might seem to be very positively socially mindful, their apparent adoption of a social agenda is more significantly driven by economic instrumentalism than by social commitment. Florida does not advocate social tolerance of gays, lesbians, varied ethnicities and even cultural workers chiefly because to do so is socially or ethically good in its own terms. For him, such tolerance is positive because it attracts the highly desired creative worker who generates prosperity and economic growth. And as much as that worker might care about living in a socially tolerant environment, Florida expects the creative worker's behaviour to be more importantly motivated by *self*-interest rather than social interest, as the creative worker moves from creative city to creative city as he or she pleases. As Peck (2007, p. 2) puts it, Florida depicts 'creative subjects as hedonistic free agents', perfect for the global neoliberal capitalist economy.

Most problematically, Florida's ideas risk exacerbating already existing privilege for the middle and higher classes and already existing disadvantage for others. His exhortation to cities to attract creative workers by providing amenable neighbourhoods explicitly prioritizes comparatively advantaged consumer desires (for example, for cafés, boutiques and other luxury resources) over basic human needs. His claim that anyone can be mobile even if not rich is patronizing or at best extremely naïve. Though he recognizes that migration is not always a result of choice, but sometimes a result of economic necessity, he pays this insufficient attention (Florida, 2008, pp. 71–2). And as Oakley points out, he apparently does not account for the fact that an '"immobility regime" of surveillance and control' presides over many 'migrants, refugees and other "undesirable aliens"' (2009b, p. 126).[9] Florida's 'talented' creative-class workers *choose* the places and work they want. Meanwhile, those workers moving from dying industries, but lacking the requisite 'talent' are barely depicted by Florida. They have little choice beyond seeking generally unsatisfying service labour even as their neighbourhoods are gentrified, pushing them out to suburban areas with, often, fewer amenities and poorer transport links as well as fewer jobs, and risking the break-up of their kinship networks as neighbourhoods and families are dispersed (Lees, Slater and Elvin Wyly, 2008, p. xxiv; Dench, Gavron and Young, 2006). Oakley concludes, 'The "non creative" class are thus marginalised twice: once because their consumption preferences and needs do not reflect that of the creative class, and secondly because the effect of an influx of the creative class may well raise land and housing prices and drive out the provision of more basic services' (2009b, pp. 130–1). 'It should come as no surprise', observes Peck, 'that the creative capitals' – such as London – 'exhibit higher rates of socioeconomic inequality than other cities' (2007, p. 10).[10]

For all the prosperity creative cities are supposed to generate, therefore, instead of solving urban social problems, the conditions produced in Florida's creative city tend not only to coexist with such problems, but to exacerbate them (Peck, 2007, p. 10; Oakley, 2009b, p. 132). The social world of creative cities is by no means entirely 'feel-good', therefore, since it is fundamentally based on and actively fuels fierce market competition between cities, nations and even neighbourhoods; exacerbates socioeconomic inequality; and privileges neoliberal ideologies and characteristics of individualism and chosen nomadism. Indeed, Peck argues that the wide global adoption of creative cities thinking and policy-making is attributable in part to the ways it fits so comfortably with 'today's neoliberalized political-economic terrain' (2007, p. 1).

Pop-ups

I now approach the idea of the creative city through arts practice by thinking about a phenomenon of city life that is becoming more common and that might also be seen as both creative and socially constructive: the pop-up. These are usually spaces such as shops, offices, workshops, factories or flats which are temporarily out of use because, for example, they are un-rented or awaiting renovation, development or demolition, and which are given over for another temporary and often creative use. Sometimes, they are temporary constructions, such as temporarily erected prefabs or shipping containers. Sometimes, they are short-term revisions to, or occupations of, existing buildings that share the pop-up's broad function; for example, cultural centres or department stores. Most frequently, pop-ups are used as restaurants or boutiques, often during periods when there is likely to be more demand for their fare – for example, in the lead-up to Christmas; on London's Southbank during the summer, when there are numerous pop-up restaurants and bars; during a festival, for example in Edinburgh in August; or on weekends in local neighbourhoods, when more city-working residents are at home.

Pop-ups are not something Florida specifically advocates, but they are appropriate to think about in relation to his creative city for at least three reasons. First, pop-ups often offer special kinds of commodities or experiences that make neighbourhoods particularly attractive to residents, perhaps especially the kind of financially secure, leisured creative class that Florida desires. Second, though the *London Plan 2011* which lays out Mayor Johnson's urban development strategy till 2031 disappointingly dedicates only about four of its 319 pages to 'Support for and enhancement of arts, culture, sport and entertainment provision' (section 4.6), within this brief section, it specifically calls on London boroughs to 'support the temporary use of vacant buildings for performance and creative work' (Greater London Authority, 2011, p. 125). Third, pop-up activities potentially leverage the gentrification which is also a risk in Florida's conception of the creative city and which has previously occurred through artists' former temporary use of places in such sites as lower Manhattan in the 1970s and, more recently, in East London's Spitalfields, Shoreditch and Hoxton.[11] This key question about pop-ups' potential to contribute to gentrification is what I concentrate on below, but first I illustrate their recent proliferation in London.

'[T]here has been an upsurge of "pop-up" shops, restaurants and theatres', observe town planners Peter Bishop and Lesley Williams in their 2012 book, *The Temporary City*. The book offers a detailed and richly illustrated overview of the trend and supports their claim with the cover image of the *Guardian*'s G2 section from October 2010 which runs the feature story, 'Is There No End to the Pop-up Revolution?' (Bishop and Williams, 2012, pp. 2–3; *Guardian*, 2010). Pop-up art practices in particular are also widespread. The London-based art commissioning company Artangel, for example, is committed to facilitating artists' creative engagement with the city, has been operating very actively since at least 1992 and frequently commissions artwork that could be seen as pop-up. A famous comparatively early example of such commissioning is Rachel Whiteread's *House* (1993–94), in which she cast an east London house in concrete (see Artangel, 2011a). More recently, Roger Hiorns's *Seizure* took place in part of a south London social housing estate that was awaiting demolition and redevelopment (see Artangel, 2011b; Harvie, 2011a). Hiorns filled an entire flat with copper sulphate solution that crystallized, completely covering the interior surface in rich blue crystals. I discuss this example in more detail later in this chapter. Artangel also commissions work for non-residential sites. A famous example discussed in detail in Chapter 2 is Michael Landy's 2001 installation *Break Down* in a department store on London's central shopping thoroughfare, Oxford Street (see Artangel, 2011c; Harvie, 2006). In the interval between its closure as a C&A and its reopening as a Primark, the site was occupied by Landy, who moved in with a conveyor belt and some collaborators and systematically destroyed all his possessions.

Examples of London pop-up theatre practice include the work of Shunt, a company which has made performance, club and bar spaces out of arches under London Bridge and a former warehouse in nearby Bermondsey. Punchdrunk, whose work I discuss in more detail in Chapter 4, has made many performances in temporary locations, perhaps most famously their 2006 production of *Faust* in a former warehouse in Wapping (Punchdrunk, 2011, *Faust* page). In summer 2009, as part of its response to the effects of the recession on the arts, Arts Council England launched the £500,000 grant programme Art in Empty Spaces, both to help artists use available spaces and to animate urban high streets (ACE, 2009b). Projects funded by the scheme included *The Uncommercial Traveller*, a collaboration by the Arcola Theatre and Punchdrunk in summer 2011 in the East London Borough of Hackney (Punchdrunk and Arcola, 2012). Sadler's Wells collaborated with Without Walls and Fuel production company to produce the dance- and audio-based 'outdoor spectacle' *Electric Hotel* in a series of stacked shipping containers behind King's Cross station in June 2010 (see Bishop and Williams, 2012, pp. 128–9; Sadler's Wells, 2012; *Electric Hotel*, 2012). Established in 2007, Theatre Delicatessen has produced theatre in vacant central London buildings – on Marylebone High Street and Regents Street for example – on short-term peppercorn rents (see Bishop and Williams, 2012, pp. 130–1; Theatre Delicatessen, 2012a, 2012b). In 2011, Folly for a Flyover literally set up shop under a flyover in East

London's Hackney Wick, providing a venue for performance, film, activities, boat hire and a café/bar (see Bishop and Williams, 2012, p. 93; Folly, 2012). Even the long-established Royal Court is in on the trend. Though famous for text-based work in its flagship Sloane Square theatres, since 2010 it has experimented with pop-ups in its Theatre Local programme, producing theatre in shop fronts in the South London Elephant and Castle mall in 2010 and in the former cricket bat factory turned cultural hub, the Bussey Building, in Peckham, South London in 2011 and 2012 (Royal Court, 2010, 2011, 2012a, 2012b).

Artistic pop-ups are also not all run or initiated by arts organizations. The property management companies Ad Hoc and Camelot find residents or 'guardians' for properties that are temporarily unoccupied; many residents make temporary arts interventions in these spaces. Space Makers Agency, similarly, facilitates use of unused or underused buildings, not specifically for art practices but, in their words, 'to create sociable spaces and sustainable local economies' (Ad Hoc, 2011; Bishop and Williams, 2012, p. 45; Space Makers Agency, 2011). They have managed a pop-up shop scheme in Brixton's indoor market, Brixton Village, and set up a street market in West Norwood, both in south London. It would also certainly be possible to call the tent communities of Occupy – in London near the London Stock Exchange (2011–12), in New York on Wall Street, and in over 1000 other places worldwide – pop-ups, as it might be possible to call forms of property squatting pop-up. The key point I want to make by listing all of these examples is that the pop-up is multiplying and thriving in London, particularly as an arts venue/event.

Pop-ups' potential benefits

There is clear creative and social value to be had from pop-up artistic venues and activities. Most importantly, they make for artists and audiences opportunities for creative expression and experience that simply do not otherwise exist. They are often thrifty and constructively opportunistic, creatively exploiting some of the more damaging effects of recession, such as an increased availability of unused commercial property, and economically securing space to make art while simultaneously alleviating the often depressing visible effects of recession. This kind of intervention has frequently been most powerful in places experiencing significant out-migration usually due to industrial change, as was the case in areas in lower Manhattan in the 1970s. But it is highly relevant in UK cities too: a study of 700 UK towns and cities found that, in June 2010, 13 per cent of shop fronts were vacant; by September 2012, 14.6 per cent of shops were reportedly vacant (Local Data Company [LDC],

2010, cited in Bishop and Williams, 2012, p. 25; LDC 2012). Pop-ups benefit not only artists but also local residents and other local businesses by animating their area. And they benefit property owners by protecting and potentially improving sites and by enabling savings on costs for security, maintenance and business rates taxed on empty buildings.

Pop-ups can also respond dynamically, flexibly and creatively to emerging opportunities and issues, arising where and when it is not only possible but also important; this is illustrated powerfully by the Occupy encampments, including Occupy London Stock Exchange. Pop-up arts venues are often more dispersed within the city than much other cultural provision that tends to be concentrated in privileged city centres. They are therefore potentially more available to a greater social range of audiences, including in areas of greater deprivation. Many of the pop-ups I have cited above have occurred in comparatively poorer areas of London. The Royal Court's Theatre Local scheme, for example, aims specifically to 'take plays to alternative spaces' and, in so doing, reach new audiences. In the press release announcing Theatre Local 2012, Jemma Read, Head of Philanthropy at Theatre Local's sponsor Bloomberg, testified to Bloomberg's commitment to 'reaching new audiences' and 'provid[ing] opportunities to those who might not otherwise have access to the arts' (Royal Court, 2012b).

Pop-ups hold out a socially micro-utopian potential, making creative interventions that are temporary, tactical, multiple and dispersed – and often deliberately social – in ways that might intervene politically in how people see and experience the world. Pop-ups thus operate as what American poet and political writer Hakim Bey influentially dubbed Temporary Autonomous Zones (TAZs), temporary sites of activity (or inactivity) which challenge conventional structures and practices and encourage alternatives to emerge. 'We recommend [the TAZ]', Bey wrote,

> because it can provide the quality of enhancement associated with the uprising without necessarily leading to violence and martyrdom. The TAZ is like an uprising which does not engage directly with the State, a guerrilla operation which liberates an area (of land, of time, of imagination) and then dissolves itself to re-form elsewhere/elsewhen, *before* the State can crush it.
>
> (Bey, 1991, p. 101, italics original)

Though not usually as deliberately oppositional as Bey's TAZs, many pop-ups offer at least temporary alternatives to what already exists. Shunt's and Punchdrunk's work has animated old and disused urban spaces in ways that implicitly question developers' frequent preference for the new and slick. Occupy London Stock Exchange radically challenged the social distribution of not only space but other material resources as well. Landy's *Break Down* disrupted the usual continuous flow of consumerism on Oxford Street. I look at the example of Hiorns's *Seizure*'s micro-utopian intervention in more detail below. In all of the ways outlined above, pop-ups potentially contribute to a liveable, creative and socially progressive city for the many, not the few.

A micro-utopian example: Roger Hiorns's *Seizure*[12]

To expand on my claim for pop-ups' potential to make micro-utopian interventions, I look here in more detail at Roger Hiorns's *Seizure*. The micro-utopian intervention of this work, I suggest, was its provocation to audiences to reconsider social housing's function, design, scale, aesthetics and changing patterns of provision and effectiveness. For me, it suggested that the scale of social housing might sometimes more significantly compromise human experience than nurture it, and might arrest and oppress development, rather than mobilize and enable it. *Seizure* drew palpable, highly affective attention to the small scale of the flat in which it was created. 'Dark and airless', observed *ArtForum* reviewer Gilda Williams, 'this tenement-housing apartment has not been rendered unlivable [*sic*] so much as exposed for how unlivable it always was, what with its oppressively low ceilings, poky rooms, minuscule hallways, and claustrophobic bathroom' (2008, pp. 311–12). *Seizure* was in many ways beautiful; head of the Arts Council Collection Caroline Douglas (in Higgins, 2012) called it 'a thing of breathtaking beauty ... the colour of the best Mediterranean sky'. Despite – or in the face of that beauty – *Seizure* turned the former home where it was sited into a decidedly unhomely, enormous, blue-toothed maw, 'somehow unnatural, uncanny' and 'disturbing' in Douglas's words. It staged a dissonance between the flat's sumptuous, jewel-like blue crystal interior and its abandoned, neglected exterior. Its title and its materials – literally chemically arrested – staged an impounding of the flat, a sort of dystopian realization of the dire consequences of failing to meet the payments on one's rent or mortgage, having one's home seized and being forced to foreclose and move out. This was a resonant reference, coming so close to the collapse of the mortgage market from 2008 on. Notably, *Seizure*'s references to the serious social limitations of such public housing, particularly its physical limits, were not only representational but also spatial and relational, bringing audiences physically together in its cramped spaces to share an experience of this site and its spatially and socially limiting conditions.

My reading of the work as an exploration of the social limitations of some social housing coincides with elements of what Hiorns has said about his own reasons for choosing to work with the particular post-war late modernist social housing typified by 151–189 Harper Road in the South London Borough of Southwark. 'These kinds of building don't work', he claimed. 'They give you very little architecture, the nominal amount of expression you're allowed to have, they were ungenerous in that respect. In the great social experiment these buildings inferred, they provided no room for movement, zero mobility to move further, they are completely static materially and emotionally' (in Lingwood, 2008). Hiorns's *Seizure* offered a sparkly celebration of the *principles* of social housing at the same as it drew attention to the failures of its *realization*, particularly its propensity to provide inadequate and insufficient space for people to move and develop, materially and emotionally. Hiorns's *Seizure* was micro-utopian because it staged not so much a visionary potential as a cautionary reality about the importance of housing to be adequate and, ideally, inspiring.[13]

Pop-ups' potential risks

Despite pop-ups' many potential and realized benefits such as the kind of social warning staged in Hiorns's *Seizure*, there are reasons to be cautious about what they do, especially how they might contribute to exacerbating rather than redressing urban social inequality, whether they do that directly or indirectly. First, advocating for pop-up cultural venues as Mayor Boris Johnson does in the *London Plan* offers him a virtually investment-free way *to be seen* to support culture with its supposedly socially ameliorating effects without having to make *actual* finance-demanding investments in state infrastructures for such things as education or housing, let alone arts and culture. Similarly, to be successful in their ambitions to 'bring' culture to those communities which participate in it comparatively less and/or have comparatively poorer access to it, schemes such as the Royal Court's Bloomberg-sponsored Theatre Local must address material issues to do with not only space but also education, to develop interest, and finance, to make ticket prices affordable.[14] They should also reflect on the ethics of their relationship to 'local' cultures. Their work may be beneficial for 'local' communities and it is no doubt motivated in part by desires to do good. But it is also almost certainly motivated by self-interest in accruing benefit to themselves through expanding markets for their work and through association with urban fringe and street cultures that bear what artist and writer Martha Rosler calls a 'lack of bourgeois polish' (2011a, p. 11) and urban theorist Sharon Zukin (2010) identifies as 'gritty', 'cool' and 'authentic'. Some forms of pop-ups – such as squatting – have more straightforwardly damaging social effects in that, however peacefully squatters practise, they risk being criminalized by legislation which is increasingly intolerant of such interstitial, often highly beneficial uses of space.[15]

Pop-ups' pernicious, and frequently direct, complicity with urban social inequality can be seen very vividly in other common pop-up forms, such as boutique restaurants and shops that deliberately insert themselves in a very high-end market of up-cycled goods, marked-up prices and designer 'capsule' collections and season launches. Such pop-ups exploit their fleeting existence as intrinsic rarity and cachet and render their products or services as desirable commodity fetishes. Their short lives urge consumers to buy now or lose out forever, while at the same time functioning as novel marketing events as much as points of sale. The high-end department store Selfridges, for example, hosts temporary pop-up boutiques consistently, but rarely enough to maintain media attention/free advertising. The first half of 2012 alone saw Selfridges pop-up shops featuring Karl Lagerfeld's 'Olympic-inspired Karl Capsule Collection' (reported in *British Vogue* and *Elle*), Californian designer Phillip Lim (heralded in *Grazia* online), and only 'twenty exclusive styles' (Selfridges & Co., 2012) by shoe designer Christian Louboutin in honour of his company's twentieth anniversary (reported in the online men's fashion and style guide *FashionBeans*) (see *British Vogue*, 2012; Kinsella, 2012; Omerod, 2012; Thornton, 2012). Admittedly, arts pop-ups are generally far less likely to cultivate either the slickness or inflated – and exclusive – price ranges of these kinds of boutiques. Indeed, arts pop-ups are frequently aesthetically rough and ready, and often offer free admission. What arts pop-ups do tend to share with their designer boutique cousins, however, is a cultivated exceptionalism – happening outside conventional arts times and places. This exceptionalism rewards and arguably requires the cultural capital of exclusive insider engagement, even if it does not require financial capital. Furthermore, by way of contrast, it devalues the common and the shared, qualities both social and experiential that are too often and too casually abandoned in the self-interested rush to pursue the 'unique experience'.[16]

Arts pop-ups' use of semi-derelict buildings can likewise have negative social effects. On one hand, this use productively retrieves the old from routine capitalist castings as redundant waste. On the other, it risks fetishizing the apparently authentic, creating a sense of neo-bohemian alternative culture that makes poorer neighbourhoods attractive to Florida's creative class. This kind of fetishization frequently leads to gentrification, 'the transformation of a working-class or vacant area of the central city into middle-class residential and/or commercial use' (Lees, Slater and Wyly, 2008, p. xv), with its twin effects of regeneration and population displacement, the latter of which is linked usually to income and often to class. In this way, and perhaps most insidiously, pop-ups risk contributing to neoliberal capitalist colonization of urban space by facilitating changes in people's perceptions of an area that then make it productive for speculative investors to move in as private developers. Admittedly, this is probably almost never an *intended* consequence of pop-up creative activities. As Martha Rosler emphasizes, following the sociologist Ann Markusen (2006, in Rosler, 2011b, p. 20), another fierce critic of Florida, 'artists are overwhelmingly to the left on the political spectrum and engage at least sporadically in political agitation and participation'. However, pop-ups often provide the kind of initial stimulus – in other words, investment – that can lead eventually to gentrification. Coming into an apparently underused site, the pop-up literally animates that site; it often improves material infrastructures, for example stripping out asbestos in old buildings as Punchdrunk Artistic Director Felix Barrett claims his company does (Eyre, 2011); it almost always develops social infrastructures such as audiences and broader social awareness of a site's interest; and it proves the site's commercial attractiveness and viability.

For example, when Space Makers began working in 2009 in Brixton Village (also known as Granville Arcade – one of several markets in Brixton), 20 shop units were empty and Space Makers' task was 'to turn this around'. Their open call for ideas (Space Makers Agency, n.d.), 'offering shops for up to three months rent free to temporary creative and community projects, or new local business start-ups with an ambition to become long-term tenants', garnered a huge response. Within a year, all 20 original empty shops were let to long-term tenants, many of which were small restaurants, and a new community arts programme was established. Writing in autumn 2011, food critic Jay Rayner (2011) lavished praise on the restaurants and hailed the development as 'thrilling and bringing lots of people to Brixton who might otherwise not think of coming here', concluding, 'That has to be a good thing.' He noted, however, that '[e]ventually, of course, the bitching will start – it always does with London food ventures. Some will complain that the soul of the market has gone, others that it has become closed off to locals. There may be rows between landlords and tenants.'

Rayner presented these anticipated criticisms about cultural change and potential conflict between existing residents and incomers and between landlords and tenants as mean-spirited, in the sense of both fussy and cynical. But they deserve more careful consideration, given that it is perhaps the holiest grail of urban regeneration practices qualitatively and sustainably to improve neighbourhoods without pricing out former residents and irretrievably erasing the neighbourhood's former character or simply exploiting that character as 'local colour'. Artist Grayson Perry (in Glinkowski, 2008, n.p.) describes this gentrification process as 'the Hoxton effect': 'the artists move in, then they get priced out and the designers come, and then the estate agents, and then the developers, and then the area is dead.' I agree with Rayner that attracting incomers to Brixton can indeed be 'a good thing'. It brings inward investment to a neighbourhood that is comparatively economically disadvantaged (34 per cent of children lived in poverty in Brixton's Borough of Lambeth in 2009, compared to 12 per cent in Richmond upon Thames) (Leeser, 2011, p. 9). And by drawing in people 'who might otherwise not think of coming here', but who then experience the pleasures Rayner (2011) details, it both celebrates Brixton local culture and potentially destigmatizes it for any who still associate it negatively with, for example, local riots, most famously those of April 1981 which responded to economic deprivation and police harassment. I would not argue that the developments enabled by Space Makers are intrinsically socially detrimental. However, I would argue that, in conducive circumstances, they can facilitate further gentrification and that this can then be socially detrimental.

Gentrification's hothouse

Pop-ups' threat of contributing to gentrification's income-linked population displacement is especially acute in the second decade of the twenty-first century in London. This is because the preservation of affordable and sufficient social housing in London itself at this time is particularly in jeopardy due to a plethora of rapidly multiplying, converging conditions, many led – or passively permitted – by government. Demand for housing – social housing in particular – vastly exceeds supply. Social housing rental costs are increasing, while housing benefits are being capped. And, from 2011, new social housing tenants' leases are not indefinite but can be reviewed – and potentially terminated – every two years. Earlier in this chapter, I suggested these conditions present a 'perfect storm' for exacerbating gentrification in London. More accurately, these conditions are better described as a hothouse; not naturally occurring, but made and actively cultivated by policy.

Demand for *all* housing in London is outstripping supply and London's significant housing shortage is set to get worse. *London Plan 2011* (Greater London Authority, 2011, p. 20) forecasts that the number of households in the capital will grow from approximately 3.32 million in 2011 to almost 4 million by 2031.[17] The resulting demand for approximately 700,000 'extra' homes will necessarily intensify the competitiveness of the housing market unless demand is satisfied, which is highly unlikely.[18] Need for social housing at affordable rents, in particular, is outstripping supply. The quantity of social housing in the United Kingdom has been deteriorating rapidly, most seriously since the Housing Act 1980, when Margaret Thatcher introduced council housing tenants' Right to Buy their properties at significant discounts on market values. This policy's impact has been enormous: between 1980 and 2000 council housing stock declined by two million properties, almost all due to the Right to Buy scheme (Lowe, 2011, p. 125). This shortage of supply does not mean that demand correspondingly shrunk. On the contrary, there were 1.84 million households on local authority housing waiting lists in England in 2011, a 4.5 per cent rise on the previous year and an 80 per cent rise in a decade (Dept. for Communities and Local Government [DCLG], 2011a; Wintour, 2012). In London alone in 2010–11, over 366,000 households were on local authority housing waiting lists, or 11.3 per cent of all households in London at the time (DCLG, 2011a, p. 24). Amongst other deleterious effects, this inadequacy of supply means that only those with the greatest need can be prioritized for accommodation, already spatially concentrating serious disadvantage (Sampson, 2008), which has been shown to bring additional disadvantage (Kintrea, 2008). Clearly, new building is needed, but what is planned is insufficient. The Conservative-led coalition government's 2010 Spending Review cut the budget for building new affordable housing by almost 60 per cent, from £8.4 billion in the three years to 2010, to £4.4 billion over the subsequent four years (Ramesh, 2010b). It pledged to build 150,000 affordable homes during its term. Not least given waiting lists, many critics view this pledge as grossly insufficient, 'less than a third of what is needed', according to the housing and homelessness charity Shelter (2012).

Furthermore, policy requiring developers to build *at least some* social housing for the privilege of being granted permission to build profitable private housing is also in jeopardy. The Conservative-led coalition government's March 2012 *National Planning Policy Framework* broadly aims 'to make the planning system less complex and more accessible, and to promote sustainable growth' (DCLG, 2011b).[19] On several occasions it emphasizes the importance of providing sufficient affordable housing (DCLG, 2012).[20] However, it insists that such required provision should not inhibit 'competitive returns' for developers.[21] The National Trust (2011), influential protector and promoter of the countryside and heritage, responded to the draft of this policy by launching a campaign headlined, 'planning is for people, not for profit', which accused the government of prioritizing economic profit rather than social concern for people, their housing and their environment. The *National Planning Policy Framework*'s suggestion that it might be time to relax requirements to sustain affordable housing development despite extraordinary need was reinforced in August 2012 by Sir Adrian Montague's high-profile government-commissioned report on perceived barriers to investment in the development of private rental accommodation. Amongst other recommended measures to increase the supply of new homes, Montague proposed that, 'In many cases, it will be appropriate for authorities to waive affordable housing requirements in relation to schemes for private rental' (2012, paragraph 49). These Conservative-led policy trends indicate the vulnerability of social housing development to the priorities of profit-led private development.

Meanwhile, rental prices on what social housing does exist are rising beyond the means of some tenants. The coalition government's wishfully-titled 'Affordable Rent' programme encourages social housing providers to charge for new tenancies prices of up to 80 per cent of local area gross market rents, far more than what is charged most existing tenants and far more than what is, for many, affordable (Homes and Communities Agency, 2011). Potentially substantial income raised through this scheme (as paid by the least wealthy) is to go into building affordable homes through funding to be distributed by the Homes and Communities Agency. One incentive for housing associations to participate in this higher rent scheme is that only those which do so will be eligible for home-building grants from that Agency. The government's message to social housing providers is: raise rents (potentially beyond affordability) if you want to increase your housing stock and make any dent in waiting lists; or do not raise rents and watch waiting lists continue to rise. Because social housing rents can rise in proportion to local private market rates, areas with the most expensive private housing will see the greatest increases in rent charges, making 'social' housing less and less affordable in the most expensive areas and leading to income-linked displacement and ghettoization. This kind of outcome is potentially further exacerbated if the government succumbs to pressures from organizations such as the right-leaning think tank Policy Exchange, which urged government in summer 2012 immediately to start selling off social housing over a median local value as it is vacated and to reinvest the income in affordable housing in less wealthy districts elsewhere (Morton, 2012). Though this measure would obviously compel income-linked displacement and concentration, Conservative MP Grant Shapps, Housing Minister at that time, admired and praised it, calling it 'blindingly obvious' (Sparrow and agencies, 2012).

As rents rise across all housing, social support for rental costs is being capped, for those both in social housing and privately rented accommodation, including many on social housing waiting lists. A cap on the housing benefit paid by the state to eligible people in the private rental sector, Local Housing Allowance (LHA), was announced by the Conservative-led government in June 2010 and introduced in stages, coming into full force at the beginning of 2012. It limited the amount of social subsidy for a one-bedroom property to £250 per week, and for a four-bedroom property to £400 per week (Curtis, 2012). Especially for families, these amounts are widely predicted to be insufficient in many cases, provoking the need to find savings on other necessities such as food, heating and clothing, and sometimes forcing people to move homes, schools, employment, registrations with local doctors' surgeries and more.[22] Alex Fenton of the Cambridge Centre for Housing and Planning Research found that reductions in LHA were likely to reduce the proportion of London neighbourhoods affordable to LHA claimants from 75 per cent to 51 per cent by 2011. By 2016, that percentage would reduce further to 36 per cent, meaning that 'almost the whole area of the traditional inner London boroughs' would be unaffordable to LHA claimant tenants (Fenton, 2011, pp. 4, 17).

Already by February 2012, in the London Borough of Westminster there were 'almost no three- or four-bedroom flats available within that price range' (Gentleman, 2012). Westminster council seems to welcome the pressure the cap places on poorer residents to move out: a council press officer claimed, 'To live in Westminster is a privilege, not a right, because so many people want to live here' (in ibid.). Many – myself included – disagree with this claim, arguing that it is intrinsically and quite violently socially damaging, eroding principles of social mixing that contribute to healthy societies; providing what the editors of *Evil Paradises: Dreamworlds of Neoliberalism* identify as 'a self-serving justification for the ... fortification of luxury lifestyles' (Davis and Monk, 2007a, p. xiv); denying some people what French urban theorist Henri

Lefebvre called simply 'the right to the city' (Lefebvre, 2003); compelling income-linked migration and ghettoization; breaking up established communities and networks, including families and relationships with schools; and displacing people from their work and livelihoods. Fenton's research shows that neighbourhoods likely to remain affordable to LHA-claiming tenants by 2016 are concentrated in outer areas of London that already have 'relatively high rates of deprivation and unemployment', accelerating the 'spatial polarisation of rich and poor' (Fenton, 2011, p. 30). Westminster is reportedly 'the borough most affected by the housing benefit cap' (Gentleman, 2012), but even some of the most economically deprived boroughs, such as East London's Newham, have felt the cap's impact, seeking to move residents on social housing waiting lists as far away as Stoke on Trent in the English midlands in the search for affordable rent and producing 'benefit ghettoes' (Ramesh and Walker, 2012).[23]

From April 2013, tenants in social housing will also see their housing benefits effectively capped, as the Universal Credit system comes into effect, gathering and replacing approximately 30 benefit schemes, including housing benefit but also Jobseeker's Allowance, Income Support and Child Tax Credits (see Bennett, 2010; Department for Work and Pensions [DWP], 2012c). Universal Credit has capped limits at £500 per week, making many council homes, especially in inner London, unaffordable to large families (Gentleman, 2012). The Department for Work and Pension's own Impact Assessment estimated that 56,000 UK households will have their benefits reduced by this policy in 2013/14, that half of affected households will be in London and that all ten of the worst affected local authorities will be in London (DWP, 2012d, p. 8). Rises in rental costs set alongside reductions in rental support will effectively drive those on low incomes from inner London due to the inflated cost of property there, 'freeing' that housing for a high-rent market as well as for gentrifying development. Though he too is Conservative, London Mayor Boris Johnson argued that the Conservative-led government's introduction of this funding cap would act as a 'Kosovo-style ethnic cleansing' because it would drive out London's poor (2010).[24] As Johnson's vocabulary suggests, this income-linked demographic displacement is also ethnically linked, disproportionately disadvantaging ethnic minorities. Furthermore, it is linked to gender and age, most seriously affecting women and children. A gender audit commissioned by Labour MP Yvette Cooper (Cooper, 2010) and completed by the House of Commons Library found that 60 per cent of those who would be affected by these housing benefit reforms were women (totalling 2.9 million women).

Alongside these conditions of scarcity and lack of affordability that contribute to gentrification, another emerging problem is the erosion of secure tenancy. Where a former principle of social housing was that it offered tenants the security of permanence if they desired and needed it, the Conservative-led coalition government's Localism Act 2011 offers what it proudly calls 'flexibility', giving Councils the right to review new tenants' eligibility for social housing every two years and, where deemed appropriate, to terminate it, destabilizing social housing tenancy by design (Lowe, 2011, p. 233; see DCLG, 2011c; BBC News, 2011). Government clearly anticipates resistance to this policy; in February 2011, it announced a sum of £5 million 'to support local authorities to pay court fees in cases where tenants refuse to leave' (Lowe, 2011, p. 235). Contributors to Shelter publication *The Future of Social Housing* show that eliminating security of tenure in social housing 'would be actively damaging to the life chances of tenants, including their ability to find and keep work' (Sampson, 2008, p. 4; see Lowe, 2011, pp. 20–2).[25]

All of this policy evidence demonstrates that the Cameron government is both actively and passively eroding and destabilizing social housing and its principles of security. By the time this book comes to print, some of these details of policy and practice will no doubt have shifted. Unfortunately, at least two things look set to persist and even to accelerate. One is UK national and civic Conservative-led governments' withdrawal of support for social housing and, more broadly, for the social distribution of good conditions for achieving good quality of life. A second is those governments' increasing facilitation of private development, private profit and the uneven distribution of wealth.

For all of these reasons arising from state policy and government ideology, as well as the kind of direct corporate incentive Florida heralds and which sees 'the post-industrial city as growth machine' (Wyly and Hammel, 2005), London is at ongoing risk of neoliberal gentrification. In *The Neoliberal City*, Jason Hackworth writes about American urbanism, but his conclusions are strikingly relevant to the UK case I have discussed here. 'Overall, gentrification is now more corporate, more state-facilitated, and less resisted than ever before', he writes.

> It could be said, in fact, that gentrification is the knife-edge neighbourhood-based manifestation of neoliberalism. Not only has it created a profit opportunity for real estate capital, but it has also created a high-profile ideological opportunity to replace physically Keynesian managerialist landscapes of old – represented by public

housing, public space and so on – with the entrepreneurial privatized landscapes of the present.

(Hackworth, 2007, p. 149)[26]

Gentrification is displacing less advantaged people and simultaneously erecting and implicitly legitimating a physical and social neoliberal landscape where private, entrepreneurial development and profit is prioritized and valued well beyond the basic human right to adequate housing. As David Harvey has trenchantly observed, 'The redistributive tactics of neoliberalism are wide-ranging, sophisticated, frequently masked by ideological gambits, but devastating for the dignity and social well-being of vulnerable populations and territories' (2007, p. 39).

To reiterate, I am not claiming that creative people and/or pop-up venues, artists or audiences inherently create gentrification. What does that is a mixture of under- and unregulated market-led development, insufficient social support for those most in need, and tolerance of social stratification and ghettoization. But I am saying that we need to be cautious about pop-ups' tendency to lead higher-income inward investment and migration by example, particularly in a political context which appears to be hell-bent on facilitating such investment and migration. Some development may be necessary and, indeed, welcome given the anticipated increase in London households; the extraordinary and growing shortage of appropriate housing in London, as in many places elsewhere in the United Kingdom; and the fact that investment in building might help to stimulate the economy and relieve effects of recession and austerity such as high levels of unemployment. But development needs to be delivered in ways that make it as fair and equitable as possible. Artists and creative people can help to protect such equitable delivery through such cautionary interventions as Hiorns's *Seizure*; through a range of other art practices which explicitly engage with home and which I look at below; and possibly also by remaining in neighbourhoods to build long-term, constructive relationships of social advocacy for their neighbours.[27] However, the equitable delivery of development must also be protected more directly through urban policy that values and prioritizes it and treats it not as an economic commodity but as a social necessity.

Neoliberalized, gentrified cities

The above two sections have explored two trends in urban culture: the 'creative cities' agenda fostered by Richard Florida and the pop-up creative venue. They have considered the ways that both trends potentially contribute valuably to urban culture, especially socially, as well as the ways they risk damaging urban culture, particularly by exacerbating urban social inequality. Both of these trends do have potential socially positive outcomes – supporting arts and culture, fostering social tolerance, potentially distributing culture beyond middle-class audiences and modelling tactical micro-utopian interventions in response to urban cultural problems. The popularity of both of these trends is very likely linked at least in part to these numerous constructive qualities.

But their disadvantages perhaps outweigh their benefits and their wide adoption risks naturalizing even their problems in ways we should be wary of. Both trends contribute to neoliberal marketization by fostering competitive markets, for creative people and for creative environments and lifestyles. Both risk instrumentalizing culture in ways set to get worse during the UK's ongoing recession and the ensuing conditions explored in Chapters 2 and 4, where Arts Council England has implemented government-imposed budget cuts of 30 per cent and warned the arts that they can no longer consider themselves intrinsically valuable or, therefore, worthy of state support; they must see themselves as part of a wider cultural economy and become more business-worthy (see Fleming and Erskine, 2011). Most problematically, both trends risk prioritizing economic growth over communities and people. The creative middle classes and the wealthiest can move where they want; disadvantaged classes are displaced or forced to move to where markets send them. Mobile capital flows, but in ways that are decidedly uneven, unstable and unregulated, reinforcing class stability rather than class mobility (Brenner and Theodore, 2010, p. 417). Cultural strategies ostensibly designed for the city's growth and liveability risk damaging its liveability, especially for the city's most disadvantaged citizens.

Art about home

As the example of Hiorns's *Seizure* discussed above indicates, some art practice is explicitly engaging with the threats to sufficient housing – social housing in particular – that are so widespread and powerful at this time. *Seizure* is part of a comparatively small, but significant trend in socially engaged arts practice in Britain that specifically addresses issues to do with housing and the nature of 'home' and often takes place in or around homes. This work highlights and interrogates a range of important issues, including the ideologies of regeneration which ignore its negative social consequences; fantasies of home ownership which have eroded social housing provision; fetishizations of 'home' that obscure its potential to be unstable, insufficient and even damaging; and fantasies of community which can act to exclude people and practices deemed undesirable or invisible. Such work includes the Institute for the Art and Practice of Dissent at Home (IAPDH), run out of a council property bedroom in Everton, Liverpool; funded by a tenth of the resident family members' collective income; and set up in response to the 'creative cities' capitalism which the members felt drove Liverpool 08 European Capital of Culture (see IAPDH, 2012). It includes the collectively titled *Home* run by the National Theatre of Scotland (NTS) for its opening in 2006 in ten different sites across Scotland, including tenement buildings in Glasgow and Aberdeen (see NTS, 2012). It includes the work of Home Live Art (HLA) (2012a), which has produced live art for free since 1999 in contexts both domestic and public. Work in the Salon Series presented in their South London house venue often explored the intimacy of relationships both typical of the home and facilitated by the spatial relations of the domestic performance space. Since 2008, their Alternative Village Fete has appeared at numerous outdoor festivals, including the National Theatre's summer event Watch This Space. Combining live art and quirky crafts to provide what Home describes as 'a sideways slant on the traditional family day out where the folk is activism and the bunting is radical!' (HLA, 2012b), the Fete challenges convention and tradition, implicitly asking who is in the 'village', whose village it is and what values it holds.

In what follows, I look in more detail at a selection of home-related art practice by Marcus Coates, Andy Hewitt and Mel Jordan, Rachel Whiteread and Michael Landy. I explore the tactics these artists use to interrogate the meanings and values of home and, in a time of acute pressure on housing, to make visible that pressure as well as the social importance of homes, while still acknowledging the complexity of homes' social value, as sites of social contest as well as security.

Marcus Coates's *A Ritual for Elephant & Castle*

Since 2004, the massive Heygate social housing estate of 1260 dwellings completed in 1974 at Elephant and Castle in South London has been scheduled by Southwark Council for 'regeneration' into 3300 dwellings, only 25 per cent of which (around 800 units) will be 'affordable' (Moss, 2011). Demolition of the estate did not start until 2011. While the Heygate awaited demolition, Marcus Coates – whose father had helped build it in the 1970s – began visiting it and getting to know residents before their eviction. He reported that 'people on the Heygate estate felt like they were being discarded. There was a huge sense of loss. I wanted to try and tap into a collective imagination, represent it and offer an alternative to the scripted, corporate vision' (in Lamont, 2012).

Coates generally makes performances and film, frequently exploring boundaries between human and animal life, often by becoming partly animal himself. Citing both 'millenniums-old traditions of "visions"; of shamen whose imaginings were used to try to solve intractable problems', and the recent appropriation of the term 'vision' into corporate discourse, Coates adopted the role of a silver-suited, horse-headed shaman and used trances and meditation to seek his own visions for the estate. Performance outcomes included a gig/trance entitled *A Ritual for Elephant & Castle* with the experimental funk band Chrome Hoof in 2009, 12 screen installations of film material of Coates's interviews and actions, and the 2012 film *Vision Quest – A Ritual for Elephant & Castle*. This film incorporated not only Coates's performance and actions but also interviews with estate 'stakeholders', including residents young and old, new and longstanding; council workers; a development consultant; and Heygate's original project architect Tim Tinker, who blamed Thatcher's Right to Buy policy for the apparent 'failure' and premature demolition of the estate (Jeffreys, 2012).

The anti-rationalism of Coates's interventions was clearly deliberate and also funny, disturbing and forceful, highlighting the failure of regeneration and development 'logic' properly to acknowledge, let alone account for the 'irrational', unquantifiable feelings and social relations of the estate that it considers failed. The anti-rationalism also resulted, however, from Coates's careful, highly rational listening. 'Getting to know people from the estate', Coates said, 'I began to understand what an intricate community existed here. Residents depended on each other, doing each other's shopping, checking in – [in] ways that you would never know if you were the council visiting to do an assessment' (Lamont, 2012). Coates's project recorded some of the deleterious effects of gentrification, such as the break-up of networks of support and the devaluation of local experience, and it parodied the self-confidence of rationalist planning and 'regeneration' 'visionaries' by modelling Coates himself as a deliberately archaic and strange shaman whose extraordinary visions would resist the assimilating drives of even the most arrogant planners.

Andy Hewitt and Mel Jordan's *SHOWFLAT*

Coates's intervention was pre-emptive in that it happened before 'regeneration' fully took hold in the Elephant and Castle. Andy Hewitt and Mel Jordan similarly made a pre-emptive intervention when they 'redeveloped' their Sheffield artists' studio in the Devonshire Quarter (branded by estate agents DQ) into *SHOWFLAT* in 2003 and invited audiences to view it as they would a 'normal' show property (Hewitt + Jordan, 2004, p. 24; 2012). The work resembled the kind of flat that housing developments typically deploy to market an unfinished project, 'exhibit[ing] the current interior design languages so essential for city living: white walls to reflect light, wood laminate floors, minimal decoration, and contemporary door furniture' (Hewitt + Jordan, 2004, p. 29).

Hewitt and Jordan's work simultaneously engaged with, and differed from, the kind of genuine housing development and marketing typical of so many British inner-city areas in the first decade of the twenty-first century, thereby drawing attention to the increasing inner-city development which aimed explicitly and proudly to gentrify the city. This development was – and continues to be – marketed to attract 'young professionals' to a chic urban lifestyle and was often built in former industrial buildings and in neighbourhoods formerly marked by a mixture of light industry and cultural activity as well as state neglect, this last feature by now replaced by state economic interest in private redevelopment. *SHOWFLAT*'s aesthetic minimalism invoked a style trend but also created an unhomely, soulless emptiness, implicitly querying the social effects that gentrifying development can produce, such as the break-up of former neighbourhood cultures; the displacement of lower-income residents and workers, including artists, whose chic appeal had been used to attract higher-earning incomers; the privileging of those higher earners in exclusive developments; and increasing social ghettoization. SHOWFLAT's presentation as part of city-wide festival Artsheffield03 and squarely in the rapidly gentrifying 'DQ' positioned it specifically 'to question culture-led regeneration' (Hewitt + Jordan, 2004) that is typical of creative cities planning. Hewitt and Jordan's 'redevelopment' of their own studio space also interrogated their own complicity, as part of an 'artist class', with culture-led gentrification (ibid., p. 49).

Rachel Whiteread's *House*

Rachel Whiteread's infamous *House* (1993), referenced in the last chapter, was an interior cast of a Victorian house on Grove Road in East London and provoked fierce debate,[28] effectively winning her the 1993 Turner Prize while also committing *House* to demolition. Detractors accused it of being 'a little entertainment for the gallery-going classes of Hampstead' (Massey, 1995, p. 46) and included local Councillor Eric Flounders (1993; rpt in Lingwood, 1995, p. 135) who called it a 'monstrosity' and 'utter rubbish'. Advocates included art historian Simon Watney, geographer Doreen Massey, architecture historian Anthony Vidler and visual culture theorist and curator Jon Bird, all of whom contributed articles to an excellent book on the work (Lingwood, 1995). As Watney put it, 'The act of casting the last surviving house of a typical terraced row had the effect of contrasting, in situ, the values we habitually attach to the concept of "home" with the actual emptiness and blankness of much domestic life, remembered or forgotten' (1995, pp. 96–109). For Watney, *House* provoked reflection on a great series of things: domestic relationships, across generations and genders; values attached to home ownership; fantasies and realities of 'neighbourhood'; and experiences of belonging and exclusion. For Massey, *House* disrupted 'normal' time-spaces, provoking reflection on relationships between past and present, private interior and public exterior and – by solidly filling the home and effectively denying social space – non-social and social space (Massey, 1995, pp. 36–7). For her and others, the work queried conventional nostalgia for home, indicating the home's potential painfulness as a site of work and drudgery, as well as rest (ibid., pp. 40–1). Bird (1995) and Vidler (1995), too, emphasized the work's denial of domestic comfort and its provocation to audiences to face, in Vidler's words, 'the fundamental terrors of exclusion and banishment, of homelessness and alienation' (1995, p. 72).

Michael Landy's *Semi-Detached*

Michael Landy's *Semi-Detached* (2004), also referenced in the last chapter, was a perfect replica of the front and back elevations of his parents' two-storey semi-detached suburban home, complete with television aerial and net curtains. Where Whiteread did not move her house from its site, Landy did his, installing the to-scale suburban home into the incongruous setting of Tate Britain's vaulting, elegant, classical Duveen galleries and foregrounding the contrasts between the literally rough (pebble-dashed) and modest, and the smooth, monumental and privileged.[29] This contrast invited viewers to compare the scale, materials and purpose of the two buildings, and to query the buildings' relative sufficiency, an idea explicitly invoked in the films projected on the exterior walls' interior surfaces and showing Landy's father's efforts at self-sufficiency following the mid-life industrial accident that ended his working life. The visible modernization and improvements of the home – its pebble-dashing, UPVC windows and door, satellite dish and kitchen extension – testified to the hard work and achievement of Landy's parents, despite the trauma of Landy Senior's accident. The work's title, and the contrast between its tidy, familiar exteriors and the intimate revelations of its interior films, spoke to common social detachments between public and private selves, as well as between neighbours, within communities and within oneself. Like so many of the other artworks discussed above, *Semi-detached* acknowledged the home's ambivalent role, here as both comfort and restraint and as the admirable achievement of ambition and, possibly, an increasingly encumbering responsibility.

As this range of examples shows, contemporary British artists are engaging actively and repeatedly with issues to do with housing and home in their work. Some of this work explicitly foregrounds the pressures of regeneration and gentrification and their ensuing effects of ghettoization and lower-income inner-city exclusion. Some of it directly indicates the collusions of artists and culture in culture-led creative city 'regeneration'. Much of it concedes to the appeal of private home ownership at the same time as it suggests the risks of that ownership – both for owners themselves and for those for whom private home development means displacement and eviction, or what the Heygate's redevelopers evasively call 'decanting' (Moss, 2011). All of it stages some of the ambivalent meanings of home – as a site of potential refuge but also of potential trouble. Through details of scale, location, irony, actions, and juxtaposition of materials and images, it repeatedly foregrounds the fundamental importance of home to lived experience and the instability and insecurity of home for so many in Britain's rapidly gentrifying contemporary cities.

Dispersed performances

If the core problems presented by creative cities ideologies and the pop-up trend is gentrification and social fragmentation, one constructive response is to model the significance of home, as work, discussed above, does, though never in ways that unreservedly romanticize home. Another response is to model, not social fragmentation, but social cohesion. While some of the work examined in the previous section tended to propose critique of problematic existing social-spatial relations – for example, in Hiorns's *Seizure*, Whiteread's *House* or Hewitt and Jordan's *SHOWFLAT* – this work often proposes somewhat utopian alternatives to existing spatial problems, extending in different ways the hopeful ambitions of, for example, Coates's *Ritual for Elephant and Castle*.

On the face of it, what unites the work I focus on in this section is that it was commissioned for the Cultural Olympiad that led up to and accompanied the London 2012 Olympics and Paralympics. The Cultural

Olympiad explicitly aimed to address large and dispersed UK audiences and implicitly sought to demonstrate and fortify a sense of community across the United Kingdom. The works I examine – by Martin Creed, the performance company Lone Twin and Alex Hartley – all clearly make efforts to reach across space and, in so doing, address a range of audiences. They also engage with issues to do with social-spatial relations, such as how to extend address and participation both spatially and socially, and how to articulate but also interrogate collectivism across space and time. They model micro-utopias of collective effort but they also query the meanings and values of public space, community, nation, territory and – in all of these contexts – art. They attempt to connect communities through participation that is both material and immaterial, sharing objects, spaces, activities, stories, sounds, time and feelings. These spatially engaged art practices help participants to understand and engage in social relations actively and in mutual support, but not uncritically and not in ways that damagingly homogenize differences.

Martin Creed's *Work No. 1197: All the Bells in a Country Rung as Quickly and Loudly as Possible for Three Minutes*

Martin Creed makes visual art, music and, sometimes, events, numbering his art pieces as composers often do.[30] Works in his prolific output are often minimal. They are made, for example, from masking tape; modest protrusions from or intrusions in walls; balloons which half-fill a space, in his oft-repeated *Half the Air in a Given Space*; vomit, in his many films of people vomiting; the lights going on and off in a room, as in his 2001 Turner Prize-winning Tate Britain exhibition; and runners intermittently sprinting the length of Tate Britain's Duveen Galleries in his 2008 *Work No. 850*.

Though the works' minimalism permits many potential meanings to rush in, some of their consistent and evident effects are playfully to alter everyday spaces and to draw attention to what we take for granted in them and in our use of them. Some of his work takes these interventions outside, as in a large neon sign reading 'EVERYTHING'S GOING TO BE ALRIGHT' that he has frequently installed on large buildings visible to passing traffic and that he notes is optimistic but 'contains the negative ... in the sense that it implies that things aren't all right' (Creed, 2002, p. 104). His 2011 *Work No. 1059* paved the 104 stairs of Edinburgh's Scotsman Steps that link the Waverley station valley with the North Bridge in 'multiple hues of marble from around the world – greens, ochre, blues and blushing pink' (Carrell and Higgins, 2012). This intervention transformed what was once 'notorious as a night-time urinal for the city's clubgoers and drunks' into not only 'a kaleidoscope of colour' (ibid.) but also what *Guardian* art and design blogger Jonathan Jones called a 'throwaway luxury for everyone' (Jones, 2012), or a general sharing of wealth, as distinct from what gentrification tends to do, redistributing space along predictable bilateral routes of wealth and poverty. Amongst many other things, therefore, a strong vein of Creed's work offers delightful surprises to a wide, public audience.

Creed's Cultural Olympiad commission, *Work No. 1197: All the Bells in a Country Rung as Quickly and Loudly as Possible for Three Minutes*, invited everyone in the United Kingdom to ring a bell for three minutes to herald in the Olympics at 8:12 am on 27 July, 2012. Its slogan was: 'Any Bell. Anyone. Anywhere' (see *All The Bells*, 2012; Creed, 2012). The work punned playfully with the Olympic rings, but also joined a tradition of bell-ringing used to herald special events. Reportedly 2.9 million people rang bells at the appointed time, including bells from bicycles, churches, ships, pubs, phones, doors, cows and Morris Dancers (Kennedy, 2012). Marching bands played. Town criers rang bells. The National Theatre rang an enormous bell from Danny Boyle's 2011 National Theatre production of *Frankenstein*. The BBC played out bells on national and local radio stations. And Big Ben struck continuously for three minutes, apparently out of its normal schedule for the first time since George VI's funeral in 1952 (Press Association, 2012b).[31] 'It's by people and for people', said Creed (*All The Bells*, 2012). Director of the Cultural Olympiad and the London 2012 Festival Ruth Mackenzie said, 'The commission shows the Festival's commitment to world-class artists and to the values of participation. Martin Creed's wonderful idea gets everyone involved in the opening day of the Games not just as an audience but as an integral part of the work' (in ibid.).

Obviously not everyone in the United Kingdom participated in the bell-ringing, and many disapproved. *Financial Times* reporter Peter Aspden (2012) called it 'infantile', 'nonsensical' and not art. In the final episode of *Twenty Twelve*, the mock documentary television comedy following the disaster-riddled preparations of the 'Olympic Deliverance Team', artists auditioned for Big Bong; one audition was uncannily similar in conception to *All the Bells* (dir. Morton, 2012, ep. 7). Describing his own response as 'resistant', Jonathan Jones (2012) argued, 'The collective is not a straightforward ideal. It means conformity as well as community. I want to know more about what Creed means by his glorification of collective acts. What does it mean to all ring bells in unison, and what does he want it to mean?' In response to Jones, I would point out that Creed did not explicitly 'glorify' collective acts, and that he said the work was by and for 'people' not a 'collective'. Furthermore, the important questions Jones asked were, for me, provoked – not obscured – by *All the Bells*. Though it clearly produced collective action, it did not necessarily or literally produce or therefore assume collective harmony; rather, in many sites it produced cacophony, demonstrating that 'collective' action can be dissonant and discordant and perhaps reinforcing Claire Bishop's (2004, 2006b, 2012) argument that the most powerfully democratic socially engaged art highlights not consensus but the dissensus upon which effective democracy relies. *All the Bells* did not prescribe participation in bell-ringing but invited it, cheaply and cheerfully extending that invitation across space, age, ability and means. What it did almost certainly mandate participation in was hearing the bells; even those who are deaf might have felt the ringing. If some wanted to ring bells, others would hear; almost by definition, *All the Bells* was most likely to 'compel' the participation of objectors such as Aspden at least as listeners. If it was 'infantile' – as Creed's balloons and vomiting videos might also be seen to be – it was by the same token playful and deliberately popular. *All the Bells*'s dispersal invited but did not mandate participation in bell-ringing, it implicitly queried the relationship between participatory action and collectivism and, rather than deferring to collective agreement, it imposed the sound of bells ringing on people throughout the United Kingdom. Its playful intervention in public space resulted in mass participation and shared endeavour that was both happy and provocative.

Lone Twin's *The Boat Project*

Lone Twin – Gregg Whelan and Gary Winters – make experimental performance for a variety of contexts including theatres but also urban and rural public spaces. Their work often has elements of absurdity and often takes the form of a journey, deliberately seeking unpredictable social encounters which result in shared stories. For most commentators, it is characterized by kindness and generosity. Theatre and performance scholars David Williams and Carl Lavery's marvellous co-edited book, *Good Luck Everybody* (2011), collects documentation and analysis of the company's work. Commentary is admittedly provided by Lone Twin's collaborators and admirers, but they are consistent in what they admire. Williams and Lavery describe the company's work as having 'participatory and optimistic energies' (ibid., p. 5). Whelan and Winters's former teacher John Hall remarks on the work's hopefulness (ibid., p. 277). Performance maker and teacher Barry Laing's contribution is subtitled, 'Avowals of Hope and Labours of Love' (Laing, 2011, pp. 155–60). Performance scholar Alan Read writes in his preface of Lone Twin's work's welcome, sensitivity, friendship, love, affections and 'the haunting sense of [the company's] optimism, their affirmation, their enthusiasm' (Read, 2011, pp. 7–8, 11). He finds in their work 'the *kindness* of strangers so familiar in the theatre, and yet, for so long it seems, a kindness treated with skepticism and suspicion' (ibid., p. 11, italics original). Following Adam Phillips and Barbara Taylor (2009, p. 2), Read defines kindness as 'instinctive sympathetic identification with the vulnerabilities and attractions of others' (Read, 2011, p. 11) and concludes, 'Compared with the habitual preoccupations of the performance terrain – sexuality, violence, and capital – it is this kindness and its expression that has a truly transgressive force today' (ibid., p. 11). Confessing that they have co-opted the title *Good Luck Everybody* from Lone Twin themselves, Williams and Lavery argue that the company's invocation of the phrase at the beginning of performances captures the sense that performance's 'shared encounter might just help a little', recognizes that 'art making is always, and before all else, a social practice' and is playfully humorous instead of earnestly monotonous (Williams and Lavery, 2011, p. 13). And though Lone Twin's work is hopeful and enthusiastic, it is nevertheless not preposterously naïve. Its heroic ambitions are generally compromised – dressed as cowboys, they attempt to haul a telegraph pole in a straight line across a town in *Totem* (Colchester, 1998); in *Spiral* (2007), they make a long spiral journey with a shopping trolley through the rectilinear landscape of the Barbican, collecting contributions along the way (see Whelan and Winters with Williams, 2011, p. 28; Williams and Lavery, 2011, pp. 115–18). And though Lone Twin is committed to collectivism, as many have noted the company's name acknowledges irreparable loss and the difficulty of knowing others (ibid., p. 118).[32]

Lone Twin won a commission from the Cultural Olympiad's public art strand, Artists Taking the Lead, to produce *The Boat Project* in Southeast England. The project would culminate in the building and maiden voyage of a 30-foot wooden sailboat – *Collective Spirit* – which would sail around Southeast England, from Emsworth in Hampshire along the Sussex and Kent coasts to Margate, over the course of three months in the Olympic summer of 2012 on one of Lone Twin's journeys, stopping off along the way. Co-director Gary Winters emphasizes that a ship launch has the capacity to 'galvanis[e] a community' (in Barnett, 2012b). This was a feature Lone Twin sought to extend through the boat's making and subsequent voyage, with the journey and shared storytelling typical of Lone Twin's work characterizing not only *The Boat Project*'s performance phase but also its production phase and its very materials. A year and a half before the boat's launch, Lone Twin put out a call inviting people to donate pieces of wood that would be incorporated into the hull. 'In the call-out', stresses Winters, 'we made it clear we didn't want any old junk but things that really mean something' (ibid.). Lone Twin received not merely over 1200 pieces of wood but as many accompanying personal stories. Materials donated ranged from the exoticness of Zebrawood to the familiarity of pine, from pencils to hockey sticks to piano, and 'from the highly personal to pieces of national importance' (ibid.). There was a tool for rope-splicing (a fid) that was rescued by a diver from the wreck of HMS Invincible, sunk in battle in the First World War in the North Sea. There was an old hairbrush donated by a woman whose father had used it as a make-up artist at one of Britain's greatest film studios, Pinewood, where classics including *Oliver Twist* (dir. David Lean, 1948), *The Red Shoes* (dir. Michael Powell and Emeric Pressburger, 1948) and a series of Bond features were made (ibid.). The resulting boat incorporated the material and emotional investment of hundreds of people and was, for Lone Twin, 'a living archive of people's stories and lives' (Lone Twin, 2012). The boat's construction techniques meant that its constituent parts form an elegant jigsaw of recognizable objects on the surface of the boat's hull, insisting on their thing-ness, visibility and history, their individualism at the same time as their important incorporation into the boat's whole.

Socially, *The Boat Project* sought and supported acts of kindness, generosity, social recognition and mutual social support. It preserved, displayed and literally toured people's emotionally important objects, invoking their stories. Its elegant and image-rich accompanying book, edited by Williams (2012), recorded those stories. Its launch, subsequent voyage and various festivals at ports of call[33] invited contributors and others to come together in celebratory events to recognize the project and its many histories and to revel in the delightful and slightly incredible success of a ship that – as the *Guardian* put it – hockey sticks built (Barnett, 2012b). The boat's grace and craftsmanship made visible the banal alongside the exceptional, erasing their conventional hierarchies. Spatially, *Collective Spirit*'s tour invited many dispersed audiences to see and visit it and to engage in its storytelling and celebration; its initial invitation to donate pieces of wood cast the invitation to participate much wider geographically. The work is deliberately optimistic about the potential of collective endeavour, effort and identity. It is nevertheless not sanctimonious; somewhat like *All the Bells*, it has a spirited playfulness, being both an elegant yacht and a game of jigsaw. Unlike *All the Bells*, but more like Creed's marble steps, it has an enduring material legacy: gifted back to the Southeast region after its maiden voyage, *Collective Spirit* will remain a mobile, serviceable and pleasurable vessel and archive for years to come as well as a material legacy of the collective endeavour of the communities who made it.

Alex Hartley's *Nowhereisland*

Alex Hartley's peripatetic Artists Taking the Lead public art commission for the Southwest of England was more a mobile island than a boat. Working with Bristol-based arts organization Situations, Hartley gathered rocks from a remote arctic region of Norway (with the permission of its government), loaded them on a boat, towed the boat into international waters and declared it a nation. He then brought this new 'visiting island nation' to Weymouth on 25 July, 2012, to coincide with the Olympic sailing there, and toured it along and up the Southwest coast, arriving in Bristol in early September, after which it was dismantled, with its rocks/territory distributed on application to its citizens (whom I shall explain below) (*Nowhereisland*, 2012a). Along its English coastal journey, *Nowhereisland* was accompanied by a 'mobile embassy' complete with ambassadors, objects and information, and it visited many ports and harbours, where it was 'hosted by choirs, bands, citizen marches, a flotilla of surfers, gig rowers, sea shanty singers[,] ... thousands of people on cliff tops, beaches, harbours and promenades' (ibid.) and intrepid swimmers (BBC News Devon, 2012). Every week in the year up to its final week, one of 52 resident thinkers posted a letter on its website. Given the 'clean slate' of this new nation, they responded to the invitation to provoke debate and test out new ideas about how we might shape society (*Nowhereisland*, 2012b). Thinkers were drawn from fields including environmentalism, peace activism, broadcasting, stand-up comedy, sustainable farming and human rights and included geographers Tim Cresswell and Doreen Massey; artists Suzanne Lacy, Tim Etchells and Yoko Ono; and civil rights activist Peter Tatchell. Their letters engaged with topics ranging from landscape to migration, environmentalism, exile, language, art, exploration, hospitality, constitutionalism, nationhood, citizenship, and national policy around arts, gender, law, economics and disability. The website offered an extensive set of resources for schools' engagement and an emerging constitution. Citizenship was available to all on application, either online or at the mobile embassy (*Nowhereisland*, 2012c).

Nowhereisland was many things; even its joined-up title could be parsed in numerous ways, admiringly as 'now here is land', with temporal emphasis as 'now here island', in despair as 'nowhere is land' and in the proper 'utopian' sense of no-place as 'nowhere island'. By its own description it was durational and nomadic, sculpture and intervention. But it was perhaps most importantly what its creators acknowledged as 'a utopian idea', combining utopian's dual meanings as both imaginary or non-existent and ideal. It was 'a conceptual nation involving thousands of people across the word shaping that nation's values and principles online' (*Nowhereisland*, 2012d). The stories it carried were to be invented by its thinkers and citizens, as *The Boat Project*'s were to be donated by its contributors. While the Olympics risks invoking national jingoism and stereotypes, *Nowhereisland* invited interrogation of ideas of nation, citizenship, migration, hospitality, globalism, territory, environment and more – without abandoning nationhood. As in *The Boat Project*, its interrogation was provoked by its materials – its 'territory' – but perhaps more by its activities – its gathering and formation, invitations, migration, debates, letter writing, ambassadorial work and dispersal.

The invitation to participate in *All the Bells, The Boat Project* and *Nowhereisland* potentially provoked emotionally and intellectually invested engagement. The projects' physical dispersal allowed them actively to seek not only dispersed audiences – as with pop-ups – but multiple dispersed audiences, extending the equality of opportunity to participate that is so at risk in the social-spatial scenarios of gentrification I discussed above. The works' explicit engagement with ideas of participation invited the formation of participatory communities but also, in varying ways, the interrogation of community – as both harmonious and discordant in *All the Bells*, as constructed rather than essential in *Nowhereisland* and as at least 'spirit' or hope in *The Boat Project*. These works – and other dispersed utopian projects like them – invited participants to engage in shared endeavour and to model collective communities. In the face of the assault on qualities of collectivism and equality generated by the neoliberal extension of urban gentrification in the United Kingdom, these works modelled those qualities, their spatial dispersal both extending the social collective (across geography, age and more) and rendering that collective elusive in ways that might preserve it from seizure.

Admittedly, the socially ameliorative effects of all of these projects had their limits. *The Boat Project* and *Nowhereisland* were 'exhibited' principally in contexts coastal and rural and so did not usually directly address issues of urban change – though both projects visited coastal towns and cities, and *Collective Spirit* was exhibited at King's College London in autumn 2012. Furthermore, the commissioning of all three projects by the Cultural Olympiad raises the question of how sustainable such work can be without the support provided by exceptional funding opportunities. It also raises questions of how complicit the work might be with David Cameron's desire to myth-make his Big Society – though I would argue that it engages with ideas of society and community with nuance and critical reflexivity rather than jingoism. It also raises questions about its complicity with the apparent desire of Cameron's government ostentatiously to show its support for the arts, despite its simultaneous serious reduction of arts funding through Arts Council England as discussed in the next chapter. And it might even raise questions about the distribution of state funds in the contexts of widespread economic hardship and pressures on social services, including social housing. Another Artists Taking the Lead commission, David Coulthard's *Forest Pitch*, for example, garnered criticism for investing in a temporary football pitch in comparatively remote forests in the Scottish borders near Selkirk when investment in public sports facilities in nearby towns was needed (McAlpine and Nicoll, 2012). In response to this criticism, I would suggest that the principle function of these artworks is not to provide sustainable *material* resources (though Lone Twin has gifted *Collective Spirit* back to the South East region), but rather to stimulate thinking, provoke emotion and nurture social relations that might ultimately be more valuable and, possibly, long-lasting.

Conclusion

Contemporary political-economic contexts of fierce neoliberalism are spatially segregating people by wealth through processes of gentrification, putting under enormous pressure the possibilities of social equality and fair and equal access to spatially distributed resources such as housing, schooling, healthcare, employment and transport as well as art and other forms of cultural practice. This chapter has explored how cultural and art practices respond to, and engage with, this pressure on spatial equality. Sometimes they work – albeit unintentionally – to collude with such pressure, for example through creative cities' policy prioritization of often comparatively advantaged creative classes, and through pop-ups' catalytic function in processes of – and contexts ripe for – gentrification. Sometimes, however, they work to respond to and resist that pressure. Recent art practices in and about homes highlight the importance of home, indicate the very ways that priorities of private capital are jeopardizing affordable housing and also interrogate some of the social fantasies attached to ideas of 'home'. Spatially dispersed art practices that model collective endeavour demonstrate that the collective itself continues to be socially effective and socially possible, despite the destructive pressures that would fragment, segregate and stratify social relations and a sense of the public. It may certainly be the case that there has been a shift in urban governance policies from those which are socially progressive to those which are fiercely growth-centred. But the examples of art practices explored in this chapter demonstrate that socially progressive arts practices are by no means eliminated in this equation. On the contrary, they are alive and well. Contemporary cultural, economic and political neoliberalizing conditions present challenges to understanding space as not only social but socially shared and, ideally, *equally* socially shared. Far from accepting these challenges as irresistible, the art practices discussed in this chapter are using and responding to space in ways that champion, preserve and interrogate its social value. They are asking what we want our cities and other communities to be and how we produce that. They are modelling spatial engagements as sites for both collaboration and the kind of dissonance that acknowledges and does not attempt to homogenize difference.

4
Public/Private Capital: Arts Funding Cuts and Mixed Economies[1]

Introduction

One of the most obvious links between the state and the arts is funding. This link clearly marks an economic relationship, but it also articulates state and social attitudes to the importance of the arts, to social responsibility for the arts, to social relations and to society itself. In the United Kingdom, there exists a long and secure history of direct government funding for the arts as part of the formation of the post-war welfare state and its social and ideological commitment to the importance of the arts and to the state's responsibility to support its citizenry by facilitating their access to participating in the arts, as audiences and makers. This chapter explores ways that this longstanding relationship between the state, the arts and people may be shifting. And if Chapter 2 focused on New Labour's 'carrot' approach to encouraging enterprise in the arts as creative, this chapter focuses on what looks dangerously like a 'stick' approach under the Conservative-led coalition government, where the apparent option of a neoliberalization of the arts looks increasingly less optional.

But before I detail that shift in approaches, a bit more context. State funding to the arts has been institutionally secure in the United Kingdom since the formation of CEMA (the Committee for the Encouragement of Music and the Arts) during the Second World War,[2] and its successor, the Arts Council of Great Britain, in 1946. In 1945, CEMA funded 46 arts organizations; by 1955, the Arts Council was funding 92 and, by 1975, 262 (ACE, 2012b). In 1994, the Arts Council of Great Britain was restructured into national arts councils, one of which was the Arts Council of England. Renamed Arts Council England (ACE) in 2003, this Council alone was regularly funding 831 organizations in 2011/12, distributing £393 million in grant-in-aid from government and £211 million from the National Lottery (ACE, 2012f, p. 8). Government also subsidizes the arts indirectly, principally through tax exemptions. According to *Compendium: Cultural Policies and Trends in Europe* (Compendium, 2011a), state funding on culture per capita in the United Kingdom as a whole in 2009 was €78.63. This is less than, for example, some continental European nations such as Germany, where per capita state funding to culture in 2009 was €112.36 (Compendium, 2011b). However, it is much more than European neighbours such as the Republic of Ireland, where, after the fall of the Celtic Tiger in 2008, per capita culture funding in 2009 was €41.22 and declining (Compendium, 2011c). And it is more than in the United States, which notoriously offers very little direct national funding to the arts. The US's major national arts granting organization, the National Endowment for the Arts (NEA, 2012), had a 2012 budget of just over $146 million (roughly £93 million or less than one-fifth of what ACE distributed in 2011/12).[3] However, the US's comparatively modest direct national funding is supplemented by funding from state and local governments and by much greater indirect subsidy through tax exemptions. Arthur C. Brooks calculates that in 1999, indirect arts subsidy through taxation in the United States totalled about $1.7 billion, a figure 16 times greater than direct subsidy (Brooks, 2006, p. 498).[4] Former director of the Institute for Philanthropy Beth Breeze notes that, in 2004, tax relief on charitable giving 'cost the US government $17bn in foregone tax' (2005, p. 52).[5]

By contrast, direct state funding to the arts in the United Kingdom since the Second World War has been supportive in its volume and its consistency. There have been shifts in volume of support across various governments, as noted above. And there have been fluctuations in governments' implicit and explicit reasons for supporting the arts – for example, to nurture excellence, to help keep arts accessible to all despite their comparative costliness to produce,[6] and/or to realize their instrumental value in developing quality of life, supporting education or raising national profile.[7] But the principle of state support for the arts has remained constant. However, following the 2007 economic crisis and the formation in 2010 of a Conservative-led coalition UK government, the arts – like other publicly funded sectors such as education and health – have taken a sizeable cut in public funding. A global figure of cuts to arts funding of almost 30 per cent was announced by the Conservative Chancellor in 2010 and the detail of these cuts for arts organizations in England was spelt out by Arts Council England (ACE) in March 2011.[8] In the face of these cuts, both the government and ACE have campaigned for arts organizations to foster new, mixed modes of funding, to realize funding that is what Dame Liz Forgan, Chair of ACE from 2009 to 2013, calls 'the three-legged stool that supports the arts: public funding, private funding and commercial income' (Forgan, 2012, p. 4). The government has particularly championed funding arts through philanthropic giving, from individuals but especially from corporations – in other words, from private as opposed to public capital. Arts organizations themselves have pursued a wide variety of initiatives to support their work; for example, using their own commercially successful productions to cross-subsidize other work, seeking micro-financing through crowdfunding and collaborating with corporate partners to make redeployable profits.

These initiatives demonstrate the ingenuity and adaptability of the arts sector. But the larger context of these shifts in arts funding raises the question of just how successful arts organizations will be at surviving and thriving in this new era of comparative austerity and mixed mode funding. And it raises questions about concurrent shifts in ideologies. Are the arts at risk of being perceived as less socially important than they were before funding cuts? Who holds social responsibility for the arts in this context of shrinking state investment in them? Does this change diminish, distribute and/or amplify social responsibility? Are new social affiliations and collective relationships emerging – for example, across arts and business, across public and private sectors or amongst fellow crowdfunders? And, if so, what are their effects? How are understandings of society recalibrated by these changes? For example, what do these changes do to ideas and practices of equality of access, participation and social responsibility, and to understandings of the relationship between public and private cultures and between the individual and the social?

In many respects I believe that, unfortunately, the Conservative-led coalition government's cuts to arts funding and its practices for stimulating philanthropy are being and will be damaging for the UK's arts ecology and for understandings and practices of society and social responsibility. This chapter aims to detail how this is so. But it also aims to identify what hope there might be in the context of diminishing public resources for sustaining both arts practice and social commitment to mutual social responsibility.

This chapter explores trends in how the arts – theatre in particular – are funded in England, focusing on the period since 2008, around roughly the start of the widespread economic recession. First, I review details of the well-publicized and often acutely felt cuts in state funding to the arts in this period. Then I explore the ways that government and Arts Council England have compelled arts organizations to develop 'mixed economies' of funding by seeking support from a diverse range of sources, including private partners alongside or instead of public ones. I focus first on the Conservative-led coalition government's campaign to advocate for and stimulate philanthropy, evaluating its initial success and future promise. Then I consider other modes of non-government funding such as cross-subsidy, crowdfunding and corporate collaboration. I examine a range of scenarios where arts organizations seek innovative ways of expanding their own or others' support. I look in some detail at the quickly emerging new social dispersed form of funding, crowdfunding. I examine the National Theatre's responsibility as an ACE National Portfolio Organization to offer leadership and support – in other words in-kind support, if not financial support – to other arts organizations and artists and its success in doing so. And I explore the strategies of highly successful London-based immersive theatre company Punchdrunk in securing audience investment and income from corporate collaborations. I propose some of the practical and ideological risks, and opportunities, of these diversifications in arts funding.

My engagement with the topic of contemporary arts funding continues and concludes my exploration in this book of shifting current dynamics between the arts, welfare state socialism, neoliberal capitalism and democracy. In England, and many places beyond, economic and ideological conditions such as state cuts to arts funding are apparently conspiring to render neoliberal capitalism widely ascendant, state socialism descendent and democracy in peril, as markets trump people in the neoliberal economy. In this context, I confess that I am rather sceptical about the 'opportunities' apparently afforded by decreased state funding to the arts in England. I recognize that cuts in arts funding – as in other areas such as health and education – have been triggered by the recession and by resulting state needs to channel decreasing tax revenues to service national debts and to prioritize other remaining areas of welfare funding. However, the cuts also risk playing into the hands of neoliberalism by legitimating the diminution of both state support for the arts and, therefore, the welfare state itself, and by contributing to the increased marketization of the arts which threatens democratic access to and participation in them.

The arts funding cuts *may* be practically necessary. They also may not be. David Harvey argues, 'The economic case for austerity is murky at best and at worst clearly counter-productive', contributing, between 2010 and 2013, to estimated job losses in the public and public-related sectors of 1.6 million that the private sector could not remotely expect to replace (Harvey, 2011, p. 266). An alternative, 'Plan B' approach to the post-2007 recession would aim to stimulate the economy and relieve hardship by investing in things such as building (homes and infrastructures) and the arts. There are, of course, precedents for such an approach: stimulus programmes recommended post-war by John Maynard Keynes in the United Kingdom, and the New Deal under US President F. D. Roosevelt in the Great Depression of the 1930s. Amongst many other things, the New Deal sponsored the Federal Theatre Project, with the US government providing, between 1935 and 1939, more than $45 million 'to pay the salaries of actors, directors, designers, technicians and others so they could produce plays' (Witham, 2003, p. 1; see Quinn, 2008).[9] 'At full tilt', the Theatre Project reportedly employed 12,700 people and performed for an estimated audience of 30 million people, many of whom attended for free (Kennedy and Larkin, 2009, p. 213).

The UK's Conservative-led coalition government is, by contrast, steadfastly – or stubbornly – pursuing a 'Plan A' strategy of spending austerity on the grounds that it is necessary. Aside from whether or not austerity measures are necessary or not, their ensuing arts cuts are ideologically fortuitous for governments and businesses which are committed to expanding neoliberal capitalism, allowing them to ride the crest of economic disaster to legitimate the dismantling of welfare state structures – including arts funding but also state education, public healthcare and social housing – and to legitimate the increasing deregulation of markets. This is a pattern that might be recognized as capitalism's creative destruction (discussed in Chapter 2) or what Naomi Klein has labelled disaster capitalism (2007), where violent destruction of the existing economic order produces a vacuum into which neoliberal market economies surge. I explore these kinds of risks in more detail later in this chapter.

Despite my scepticism about 'opportunities' presented by arts funding cuts, however, I also attempt to explore these. I do not want to be an apologist for neoliberal capitalism nor for cuts to the arts, but I do want to seek some potential value in the current conditions. I explore how neoliberalism's growth need not spell its unilateral triumph; how socially progressive, democratic opportunities persist and thrive despite the circumstances; and how artists keep making aesthetically and politically progressive work in changing and challenging conditions. What I want to imagine is not only the risks of neoliberalism, but also the resilience of models of social practice and support. And I want to imagine the resilience of arts and artists to keep making culturally and politically progressive arts, despite the constraints of their circumstances.

Cuts to arts funding in England

After some cuts to English arts funding in 2009/10,[10] a very serious blow came on 20 October 2010, when George Osborne, Chancellor of the Conservative-led coalition government elected in May that year, announced in the Spending Review that the government was cutting the previously agreed settlement to ACE for 2011–15 by almost 30 per cent, almost 15 per cent of which had to be passed on to arts organizations (Higgins, 2010). ACE's annual budget was cut by over £100m, in real terms, from £449.5m in the 2010 financial year to £349m by 2014 (ibid.), with the biggest proportion of this cut implemented immediately in 2011, when ACE's budget was cut by £71 million (Hill, 2012). ACE duly passed half of its budget on to arts organizations in funding cuts announced in March 2011. 206 arts organizations had 100 per cent of their funding cut; 18.4 per cent (or 38) of those were theatre companies (Rogers, 2011a), including such well known and established organizations as Shared Experience (which specializes in combining text and physical theatre); the major regional touring venue Theatre Royal Newcastle; and British East Asian theatre company Yellow Earth (Rogers, 2011b; ACE, 2012c). Many more companies lost large portions of their funding and again included high-profile organizations: the high-quality North London literary theatre, the Almeida, had a 33 per cent cut, with a real terms effect of 39 per cent; new play touring company Out of Joint had a cut of 20.8 per cent (27.9 per cent in real terms); central London new writing, cabaret and comedy venue the Soho Theatre lost 9.5 per cent (17.6 per cent in real terms); Black-led company Talawa Theatre lost 14.2 per cent (real terms, 20.9 per cent); pioneering experimental theatre company, Sheffield-based Forced Entertainment lost 6.5 per cent (14.9 per cent in real terms); and even such major national organizations as the Royal Shakespeare Company and the National Theatre each suffered cuts of 6.6 per cent (15 per cent in real terms) (see Rogers, 2011b).

Alongside these extensive and deep cuts at national level, English organizations experienced arts funding cuts from other state sources. The National Lottery is normally one of the greatest funders of arts in the United Kingdom, but funds totalling a whopping £2.175 billion were diverted from its usual commitments to subsidize the 2012 London Olympics (though around half a billion of this may eventually be repaid) (DCMS, n.d.). Local authorities' available funds have also been squeezed by reduced allocations from Westminster and are similarly reducing their support for the arts, sometimes drastically (see Davey, 2010, p. 3).

In November 2012, Newcastle City Council (2012) published proposals for a 2013–16 budget which will cut all arts funding, making Newcastle 'a test case for the survival of the arts in a harsh climate, rather than a shining example of the positive impact of cultural investment' (Thorpe, 2012) which, until recently, it had been.

Admittedly, these cuts followed what many – including former Prime Minister Tony Blair (2007) – have called a 'golden age' in arts funding under New Labour. ACE's total investment in regularly funded organizations grew in cash terms by 130 per cent over the course of New Labour's periods of government, from £149 million in 1996/7 to £344 million in 2009/10 alongside project awards from the Grants for the Arts programme totalling almost £65 million (ACE, 2010a; see Knell and Taylor, 2011, p. 10).[11] And, as mentioned above, in 2009, state funding on culture per capita in the United Kingdom as a whole was €78.63 (Compendium, 2011a). Nevertheless, and perhaps especially because of these comparatively well-supported contexts that directly preceded arts cuts in England, the cuts announced in March 2011 were acutely felt.

'Mixed economies' of arts funding: philanthropy[12]

As noted above, these cuts to arts funding in England coincided with the 2010 formation of a Conservative-led coalition government. If the cultural legacy of New Labour was its support and development of creative industries (as explored in Chapter 2), the Conservative-led coalition government wants its legacy to be a 'culture of giving', particularly giving by large corporate sponsors. A major plank of the UK Conservative Party's election campaign in spring 2010 was its advocacy of the 'Big Society', in which government would relinquish control in certain areas and people would take on more social responsibility.[13] The 'Big Society' rather quickly fell into disrepute, first because many, including opposition Labour MPs, criticized it as being indicative of the government's disavowal of *its own* social responsibility and the government's reliance on citizens to provide '"do-it-yourself" services', and second because the government mostly failed to follow up this so-called '"only big idea" on offer' with any detailed policy or programming (BBC, 2010b). However, in the arts, the Conservative-led coalition government did actually follow up the Big Society idea with policy around philanthropy.

Here I examine, interrogate and challenge this government's practice in relation to philanthropy, its appropriation of the term's positive implications and the artistic and social damage it risks promulgating under the banner of social good. Philanthropy literally means love of humanity; practically, it is commonly interpreted as 'voluntary action for the public good' (Moody, 2011, p. 145; Payton and Moody, 2008, pp. 27ff.). It should stand for basic, good human values of generosity, social care and the fair distribution of wealth through the divestment of those with 'too much' to those with 'too little'. However, philanthropy risks reinforcing social imbalances rather than challenging them in at least four ways. It risks being, literally, patronizing, the negative incarnation of patronage.[14] It risks allowing those with 'too much' actually to garner more through giving, for example in accruing the social capital of munificence. It risks producing the 'opportunity cost' of many arts organizations suffering from neglect when philanthropists invest exclusively in their selected – sometimes pet – projects. And it risks legitimating government withdrawal from arts funding. I argue that the Conservative-led coalition government's emphasis on philanthropy in arts policy is and will be profoundly damaging to the UK's arts ecology because, first, it has been relatively unsuccessful in stimulating philanthropy and supporting the arts and, second, it tends to privilege the most conservative arts forms and organizations. I argue further that this emphasis on philanthropy is damaging for UK culture more broadly because rather than facilitating the social distribution of power – which the government implies is one of the benefits of philanthropy – it tends to entrench power in the hands of an unelected and in many respects unaccountable financial elite.

The 'Year of Corporate Philanthropy'

Less than two months after the October 2010 Spending Review in which Conservative Chancellor George Osborne announced cuts of 30 per cent to arts funding, the Conservative-led coalition government began to detail its chief solution to these cuts: philanthropy. On 8 December 2010, the then Secretary of State for Culture, Media and Sport (DCMS), Conservative MP Jeremy Hunt, gave a keynote address to the European Association for Philanthropy & Giving in London. There, Hunt outlined a ten-point plan for cultural philanthropy (see DCMS, 2010); he launched two DCMS-commissioned publications advocating philanthropy, one written by British Museum Director Neil MacGregor (2010) and one by the Arts Council, *Endowments in the Arts* (2010b); and he announced his government's designation of 2011 as 'the Year of Corporate Philanthropy' (Hunt, 2010). He emphasized that his government's 'approach to philanthropy' did not aim to replace state funding with private support, but rather 'to combine the best of US-style philanthropic support with the best of European-style public support' with an emphasis, nevertheless, on private support. '[S]urely we must ask ourselves', he implored, 'what we can learn from a country [the USA] in which cultural giving per capita is £37 a year compared to just £6 in the United Kingdom? The best model for financing the arts – one that secures not just financial independence but artistic independence too – is one in which cultural organisations can count on a plurality and diversity of funding sources.'[15] For its part, ACE's 48-page booklet *Endowments in the Arts* set out to debunk the myth that only large, metropolitan arts organizations are successful in securing private funding and it encouraged other – presumably smaller and non-metropolitan – arts organizations to do likewise. The rhetoric of *Endowments in the Arts* was supported by practical activities (ACE, 2010b). In spring 2011, for example, ACE offered six classes nationwide with Michael Kaiser whom they described in this glowing biography (ACE, 2011b) of private funding success: 'He was Chief Executive of the Royal Opera House from 1998–2000 and, during his tenure, the organisation erased its historic accumulated deficit, completed a £214 million redevelopment of the facility, created an endowment fund, and greatly increased its level of support from the private and public sectors.' (They fail to mention how big and metropolitan the Royal Opera House is, slightly undermining their own attempts at myth-debunking.)

In March 2011, Osborne (2011) delivered a budget that he claimed represented the 'most radical and most generous reforms to charitable giving for more than twenty years'. Many of these reforms were elaborated in more detail in the government's *Giving White Paper* published in May 2011 which noted that though 'evidence shows that the United Kingdom is a relatively generous society ... we cannot afford to be complacent – levels of giving have flat-lined in recent years' (HM Government, 2011, p. 8). Reforms included a simplification of a digital platform for Gift Aid to make more efficient and productive this scheme allowing charities to reclaim basic tax on donations and higher rate tax-paying donors to claim extra tax relief on donations (see HM Revenue & Customs, 2012); increased Gift Aid benefit limits, so that charities and museums can thank donors by giving them a gift worth up to £2500, instead of the former limit of £500; a then-forthcoming consultation on art donations in lieu of taxation; and a '10% cut in inheritance tax for those leaving 10% or more of their estate to charity' (Chapman, 2011). The *Giving White Paper* (HM Govt., 2011, p. 9) argued for a 'mix of approaches' to 'make giving easier and more compelling without "interfering"': 'more traditional policy levers such as tax incentives, funding, policy programmes and removing regulatory barriers' as well as '"softer" approaches such as setting a good example and bringing people and organisations together to share ideas and celebrate success'.

Though Osborne boasted the introduction of many reforms, they were mostly passive, meant to leverage and incentivize rather than actually require investment or giving. And since many of the reforms offered were tax breaks, they sacrificed the collection of tax revenue for the public treasury, revenue which might at least partially have gone to arts funding. When Osborne proposed capping tax breaks on charitable giving in his March 2012 budget there was a vociferous outcry heralded by Twitter campaign #giveitbackgeorge (see GIB, 2012a; 2012b). That campaign drew attention to how large the sacrificed tax revenue might have been – £50–80 million according to *The Independent* (Morris and Grice, 2012), though this seems an underestimate given that, according to former director of the Institute for Philanthropy Beth Breeze (2005, p. 52), 'tax relief on charitable donations cost the British government £1.3bn' in 2003. Incidentally, George did 'give it back' in May 2012, u-turning on this proposal (amongst several others at the same time) and not capping tax relief on charitable giving (see Ramesh and Jowit, 2012).[16]

Catalyst

The biggest direct investment the Conservative-led coalition government has made in stimulating philanthropy in the arts is its three-part Catalyst funding scheme, announced in spring 2011 and worth £100 million. The scheme aims 'to boost private giving to the cultural sector and build long-term resilience, sustainability and innovation' through three streams designed to develop endowments and other forms of 'match' private funding (ACE, 2011c). The largest share of Catalyst's £100 million total – £56 million – goes to the 'Catalyst: Endowment' scheme which 'offers match funding for the purpose of building a new endowment fund, or increasing an existing one' (Catalyst, 2012). Endowments must 'be managed by the [recipient] organisations for a minimum of 25 years', and they must support 'additional arts activity ... not core funding' (DCMS, 2012a; see also DCMS, 2011, p. 3). An endowment is usually a large financial sum held by an institution over a long period; the institution aims not to deplete the endowment's capital, drawing instead on its *interest* as a source of consistent support. Demand for the Catalyst: Endowment fund vastly exceeded expectations: ACE reportedly received 350 applications (Hill, 2012).[17] However, ACE made awards to only 18 organizations in June 2012, worth a cumulative total of £30.5 million, while the Heritage Lottery Fund simultaneously made awards to 16 museums, galleries and other organizations to a total of £25.5 million. Of the 18 ACE-funded organizations, 11 shared as their principle art form music. A mere two were theatres: the Royal Shakespeare Company received £1 million, with a match funding target of £1 million; and the Old Vic Theatre Trust 2000 received £5 million, with a match funding target of £15 million. Three of the ACE-funded Catalyst Endowment recipients were art galleries: the contemporary-focused Serpentine Gallery in Hyde Park (awarded £3 million, with a target of £6 million match funding) and East London's Whitechapel Gallery and Margate's Turner Contemporary, both awarded £1 million (and the same matching target). While state funding contributed £56 million across arts and heritage, the scheme was hailed as 'set to unlock £162 million', with 'successful projects ... expected to attract an additional £106 million from private and corporate donors' (DCMS, 2012a).

The second Catalyst scheme, 'Catalyst Arts: Capacity building and match funding scheme', supports organizations in 'building their fundraising capacity and capability over a three-year period' (DCMS, 2012b) with individual grants of between £120,000 and £240,000 made on 17 May 2012 to a total of 173 organizations and a total sum of almost £30.5 million (see ACE, 2012d). This scheme's funding was – predictably – less conservatively distributed than was that of the Endowment scheme. Of these 173 funded organizations, 46 – or over a quarter – were theatres; 32, or almost 18 per cent, were visual arts organizations. Funded organizations include East London's Hackney Empire (£196,750); theatre, installation and site-specific performance company Fevered Sleep (£166,500); London's Institute of Contemporary Arts (or ICA, £180,000); dance venue Sadler's Wells (£226,000); contemporary dance organization Siobhan Davies Dance and Independent Dance (£120,000); North London music, performance and new media venue the Roundhouse (£234,438); Manchester's Royal Exchange Theatre (£236,500); and theatre/performance company dreamthinkspeak (£145,305). Each receiving the maximum allocation of £240,000 were the Battersea Arts Centre (BAC); leading South West England producing venue, Theatre Royal Plymouth; Yorkshire Sculpture Park; North London's Tricycle Theatre Company; site-specific arts producers Artangel; Manchester International Festival; Brighton Dome and Festival; and the East London combined arts venue Rich Mix (ibid.). The range of funded companies was geographically spread and artistically dynamic.

The third strand, 'Catalyst Arts and Catalyst Heritage: fundraising capacity building grants', aims to 'support arts organisations with little or no fundraising experience who would like to build their fundraising capacity and capability to attract new donors and strengthen their financial resilience to enhance their artistic output or engagement with the public' (ACE, 2012d). This strand was initially intended to launch in April 2012, but was delayed until autumn 2012 (Catalyst, 2012); it will distribute £7 million to the arts (and £5 million via the Heritage Lottery Fund) and ACE will distribute a further £3 million 'in a programme of learning and knowledge sharing' (DCMS, 2012a).

Catalyst's benefits

It is impossible to assess the real long-term benefits of the Catalyst schemes when, at the time of writing, one programme is not yet launched and two programmes have only just announced their awards. However, it is possible to imagine some of their benefits if they work as planned. First, they aim to support long-term planning, sustainability and resilience by helping to support arts organizations in building endowment funds – or plans for endowment funds – that the organization can then draw on for years to come, even when public funding is insecure, as it has been since 2008. Jeremy Hunt's iconic example of the successfully endowed arts organization is New York's Metropolitan Museum of Art which, he observes, took 'over a century to build up its multi-billion dollar endowment'. Hunt (2010) enthuses, 'In a hundred years time, I want people to look back and say that the multi-billion pound endowments owned by our national cultural organisations put their first roots in the ground back in 2010.' Though only the 'national cultural organizations' of the RSC and the Old Vic are Endowment-funded through Catalyst, many great, dynamic and important smaller organizations have also been funded, such as the Battersea Arts Centre and Sadler's Wells. Second, the Catalyst schemes potentially 'unlock', as the government likes to say, large sums of private funding in support of the arts (see DCMS, 2012a). Unquestionably, there is excessive wealth in some quarters of the UK economy: the 2012 *Sunday Times* 'Rich List' reported that, despite the post-2008 financial crisis and government spending austerity, the UK's 1000 wealthiest people included 77 billionaires (two more than in 2008's previous record) and were worth a combined total of more than £414 billion, almost five per cent more than in 2011 (*Sunday Times*, 2012; *Guardian*, 2012). With this kind of personal wealth in the United Kingdom, it is just and appropriate that it is redistributed, though it might certainly be argued that this redistribution is the proper function and domain of taxation and treasury allocation. Third, Catalyst can do a welcome job of stimulating, supporting and publicly acknowledging individuals' and corporations' acts of social responsibility, possibly contributing to a culture change around attitudes towards giving, including senses of responsibility to give, of the value of giving, and of the value of social economies of altruistic generosity and giving over market economies of profit.[18] Sociologist Marcel Mauss (2002) famously argued that gift economies are rarely entirely altruistic and most gift-givers seek reward. However, what might be possible in a gift economy – including that sought by Catalyst – is at least some recalibration of the social and market dominance of profit-making and some engagement with *active* giving, as distinct from the giving required through statutory taxation.

Catalyst's problems

However, the potential risks of the Catalyst scheme and its framing ideologies are much greater than those potential benefits. The first great risk is that these schemes prove both insecure and insufficient as they fail to stimulate corporate and individual giving. Evidence suggests this is already a problem, as the recession has hit not only state purses, but also those of businesses and individuals: 2008/09 saw a seven per cent decline in charitable giving in the arts in England (ACE, 2010b, p. 31). In 2010, donations to the UK's top 500 charities fell by £70 million, with seven major causes – including arts and culture – experiencing a 'real terms fall in their income' (Pharoah, 2011). In 2010/11, 'Corporate investment in the arts dropped to its lowest level for seven years' (Hill, 2012), including a whopping '20% decline of business involvement with the arts over the last five years' (Eyre, 2012). Voluntary sector analyst Diana Leat (Leat, 2012, p. 15) observes that 'Foundations are not – and show no signs of wishing to be – a substitute, supplement, or back pocket for the provision of public services.' All this despite the government's claim (or, perhaps more accurately, hope, fantasy or myth), that 2011 would be the 'Year of Corporate Philanthropy'.[19]

In a global context, we may be in what cultural sociologist Michael Moody (2011, p. 147) identifies as an 'historic era for philanthropy' due to the establishment in the 1990s of the Bill and Melinda Gates Foundation, enhanced since 2006 with the philanthropic investments of Warren Buffett, making it 'the largest foundation in the history of the world, by far' with, in 2008, 'nearly $30 billion in assets, and annual grants of more than $3.6 billion'. However, that broader context appears neither to translate into arts giving nor to transfer to the United Kingdom. Helen Burrows and Kitty Ussher's 2011 Demos think-tank paper on giving to and investment in the arts, *Risky Business*, argues that investors generally consider the arts too risky for investment. In the United Kingdom, no super-rich Briton on the scale of the Gates or

Buffett has recently formed or contributed to enormous foundations;[20] and almost certainly the post-2007 recession and crises in sectors such as banking have detrimentally affected philanthropic giving. In 2010, the Royal Bank of Scotland Group PLC 'reduced its [charitable] spending slightly', and this may be the shape of things to come in the context of ongoing European economic uncertainty (Hill, 2011). In Spain, for example, savings banks were formerly 'the main sponsors of culture, even more than government';[21] not anymore. In the Spanish region of Castilla-León, for instance, local savings banks' investment in culture and good works has fallen by almost two-thirds between 2005 and 2012, from €92 million to €34 million. Research by the Swiss bank UBS indicates that five of Spain's major savings banks will have 'no social budget at all in 2013' (Burgen, 2012).

Even that apparent Eden of arts philanthropy, the United States, has seen philanthropy hit hard by recession. In 2010, some estimates indicated that 'one in 10 of the country's 100,000 arts organisations are in such financial straits they have been forced to make swingeing cuts or consider closing' (Pilkington, Davies and McDonald, 2010). Arts organizations affected included large institutions: Minneapolis's Guthrie Theater cut its budget by nearly $4 million in 2009–10, for example (Donahue and Patterson, 2010, p. 151).[22] Jeremy Hunt may lionize the Metropolitan Museum of Art's endowment fund, but even it has proven vulnerable to the recession, even before Hunt launched his 'Year of Philanthropy': in February 2010, the Met 'shed 14% of its staff after the value of its investments fell $600m (£388m)' (Pilkington, Davies and McDonald, 2010).

During an era of historically low interest rates, Catalyst will see annual returns on endowments of 'peanuts', in the terminology of John Nicholls (in Chapman, 2011), managing partner of UK cultural agency Arts Quarter. In 2010, for example, though the value of UK endowment funds reportedly increased by 17.2 per cent, their income from investments actually fell by ten per cent (Hill, 2011). On the day the Catalyst endowment fund was launched, Nicolas Kent, former artistic director of Kilburn's Tricycle Theatre, reportedly 'stood down after 27 years as a direct result of arts cuts' (Chapman, 2011). He has called the Catalyst: Endowment scheme 'ridiculous', pointing out, 'At the lowest level regional organisations are going to have to raise 500k that will have to be matched by their donors. If they can achieve that, though most of the smaller ones won't, then they will earn about £10,000 a year interest – how is that going to help regional organisations?' (ibid.). The funding hypothetically leveraged by Catalyst is insufficient.

Second, there is the risk that, even where private sources of funding can be found, it will be difficult to leverage that funding to arts organizations through *these* schemes. One reason for this is that Catalyst's pay-off lacks immediate, high-visibility impact so is comparatively unattractive to funders. American cultural economist Diane Ragsdale has observed that 'Few funders and donors in the US appear to have the trust, lack of ego, and long-term vision to patiently support organisations and seek results not in one year, or five, but 50' (2011, p. 5). British philanthropic analyst and adviser Teresa Lloyd (in Chapman, 2011) says of the Catalyst scheme in particular, 'It is a very sophisticated ask [even] for people who know the organisation [they might fund] and have confidence in its longevity.'[23] Given that this scheme is designed to 'support additional arts activity' and 'is not core funding' (DCMS, 2012a), many arts organizations will not have the resources to pursue it when they must prioritize current work, without which there will be no 'additional' future activity. Furthermore, many arts organizations will struggle to match donors with the new funding stream. From February to March 2012, Arts Quarter surveyed 361 arts organizations on their perceptions of the success – or otherwise – of the Conservative-led coalition government philanthropy agenda. They found that 'some 68% of ... respondents ... feel they will be unlikely to find suitable candidates to [*sic*] newly created fundraising roles under Catalyst' (Nicholls, 2012, p. 6; see artsquarter, 2012).

Thirdly, the demands that Catalyst makes on private funding are great and perhaps too steep. In principle, Catalyst works on a 'match' funding system, where the arts organization aims to 'match' a funding contribution from government with a contribution from a private source. In practice, however, Catalyst often requires more-than-matching funding from 'private philanthropic sources', 'on average ... £2 from private sources for every £1 of public funding' (ACE, 2011d). Where Catalyst: Endowment government agency contributions are for £5 million – as is the case for the Old Vic Theatre's award – the required 'match' funding is a rather colossal three times that sum (DCMS, 2011, p. 2). Without securing match funding, arts organizations provisionally awarded Catalyst funds will not be eligible to receive those funds (ACE, 2012e). Catalyst may very well therefore end up distributing much less funding that its headlines and champions claim.

As well as those conditions that suggest Catalyst schemes will be unsuccessful in generating private funding, there is also the risk that what funding is generated will tend to travel in conservative, predictable ways, favouring companies which are large, long-established and consistent in their outputs, 'safe brands', as commentator Dany Louise (2012) puts it, with 'excellent but not-too-challenging art' (see ACE, 2010b, p. 20; Moody, 2011, p. 156; Quine, 1998, p. 708). Catalyst has so far broadly failed to break the link of endowments with larger organizations and it tends to favour organizations which make music, usually symphonic or operatic music. As noted above, 11 out of 18 Catalyst: Endowment award recipients were music organizations and/or venues. Endowment funding does not favour arts organizations whose output is live and/or particularly unpredictable. To reiterate, out of the 18 arts organizations supported by the Catalyst: Endowment fund, only two were theatres – the RSC and the Old Vic – and, whatever the quality of their work, institutionally, both are established organizations, and formally, both produce classical texts. Lloyd observes that the Catalyst: Endowment scheme asks

> donors to put their faith in [companies'] future vision and artistic and management leadership. This may not be a problem for national collections such as the V&A or The Wordsworth Trust, but may be more difficult for performing arts organisations, because of the artistic ups and downs every long-term donor (and it is loyal donors and audience members who will be the focus of the promotion of endowment) has experienced.
>
> (in Eyre, 2012)

Likewise in the United States, Ragsdale notes, 'support from private foundations has tended, on average, to gravitate to larger, high profile, "fine arts" institutions' (2011, p. 4).

There is, therefore, a real opportunity cost for those smaller, more dynamic and performance-based organizations that would struggle ever to get into the running for major endowment funding. As Louise (2012) puts it, 'organisations that are politically challenging, socially radical or just plain unsexy are unlikely to benefit' from the endowment scheme. It is encouraging to see organizations such as BAC, Hackney Empire, Sadler's Wells, the Tricycle Theatre and the Roundhouse, for example, receiving significant 'Catalyst Arts: Capacity building and match funding scheme' grants; but it is also frustrating to recognize how difficult it would be for such companies to 'graduate' to the top-tier endowment scheme funding. For Louise (ibid.), this trend is symptomatic of 'a lessening of opportunities for the edgier, the experimental and the new, and for those organisations championing and nurturing the next generation of emerging artists'.

Not surprisingly, given such problems with endowments in particular, there appears to be widespread dissatisfaction in the cultural sector with what Arts Quarter called the government's 'Philanthropy in the Arts Agenda' in its early 2012 survey with 361 cultural organizations on the perceived success of that agenda.

> [O]verall, our respondents feel that implementation of all but three [out of thirteen] aspects of the Agenda has been disappointingly slow .... Even of the three elements on which a majority of respondents felt there had been the greatest degrees of delivery – building fundraising skills (58%), promoting legacies (50.2%) and defining and launching a matched fund programme (60%) – [...] significant proportions of respondents still feel there remains a significant way to go to deliver the aspirations of the Agenda .... [T]he three areas in which respondents felt there had been the least degree of delivery were in fostering and extending corporate giving (70%), promoting support from international donors (90%) and in the sharing of knowledge about endowments (76%).
>
> (Nicholls, 2012a, p. 4)

The report also records an acute lack of confidence in the government's tax changes affecting charitable giving, with 100 per cent of respondents from the music, opera and dance communities indicating that they 'believe or are unsure that the current tax changes will have any impact on giving to the arts while across all other respondent constituencies levels of negative feeling lie within the 88%–95% threshold' (ibid., p. 6). And this lack of confidence was recorded even before the government made a series of u-turns in May 2012 on taxation plans announced in its March 2012 budget, including the u-turn mentioned above on imposing caps of £50,000 or 25 per cent of income, whichever was higher, on making charitable donations instead of payment in taxes (see BBC, 2012c). Arts Quarter's survey's respondents reported satisfaction with the Catalyst programme; nevertheless,

> clear majorities of respondents feel that Catalyst of itself, will be insufficient to develop fundraising capacity and encourage higher levels of giving through its matched funding element. Among theatre respondents in particular, 88% of respondents do not believe or are unsure whether Catalyst will develop fundraising capacities and 84% of theatre respondents also believe that the matched funding of Catalyst will not work effectively to incentivise greater levels of giving to the arts.
>
> (Nicholls, 2012a, p. 5)

The report's author John Nicholls notes further that 'fundraising *competition* within the arts is about to enter a phase unimagined up until this point as more organisations compete with each other and with other non-arts causes' (ibid., p. 14, italics added). For a government that wants to stimulate market culture, such competition may be a happy symptom. But for the arts ecology, it may prove damaging and destructive.

There are, therefore, many specific problems with the Catalyst programmes' impact on the arts, caused by inopportune timing; a disincentivizing emphasis on the long-term; tendencies to support established companies and comparatively conservative, or at least static, artistic forms; and a failure to earn the confidence and trust of the cultural sector. But as well as those problems, the Conservative-led coalition government's promotion of philanthropy has problematic implications for UK culture and sociality more broadly; specifically, it risks reinforcing and exacerbating elitism and class privilege. This government's emphasis on stimulating specifically *large*-scale philanthropic giving means that giving will remain chiefly the province and privilege of the wealthy. This alignment of the wealthy with the privilege of giving is further enforced through the government's many measures to incentivize giving through tax breaks – for example, through Gift Aid, tax breaks on philanthropic donations, tax breaks on inheritance, and the possibility of making art donations in lieu of tax. Tax breaks act as the greatest incentive to those who might otherwise either pay most tax and/or might most want to avoid or at least self-direct their 'tax' pounds. Such 'givers' give, but they enjoy the privilege of self-selecting where their 'tax' contributions go; other tax-payers, of course, contribute taxes to the state treasury and rely on government to distribute that money in the nation's best collective interests. This government's enactment of philanthropy entrenches financial and cultural power in the hands of an unelected and unaccountable financial elite.

There are some reasons to be cheerful about this government's approach to philanthropy and the arts. Some great, important organizations, including those with comparatively short histories and dedication to new and emerging arts, such as the Turner Contemporary in Margate and BAC in South West London, have received significant Catalyst funding. With the third Catalyst programme yet to be revealed let alone distributed, more important arts organizations stand yet to profit.

But there remain many reasons to be sceptical about this government's approach to philanthropy, the arts and, indeed, contemporary social relations. The diversity of Britain's arts ecology – and especially its emerging new arts practices – is at risk. Though there is Catalyst funding for a great range of arts organizations, the largest shares continue to go to established and comparatively conservative arts organizations and to very few theatre organizations. Because Catalyst funding cannot, by definition, replace core arts funding, it is unlikely to help preserve any companies that are at serious financial risk, and there are likely to emerge several or many of those in the financial context of austerity and cutbacks to arts funding. Also at risk is the social democracy of contemporary British culture. Though Cameron and his fellow Conservative Party members may claim that the Big Society is meant to *distribute* power more extensively across society in a kind of people-power movement, his government's practices in the contexts of philanthropy are, on the contrary, further concentrating cultural and financial capital and authority and legitimating that concentration. A culture of giving is a good thing, and is important to social welfare. What is bad in this government's enactment is the suggestion that giving is both optional and ideally individually determined. This government's approach to philanthropic giving to the arts is, sadly, typical of its approach to distributing power in the 'Big Society' more broadly. It is both tokenist – offering comparatively small amounts of money to comparatively few – and elitist – enhancing the interests of a wealthy elite.

Other mixed modes of arts funding

Philanthropic donations are not the only kind of non-state funding the DCMS, ACE and arts organizations themselves are trying to cultivate. The next section enumerates some of these alternative modes of support and then offers some closer examination of a selection of case studies, namely crowdfunding as an emerging and growing form of non-state funding for the arts; the National Theatre's support of 'outside' individuals and organizations; and Punchdrunk's activities cultivating individual sponsorship and corporate collaboration. I evaluate the success of these various modes of support as well as their effects for social relations and arts practice. Though I admire the dynamism and inventiveness that they often indicate in arts organizations' efforts to keep making work, I am wary of their potential insufficiency and the ways they potentially naturalize hierarchical social relations and the dominance of consumer culture.

ACE encourages theatres and artists effectively to co-sponsor one another with, if not hard funds, in-kind support including free labour provided through mentoring, interning or volunteering. The influential 2008 DCMS publication, *Supporting Excellence in the Arts*, otherwise known as the McMaster Report after its author, the former Edinburgh International Festival Director Sir Brian McMaster (2008, p. 13), recommended the establishment of a 'Knowledge Bank' of experts. These specialists in arts management would share their expertise across the sector. It also recommended 'that practitioners take responsibility for the cultural ecology and actively engage with the development of their peers and the next generation' (ibid.). The National Portfolio Organization (NPO) funding programme launched by ACE in April, 2012 (replacing its former Regularly Funded Organizations programme), explicitly requires NPOs to support the broader arts network. ACE's document on *The Relationship Between the Arts Council and Funded Organisations*, published in April 2012, emphasizes, 'The organisations in our portfolios [*sic*] represent the backbone of the arts and culture in this country, and we want them to lead the way in terms of achievement, accountability and performance' (p. 3). Beyond this expectation, ACE writes, 'it is the *responsibility* of all National portfolio organisations to work with the Arts Council and other organisations to share skills and expertise, as together we deliver great art for everyone' (ibid., p. 21, italics added). Below, I look in more detail at such work supporting a wider arts ecology by London's National Theatre (NT) which has, for example, co-produced with Shunt, Headlong, DV8 and Punchdrunk.

Arts organizations are also seeking to cross-subsidize their own work through combining successful commercial production alongside state subsidized productions. The NT consistently cross-subsidizes its own work through the success of such shows as *The History Boys* and the mega-hit *War Horse*, which accounted for almost 20 per cent of the NT's income in 2010/11 (NT, n.d.a, p. 42). *War Horse* opened in 2007 on the National's Olivier stage; it transferred to London's West End in 2009, Broadway in 2011 and Toronto and Melbourne in 2012; it went on a US tour in 2012; a UK tour and a Berlin production are planned for 2013; and further future plans include tours around Australia, South Africa and Japan (see War Horse, 2012; NT, 2012). 'It is our intention', says the NT's website, 'that within two years, eight concurrent productions of *War Horse* will be running on five continents' (NT, 2012). In the NT's 2010/11 Annual Report, Chairman John Makinson observes, 'it looks likely that box office receipts from *War Horse* will exceed the total income from the three theatres on the South Bank combined in this financial year. We are being careful not to mortgage our future to a single show with a limited life but for now *War Horse* (2012) provides a cushion against financial risk and a platform from which to take creative risk' (NT, n.d.a, p. 6). I discuss Punchdrunk's cross-subsidy of its work through commercial collaboration in particular in more detail below.

Finally, the DCMS and ACE encourage arts organizations not only to find new sources of funding but to save money by economizing. ACE's DCMS-commissioned *Endowments in the Arts* encouraged arts organizations simply to take 'steps to improve ... financial management capabilities' (Davey, 2010, p. 4) to save money – though one would expect that savings achieved through economizing would struggle to match the cuts companies received. All these are just some of the many strategies that state and arts organizations in England have developed to diversify support for arts-making in the context of cuts in state-granted arts funding. I offer a summary analysis of the effectiveness and effects of these strategies below, but first I look in some detail at a few examples of modes of arts funding devolved from or effectively privatized by government to evaluate these modes' success and implications.

Crowdfunding

The mixed economy model is also delighted to see the growth of crowdfunding. For example, it was specifically recommended by the DCMS: on a very short webpage dedicated to 'Philanthropy and Fundraising' that existed in 2012 but is gone in 2013, the DCMS pointed out, 'There are a number of innovative fundraising and crowdfunding websites, which can prove useful portals for fundraising activities', citing websites for We Fund, We Did This and Sponsume. Like crowd sourcing, crowdfunding seeks contributions from a large group of people, whether those contributions take the form of expertise, feedback or solutions to problems as in the case of crowd sourcing, or money as in the case of crowdfunding. Through a web portal such as Sponsume or Kickstarter, artists or companies make a pitch to potential funders to support a project, normally aiming to raise a targeted amount of money within a limited time.[24] If the funding target is not reached, no money is drawn from investors. The pitch invites funders to participate in 'micro-patronage', where many people give a little, as distinct from patronage, where few people give a lot. Funders' contributions can take the form of equity purchase, loan, donation or pre-ordering of the forthcoming product (Belleflamme, Lambert and Schwienbacher, 2012, p. 2), though in theatre and performing arts contexts, contributions are normally donations for which funders only receive a small perk, such as a signed photograph or recognition as a benefactor in a production programme. Examples of theatre projects successfully funded through Sponsume in England include the Belarus Free Theatre, which raised over £9000 from 152 contributors – or backers – in 2011 to start a full UK office (Sponsume, 2012b); and GO OPERA, which raised £6000 from 34 backers in spring 2011 to produce a condensed, immersive *GO TRAVIATA* in a warehouse in East London (Sponsume, 2012c). Though both those projects raised several thousand pounds, funding sought for performing arts projects in the United Kingdom is often for much smaller amounts, often below £2000, and it is often for the work of very small and new companies, for example groups taking shows to the annual Edinburgh Festival Fringe.

Given its success elsewhere (such as in the United States) and in other art forms (for example, music production) (see Belleflamme, Lambert and Schwienbacher, 2012), it seems likely that crowdfunding will grow as a source of theatre funding in the United Kingdom. In Ireland, for example, through the website Fundit (2012b), Landmark Productions and Galway Arts Festival secured over €16,000 in spring 2011 to patch the budget shortfall for their summer production of Enda Walsh's *Misterman* starring Cillian Murphy. In the UK theatre sector there is evidence of qualified confidence in crowdfunding; Arts Quarter's 2012 consultation with 361 cultural organizations found that, among theatre respondents (81 organizations), '48% regard[ed] [crowdfunding] as a viable means of generating support over the next three years' (Nicholls, 2012a, p. 10). This somewhat cautious sectoral confidence may be justified by crowdfunding's exponential growth. *The Economist* reports that in February 2012, no crowdfunded project on one of the biggest platforms, Kickstarter, had yet raised $1 million, but by June 2012, seven had (*Economist*, 2012). Across its various forms (donations, investing, and so on), crowdfunding raised $1.5 billion in 2011 and is forecast to raise almost double that – $2.8 billion – in 2012 (ibid.). In 2007, there were 100 crowdfunding platforms; in mid-2012, there are over 450 and there are forecast to be 536 by the end of 2012 (ibid.).

There are many potential social and cultural advantages to this fast-growing form of arts funding, especially in its apparent democratization of philanthropic arts giving and receiving. For audiences, it specifically invites and thereby legitimates small contributions, enabling the 'crowd', popularizing philanthropic giving and facilitating active participation in supporting artists and artwork that a funder admires, even if the funder has little money. For artists, crowdfunding potentially democratizes opportunities to benefit from philanthropy and to work comparatively independently. Allowing artists to produce themselves, it reduces artists' potential reliance on big producing organizations. It enables smaller, start-up organizations at comparatively little expense: the cost of posting an online pitch is generally free and sites usually charge 'between 3–12.5% for processing donated monies' (Speed, 2012). Artists generally retain copyright, so there is little cost or risk. And arts crowdfunding is reportedly quite successful: 'Kickstarter claim that around half the projects they feature make their funding goal – a figure that is comparable to, or higher than some UK regions in the Arts Council England "Grants for the Arts" success rates' (ibid.). Founder of the crowdfunding platform WeDidThis.org.uk Ed Whiting (in Healey, 2011) claims that these benefits for audiences and artists also produce benefits for art: 'We think that by creating a "critical mass" of these micro-philanthropists we can strengthen the bond between artists and their audiences and make the arts stronger and more open'.

But are the crowdfunded arts really more open and more beneficial for audiences, artists and arts? Research indicates that crowdfunding in the arts often finds significant *initial* investment from friends and family, with other people tending to invest more significantly later in the funding window, their confidence secured by the friends' and family's initial 'entrepreneurial commitment' (Agrawal, Catalini and Goldfarb, 2011, p. 20) of between 20 and 40 per cent of the targeted amount (*Economist*, 2012). This suggests that *successful* crowdfunding benefits from nepotism and is possibly elitist, that it is a sphere in which those with friends and family with the material resources and cultural capital to 'kickstart' the appeal will most likely – as usual – prove the most successful. Crowdfunding's emphasis on rewards for the funder also risks marketizing the donor/recipient relationship so fully that the donor becomes, more accurately and/or fully, the consumer. Though it may be a popular myth that crowdfunded donations 'arise because individuals are assumed to be altruistic', the academic authors of 'Crowdfunding: Tapping the Right Crowd' suggest rather that 'crowdfunders donate because they expect to be consumers' (Belleflamme, Lambert and Schwienbacher, 2012, pp. 4–5). WeDidThis's Whiting (in Healey, 2011) advises those planning pitches to seek funding to '[t]hink about rewards that will be really valuable and attractive for your funders.' Whiting (2011) observes that though 'more than half of the online population have used the internet to engage with the arts and cultural sector and while 58% of adults shop online, only 7% give online'. He assures artists that 'WeDidThis is bridging the divide between the online shopping and donating experience by offering shoppers the opportunity to become philanthropists at the same time, through hosting each WeDidThis project reward on culturelabel.com, an online gift shop featuring products from a wide range of galleries and cultural institutions.'

I do not mean to suggest that crowdfunders having a consumer relationship to giving is either disastrous or unpredictable. But I do mean to suggest that crowdfunding appears to normalize philanthropic giving as consuming in ways that might, simultaneously, limit the altruistic potential of giving, risk commoditizing the arts organization and/or the artist and make the arts organization beholden to prioritizing funders' expectations, requests or demands more extensively than it might otherwise wish. This distortion of the benevolent social relationship that might exist between giver and receiver can run both ways. Crowdfunding appears to form beneficent communities because funders share an interest in the funded organization. But the value and integrity of these communities is questionable. Though the online, virtual nature of the 'crowd' need not prevent it from being a strong, supportive organization, what does at least jeopardize such an achievement is the fact that often little or no communication occurs amongst crowdfunders supporting the same project. Furthermore, the communication of the recipient with the funders is at least partially opportunistic since, by definition, '[u]nder crowdfunding, entrepreneurs form ties with the "crowd" for strategic purposes of raising money' (Belleflamme, Lambert and Armin Schwienbacher, 2012, p. 5). Fundamentally, though crowdfunding enables individuals to act with self-determining agency in deciding what arts to choose to fund, it destabilizes mutual social responsibility. Funders are not a socially connected crowd but a crowd of individuals who act the same way; social connection is neither necessary nor necessarily achieved, despite the intimation of co-activity and potential collectivism in the word 'crowd'. Crowdfunding also risks, again, legitimating the rolling back of state support for the arts by stepping in to fill its gaps.

The National Theatre

As mentioned above, ACE expects NPOs to 'provide collective leadership in the arts sector' and 'those organisations with the largest turnovers, or those in receipt of the largest amounts of public funding,' to provide 'greatest leadership' (2012a, p. 21). This is especially urgent given that ACE itself is being required to shrink dramatically: of the 30 per cent cuts in allocation to ACE announced by government in 2010, half of those cuts had to be absorbed by ACE itself; in 2011–12, ACE was required by government to shrink its administrative budget by another whopping 50 per cent (Davey, 2013, p. 6). In this section I therefore examine how the National Theatre, a major national company in receipt of one of the highest levels of public arts subsidy, fulfils its responsibility effectively to share its wealth across the arts ecology, helping to develop a broader range of artists and companies than are formally part of the NT itself. I ask what it does to share its resources and what more it could and should do.

First, I provide context on the NT's comparative wealth, concentrating on the financial year 2010/11 which offers the most recent annual report and financial statement at the time of writing. In that year, the NT's total income was £70.64 million and its expenditure over £64 million (NT, n.d.b, p. 2). Its annual ACE grant as a Regularly Funded Organization was £19,641,009, making up approximately 28 per cent of its income (see ACE, 2012c; NT, n.d.a, p. 42). This ACE grant was the third highest in England that year, following the Royal Opera House (ROH) which received £28,294,806 and the Southbank Centre which received £22,173,370; the Royal Shakespeare Company (RSC) received the fourth largest grant, £17,639,392.[25] Like those three other highest funded organizations, and many other arts organizations besides, the NT took a 6.6 per cent cut in its funding, or almost 15 per cent in real terms, beginning in 2011. Also in 2010/11, the NT received over £6 million in private funding, or 8.5 per cent of its annual income. Around half of this was from individuals (NT, n.d.a, p. 44). Major corporate sponsors included Accenture, American Airlines, American Express, Aviva and Bank of America Merrill Lynch, somewhat begging the question of which nation this National Theatre serves or is perceived to serve in globalized times. Another major sponsor is Travelex (ibid., p. 54), which has funded the Travelex ticket scheme since 2003, making a significant number of tickets available at the reduced price of £10 until 2011 and £12 since. Travelex's Chairman and Chief Executive Lloyd Dorfman is also a trustee of the NT and the Dorfman Foundation. In October 2010, the Dorfman Foundation pledged £10 million to NT Future, a major building upgrade and development project with an anticipated budget of £70 million (NT, 2010). The Cottesloe Theatre is to be renamed the Dorfman Theatre (NT, n.d.a, p. 12). The NT is comparatively a very wealthy theatre and has the kind of status, track record and infrastructure that helps it consistently to secure substantial privately donated funds.

Appropriately, the NT does share its resources with the broader theatre and arts sector, though we might ask whether its efforts are sufficient. 'As a *national* company', the NT's 2010/11 *Annual Report* claims, 'the NT takes responsibility for fostering the health and renewal of the wider British theatre community by sharing our expertise and resources with emerging talent, freelance artists and other theatre companies and providing appropriate levels of support across artistic and administrative areas of theatre-making' (NT, n.d.a, p. 41; italics original). One of its five company objectives states, 'As a *national* theatre, the NT takes responsibility for fostering the health of the wider British theatre' (ibid., p. 4, italics original). Of five objectives specifically for 2010/11, one was to pursue '[c]ollaborative initiatives to help sustain theatre-making in difficult times' (ibid., p. 10). What collaborative initiatives does it pursue? It shares profile, material resources, space, location, expertise, experience, infrastructures (for example, for ticket booking) and opportunities for performance.

Perhaps most visible of the NT's collaborations are its co-productions with smaller companies and individual artists. It has co-produced shows with, amongst others, Punchdrunk (*Faust*, 2006–7), Shunt (*Tropicana*, 2004–5) and DV8 (*Can We Talk About This*, 2012). In the 2010–11 season it co-produced with Headlong the premiere of a new play, *Earthquakes in London* by Mike Bartlett, which showed in the Cottesloe Theatre. Alongside these building-based collaborations, the NT hosts dozens of companies at its outdoor space facing the Thames, Theatre Square, in summer festivals such as Watch This Space, Square2 and Inside Out. In 2010, Watch This Space 'produced 323 shows and 30 workshops by presenting the work of 342 visiting performers and technicians and 72 different companies (27 international)' (NT, n.d.a, p. 30). The NT also supports the work of visual artists and musicians by hosting gallery exhibitions and jazz performance in its lobbies.

The NT provides not only performance opportunities for its collaborators, but also administrative support and expertise in administration, design and technology. Artists performing at Watch This Space could avail themselves of 'the expertise of the NT's professional staff in developing sets and lighting for their performances in Theatre Square' (NT, n.d.a, p. 30). In 2010–11, the NT offered other theatres 'ad hoc support and advice on HR issues [and] diversity training' and members of the NT Development department reportedly offered fundraising advice programmes to two theatres (ibid., p. 41). The NT also shared box-office services, an especially helpful support for companies which lack the kind of online infrastructure the NT has and which consumers increasingly expect.

The NT also offers more formal development programmes for individuals. In January 2012, it offered spaces for two people on a two-year paid apprenticeship scheme in technical aspects of theatre production leading to certification (NT, n.d.a, p. 41). Along with the ROH, with in-kind support from small- to mid-sized theatre and performance companies BAC, Nitro and the Young Vic, the NT participates in the

Step Change programme, which offers 'early–mid career professional development for talented individuals in need of additional experiences to make a "change" in direction or area of work' (ibid.). And the NT runs an attachment scheme, in 2010–11 offering 24 artists – 17 writers, three directors and four others – the opportunity to work temporarily at the NT, sometimes developing shows that then play elsewhere (for example, Leeds' West Yorkshire Playhouse and London's Finborough Theatre) (ibid., p. 24).

Besides the development work the NT does with all staff who then work elsewhere and productions that then transfer, likely the most significant feature of the NT's contribution to the broader arts ecology is the work it does in and through the NT Studio. With its own staff, building (substantially renovated in 2008), and research and development budget (£1.1 million in 2010–11) (NT, n.d.b, p. 5), the NT Studio is a laboratory for the development of new theatre work including, in 2010–11, '14 play readings and 53 development workshops for projects outside the NT repertoire' (NT, n.d.a, p. 24). Sometimes work developed here makes it into production at the NT; in 2010–11 this was the case of five productions (ibid.). In 2010–11, the Studio also collaborated with international partners and had five affiliated external and emerging companies with which it worked regularly: Ontroerend Goed, Made in China, Tangled Feet, Analogue and Theatre O (ibid.).

Finally, the NT provides research resources for the broader community. This includes the NT's extensive archive of its own work. But it also includes the new Black British Play Archive, a collection initiated by playwright and NT Associate Kwame Kwei-Armah of 'every play produced or published in the United Kingdom by a Black British writer in the last 100 years' totalling 646 plays by 132 playwrights (NT, n.d.a, p. 24). The NT is working on developing an accompanying public digital resource to include complementary recorded visual and audio material.[26] Provided it develops fully, this is a resource which might help to foster production of some of the plays the archive holds far beyond the National Theatre itself.

I admire the range of collaborative and leadership initiatives that the NT pursues in sharing and developing productions, skills and resources. I also admire the fact that, though ACE only encourages NPOs to provide leadership, the NT leads quite actively. However, given the scale of public funding that the NT receives – not to mention the scale of private funding it can leverage – I do wonder if its leadership initiatives could be more extensive. The NT Studio's activities are exciting, for example, but its budget is only about one-seventieth of the NT's total annual budget. Might not more of the budget contribute to development through the Studio? Might it also be constructive if ACE were not only to encourage leadership but to be more specific about what kind of leadership it would especially like to see and, even, to mandate its delivery in certain quotas by the best funded NPOs? 'Target culture' is often (negatively) associated with the days of New Labour and instrumentalist funding regimes that were perceived to require particular targeted levels of audience attendance, demographic distribution and social impact; and it has often been vigorously derided for subordinating quality to issues of access and social impact. But in the face of the wider 'difficult times' that the NT itself acknowledges (NT, n.d.a, p. 12), and given that the NT and other major national institutions such as the ROH and RSC are apparently 'too big to fail' – by which I mean, perceived by themselves and ACE as too big to lose their ACE funding – I believe it would be reasonable and productive to mandate companies in receipt of major ACE NPO grants to dedicate a significant portion of their state funding – say 15 to 20 per cent – to developing the wider arts ecology.

Punchdrunk

Highly successful London-based performance company Punchdrunk actively and notoriously cultivates mixed sources of income to make its work (see McGinn, 2011; Espinoza, 2010). Its overt corporate alignment in particular makes it an important company to examine to better understand contemporary mixed arts funding economies in the United Kingdom and their ideological effects. Amongst its many benefits, Punchdrunk's mixed funding enables arts practice that is often highly innovative, enjoyable, creatively stimulating and creatively collaborative and that contributes to re-calibrating expectations of theatre so that they value sensual engagement. However, Punchdrunk's mixed economies also risk monetizing social relationships and intimacies, reinforcing elitist market hierarchies and reifying the understanding of the supremacy of the individual over the group that is so crucial to neoliberal ideology. The best resistance Punchdrunk perhaps offers to these problems is rarely wholly to capitulate to them.

Punchdrunk was founded in 2000 by Felix Barrett and, since 2003, has been run by him and associate director and choreographer Maxine Doyle.[27] The company self-describes as having 'pioneered a game changing form of immersive theatre in which roaming audiences experience epic storytelling inside sensory theatrical worlds. Blending classic texts, physical performance, award-winning design installation and unexpected sites, the company's infectious format rejects the passive obedience usually expected of audiences' and 'focus[es] as much on the audience and the performance space as on the performers and narrative' (Punchdrunk, 2011). Punchdrunk's production of *Faust*, set over five storeys in a disused warehouse in Wapping, East London, brought it huge prominence, played for six months from October 2006 to March 2007, and is in many respects typical of the ambience it aims to create, the ways it uses space and the invitations it offers audiences. As I discuss in more detail in Chapter 1, an audience experience of disorientation was cultivated even before the show began, with little signage en route to the venue and requiring a journey through a scruffy, walled yard. Inside, audiences waited in a bar area before being handed Venetian masks and taken in small groups in an elevator to be let loose to roam the building and its various ambient spaces, including an eerily abandoned archive, a fragrant pine forest, a cornfield, a diner, a row of shops, a small cinema and a dance hall. While it is unlikely – perhaps even impossible – that any roaming audience member would happen upon all the performed narrative of this *Faust*, it is certainly the case that audiences would experience ambient environments and also the opportunity to choose where to go, when to do so, what to look at, what to listen to and so on. Punchdrunk followed *Faust* with an adaptation of a series of stories by Edgar Allen Poe, *The Masque of the Red Death*, performed throughout the Battersea Arts Centre in South West London from January to April in 2008. Its adaptation of *Macbeth*, *Sleep No More*, was first produced in London in 2003, then Boston in 2009 and became a sell-out, long-extended hit at the fictional McKittrick Hotel (really three adjoining warehouses) in Chelsea, New York, from March 2011. And in July 2011, Punchdrunk collaborated with the BBC's *Dr Who* team at the Manchester International Festival to make *The Crash of the Elysium*, a 'spectacular, live Doctor Who adventure for children aged 6–12 and their families' (MIF, 2012).

What I particularly want to emphasize in this brief and partial review of the company's history is their innovative efforts to cultivate audience experiences that are as unusual and individual as possible and, wherever possible, unique. In this important respect, Punchdrunk is an almost-textbook example of the kind of business advocated by Joseph Pine II and James H. Gilmore in their 1999 book, *The Experience Economy* (published in a revised version in 2011). Pine and Gilmore (2011, pp. ix–xiii) argue that economies can no longer rely on supplying goods and services to thrive; instead, they must offer mass-customized staged experiences to engage and seduce consumers. I say Punchdrunk is an *almost*-textbook example because, where many of the 'experiences' Pine and Gilmore admire come across – to me – as profitable for business but superfluous for consumers, Punchdrunk's shows might offer more value for audiences – chances to explore, opportunities to develop their own versions of the shows, exciting encounters with characters and environments and the possibility of a unique experience. However, the precise value of Punchdrunk's audience experience – as, at one end, genuinely unique, rewarding and moving and, at another, full of false promises, superficial and disappointing – is part of what I aim to interrogate here.

Putting temporarily aside the question of how genuine and/or substantial are audiences' experiences of Punchdrunk's shows, the company's *efforts* to create unusual audience experiences have proved crucial to its success in securing income from a range of organizations, including ACE, independent grant-making organizations such as the Paul Hamlyn and Esmée Fairbairn Foundations, individuals and businesses. Punchdrunk is an ACE National Portfolio Organization and is comparatively very well funded. In 2011, on the day when ACE announced 15 per cent cuts across its budgets to arts organizations, Punchdrunk received news of an exponential *increase* in its funding of 141 per cent in real terms, from just over £83,000 in 2011–12 to £225,000 in 2012–13 (see ACE, 2012c). This speaks to the ways Punchdrunk is seen to fulfil ACE ambitions to combine arts access and excellence – as articulated in ACE's 2010 ten-year vision document, *Achieving Great Art for Everyone*. In a 2007 interview, then-Secretary of State for Culture, Media and Sport, Labour's James Purnell singled out Punchdrunk for praise for its achievement of both access and excellence, claiming it 'took a canonical subject, "completely reinvented the genre", and attracted an "audience of every single age and background"' (in Higgins, 2007). In a round-up of 'great' artwork she had experienced over 2011–12, ACE's Chair Dame Liz Forgan wrote of being 'bamboozled by Punchdrunk' (2012, p. 5). Despite its popularity, however, Punchdrunk's work is generally grossly uneconomical; 'we're never going to make money', admits Barrett (in Eyre, 2011). '[T]he "majority" of the budget' reportedly goes on making Punchdrunk's found spaces safe: 'We spend a lot getting rid of asbestos', says Barrett (ibid.). Also expensive is what one journalist refers to as the company's 'ruinously wonky ratio of huge production staff and performers to small audiences' (ibid.). On top of its ACE funding, therefore, Punchdrunk seeks to finance its work with income from numerous other sources.

These sources include individuals. A former 'friends' scheme gave those who paid a modest fee advance notice about forthcoming productions. In 2010, Punchdrunk launched its more complex and ambitious

Key Holder scheme, with six graduated ranks of key holder fees, statuses and privileges (see Reeve, 2010). For £30 annually, the Valet Key 'unlocks limited access to the company's plans with priority booking for some Punchdrunk productions and an occasional newsletter' plus, stock-permitting, a 'complimentary limited edition DVD' of their production of *Faust* (Punchdrunk, 2012a). At £250 annually, the Bow Key buys Valet Key privileges plus a 'one-to-one experience at some point during your year of membership' and 'exclusive dialogue with the company regarding future activity'. For annual contributions between £1000 and £4999, the Zeiss Key additionally offers 'an exclusive private party'. For annual contributions between £5000 and £10,000, the Abloy Key buys the above plus 'access to an exclusive dinner with the artistic team' and 'a personalised service from the Punchdrunk team' during which the key holder can 'develop and nurture a close relationship with the company'. For £25,000 biennially, the Skeleton Key holder will have all of the above plus 'a bespoke opportunity of the most exclusive and exhilarating nature, a once in a lifetime trip with Punchdrunk Travel Company' (ibid.).[28] Finally, the Master Key is an 'access all areas key that is available to anyone who wishes to support the company at a higher level' (ibid.).

While Punchdrunk's Key Holder scheme resembles a typical theatre subscription scheme by offering priority information and booking, unlike most such schemes, no key (except perhaps the Master) actually secures show tickets, which can be notoriously difficult to get. What the various keys do offer is an invitation to be an entrepreneurial philanthro-capitalist who invests in a company which 'continues to innovate and push the boundaries of theatrical experiment' and who thereby supports its 'artistic freedom to continue to break new ground' (Punchdrunk, 2012a). The Key Holder scheme is a bit like a Punchdrunk-only crowdfunding platform; however, unlike other crowdfunding platforms, for potential Punchdrunk key holders, giving is neither time-limited nor project-specific. The scheme also offers graduating levels of intimacy with the company, moving from access to Punchdrunk's work and its planning to increasingly exclusive access to its people. The £250 Bow Key holder travels 'beyond the veil of secrecy that surrounds Punchdrunk's work' and has 'an exclusive dialogue with the company regarding future activity' (ibid.). While the £1000 (minimum) Zeiss Key promises 'the opportunity to get to know the artists behind Punchdrunk creations' at an 'exclusive private party', the £5000 (minimum) Abloy Key further rarefies this personal intimacy, offering 'an exclusive dinner with the artistic team', 'personalised service from the

Punchdrunk team' and 'a close relationship with the company' (ibid.). For Punchdrunk, the Key Holder scheme stands to garner important new sources of funding. For the Key Holder, it offers precisely the pay-offs Punchdrunk most celebrates in its shows – individual attention and individuated experiences – even while it does not precisely offer tickets to the shows. Alongside these apparent benefits, however, the scheme's steep fees make its privileges increasingly elitist; its emphasis on the importance of being able to seek exclusive individual experiences reinforces neoliberal ideology; and its pay-off of offering increasingly intimate levels of access to the company (levels that are also sexually charged, through suggestions of keys, dates and secret get-aways), monetizes and fetishizes knowledge, sociality and intimacy.

Punchdrunk is also innovating collaborations with industry. As early as 2006, it formed what *Guardian* theatre critic Lyn Gardner (2006) described as its 'sister company' Gideon Reeling (2012), 'purveyor of bespoke interactive experiences', including performances at festivals such as Glastonbury, Bestival and Big Chill, parties for Southern Comfort and work for other clients including Google, Bacardi/Agent Provocateur and Red Bull. At least since 2010, Punchdrunk has brought some corporate collaboration directly in-house, making immersive shows which aim straightforwardly to enhance the brand identity of the corporate partner and/or its product in work supported by its Brand Partnership Director (Punchdrunk, 2011, Partnerships page). In June 2010, Punchdrunk contributed a show to the opening party of Louis Vuitton's new flagship store in London. In 2010 and 2011, it made two different theatre events to launch the new lager, Stella Artois Black (see Alston, 2012). In September 2011, it made a show to launch Sony PlayStation's new game, *Resistance 3*. As noted above, in July 2011, it collaborated with the BBC to produce an interactive *Dr Who* children's show. And for London Fashion Week in February 2012, it collaborated to produce the catwalk show for the eminent British fashion design company formerly led by Alexander McQueen, McQ.

Reviewers are generally gushing in their praise of these events' excitement, attention to detail, surprises and specialness. For the 2010 launch of Stella Artois Black, customers at a handful of London pubs and bars found those venues 'transformed into a 1960s Parisian nightspot, complete with jazz band' (Caird, 2010). On purchasing the new beer, customers could win one of approximately 100 tickets to experience the 15-minute Punchdrunk performance *Night Chauffeur*, wherein '"Passengers" are welcomed by glamorously dressed and perfectly pouting "femme fatale" hostesses and invited to make themselves comfortable before the arrival of the eponymous chauffeur with his purring 1960s Citroen DS' (ibid.). Writing about the launch of *Resistance 3, Guardian* blogger Jack Arnott (2011) credits Punchdrunk with creating 'a terrifying and brilliantly authentic-feeling world beneath the railway arches at Waterloo station', warning, 'Enter at your peril'. For *Grazia* journalist Siobhan Mallen,

> The hands-down fashion moment of [2012's] London Fashion Week was the incredible finale to the McQ show, which not only featured the legendary model Kristen McMenamy bathed in light as cascades of autumnal leaves swirled around her, but also included some post-show audience participation when we all had to exit the show space via the live wood that was the set, and drop in at a broken down shack where McMenamy was holding court!
>
> (2010)

She notes that McQueen creative director Sarah Burton 'had collaborated with the pioneering theatre group Punchdrunk to create the whole spectacle – from the concept, to the music and that incredible set'.

Again, there are impressive benefits to these industry collaborations that Punchdrunk has forged. They can profit Punchdrunk's less commercial performance work, both through generating revenue that then cross-subsidizes other work and through allowing Punchdrunk to experiment with performance strategies it might subsequently develop and incorporate artistically (see Gardner, 2006). They allow collaborations with some extraordinary, imaginative and often well-resourced innovators in compelling characterization and narrative (*Dr Who*), audience interaction and mood generation (PlayStation) and design (Louis Vuitton and McQ). Vuitton's leaders, for example, claimed they wanted to give something back to London's artistic culture (Chamberlain, 2010). Punchdrunk corporate collaborations can offer wonderful experiences for audiences, empower those audiences – children were called on to save the world in *The Crash of the Elysium* – and possibly cultivate new audiences for Punchdrunk's theatre work. And they are impressively innovative in generating new sources of income in an age of public arts funding austerity.

Again, however, these innovations also pose ideological and social problems. Almost none of these industry collaborations were broadly open to a paying public so the exclusivity of experience on which Punchdrunk bases its brand is here taken to a rather compromising extreme. Punchdrunk no longer rewards simply any ticket-holder's adventurous spirit; instead, its pleasures are available principally to those with privileged economic access, however great their level of participation – or rather of distraction. At the Punchdrunk element of the London Louis Vuitton store launch, for example, journalist Vassi Chamberlain notes that fellow audience member and eminent artist Chris Ofili appeared to enjoy a glass of absinthe particularly (rather than other elements of the show), while celebrity Jerry Hall let Chamberlain go ahead on a rickshaw ride because Hall was 'deep in conversation with a friend' (Chamberlain, 2010). Where audiences do register excited engagement, it is often in response to experiences of sexual frisson and opportunities to be a voyeur and to star-spot. Both Chamberlain and *Telegraph* journalist Sheryl Garratt write at comparative length about their respective moments of near-sexual encounter following their rickshaw journeys at the Vuitton store opening. In Garratt's telling, she is guided

> behind a pillar where a woman straight out of a film noir ... barks at me to sit down at a table for two. She pours two brandies ... and commands, 'Drink!' Then suddenly we're standing again, she has me pinned against the wall, gloved hand at my throat and her lips brushing my cheek. 'I think you should go now!' she hisses, menacingly, into my ear. I think she's right.
>
> (2010)

In Chamberlain's account,

> A man in drag gives me his hand and guides me to a woman (or is it a man?) sitting on a club chair wearing black fishnets and a corset. It is dark, I am disorientated .... What follows is the closest I come to a multi-partner near-sexual encounter as two women and a man snog, caress and writhe within millimetres of my mouth and body. I am too shocked to breathe, too embarrassed to laugh. ... When a burlesque dancer takes my hand to escort me into dinner all I can do is giggle with relief — or is it repressed excitement?
>
> (2010)

There is nothing intrinsically wrong with the thrills of sexual excitement or voyeurism; indeed, in some of Punchdrunk's performance contexts, I admire its commitment to stimulating and valuing sensual experience in performance. However, such thrills can also indicate superficiality in the engagements on offer in what Guy Debord (1994 [1967]) called the society of the spectacle, where *social interaction* is abandoned and replaced by its representation. And this kind of reduction to spectacle seems especially likely in these contexts which aim to cultivate luxury brands in scenarios of unadulterated commodity and celebrity fetishism where, as Chamberlain (2010) observes, 'greed [makes] a comeback', and, incidentally, gender stereotyping apparently comes as standard (despite Chamberlain's confusion).

At their best, Punchdrunk's adventures in fundraising and corporate collaboration demonstrate impressive and frankly rewarding creativity and inventiveness in securing funding for theatre work that by its very nature is expensive to produce. Punchdrunk's collaborations with extraordinary design companies such as McQ also demonstrate that interdisciplinary creative collaboration can be mutually rewarding, giving the fashion company a stand-out show and Punchdrunk an opportunity to experiment with fashion's extraordinary bodies, rituals and budgets. Also promising is that, whatever corporate experiments Punchdrunk pursues, it maintains work which is non-corporate in activities that it calls 'enrichment' and that others might call outreach or education, such as its school-based storytelling project *Under the Eiderdown* and its 2011 show with East London Arcola theatre's over-fifties group, *The Uncommercial Traveller* (see Punchdrunk 2012b; McGinn, 2011). What Punchdrunk's corporate collaborations risk – and what it and fellow arts companies seeking corporate funding must beware of – is compromising the principles of engagement and participation that form crucial parts of its identity, pleasure and practices. Though it might seek to be known for extraordinary moments of social encounter and opportunities to pursue adventure, its corporate work risks closing down adventure to the most wealthy and simply exploiting residues of social intimacy by exploiting them.

Risks of arts' mixed economies

While Jeremy Hunt, the DCMS and ACE may be especially keen on private endowments because they represent investment that is secure and long-term, many donated funds – including those provided through the micropatronage of crowdfunding – are instead temporary and modest, often one-off donations linked to projects rather than to infrastructure. Structures of support that ACE used to offer are eroding and are not being replaced. Significantly, ACE no longer calls long-term funded organizations 'Regularly funded organisations' or RFOs, but instead organizations in its 'national portfolio funding programme', a name change that not only removes the security of regularly funded status for arts organizations, but recasts them as ACE's portfolio of purchased stocks and shares that might just as easily be sold again. This erosion of structural support jeopardizes planning, security and professionalism for both arts institutions and artists.[29]

The state is thus diminishing its responsibility for the arts, even as it continues to want to exploit them through a wide variety of instrumentalist agendas. The arts are called on to support national brand identity and its dissemination in the global market, for example during the enormous Cultural Olympiad organized in anticipation of and alongside the Olympics in 2012 (see London 2012 Festival, 2012). The arts are at risk of instrumentalization not only by public funders but also by private funders, possibly increasingly so with the growth of so-called 'venture philanthropy' or 'philanthro-capitalism' as practised by super-wealthy entrepreneurs. (In 2008, the United Kingdom reportedly had 385,000 millionaires and 68 billionaires [Glinkowski, 2008, n.p.].[30] As noted above, by 2012, the United Kingdom had 77 billionaires.) Arts funding researcher Paul Glinkowski explains that 'Where the traditional model of philanthropy is based on gift-giving, the new model implies a more active form of engagement in which the philanthropist develops a more hands-on relationship with the recipient of his or her funding (which is often referred to as "investment")' (Glinkowski, 2007; see also Anheier and Leat, 2002, pp. 154–7). Such a hands-on approach may be constructive, but that depends on what aspect of impact the investor is most keen to maximize, for example artistic impact, social impact or financial gain. Even if the investor's engagement is part of a corporate social responsibility campaign, which might seem to protect it from focusing on capital gain, research suggests such investment is more likely to favour social impact than artistic impact (Glinkowski, 2007, p. 21). And frankly, investors often principally seek visibility, with the result that arts organizations can end up prioritizing blockbuster events and sacrificing other priorities. Shortly after taking over as Director of the Tate, Nicholas Serota expressed his fear that important museum activities of 'scholarship, conservation, and education, as well as "academic shows", might be "squeezed out" in circumstances of cash crisis' (Wu, 2002, p. 137; Wu cites Beck, 1989, p. 118).

Furthermore, arts organizations' forced reliance on private funding marketizes and privatizes theatre and other arts in ways that put them at risk of producing some of the worst effects of the neoliberal market, such as intensifying the precarity of arts labour and making it labour that is increasingly only affordable to the independently wealthy, in other words, those who can afford to work for free. Theatre's capacity to risk labour exploitation, especially through unpaid internships and volunteering, is well known and age-old but is at risk of dramatic growth in the context of ACE's search for 'in-kind' support. In his 2008 report, Brian McMaster's advocacy of unpaid artists' peer review and mentoring systems implicitly argued for more free labour in theatre. This shift to precarious funding has happened despite ACE's recognition of theatre workers' precarity. As noted in Chapter 2, ACE's *Theatre Assessment 2009* found that people working in the industry 'expressed worries about the proliferation of unpaid internships' and about workers' reliance on 'some sort of family or other support' over a decade that saw a 100 per cent increase in the number of volunteer workers in the sector (ACE, 2009a, pp. 51, 65, fig. 15).

Another problem with this apparently requisite diversification of arts funding is that the onus on diversification is placed much more heavily on arts organizations as 'askers' than on the private sources as 'givers'. ACE's DCMS-commissioned *Endowments in the Arts* exhorts arts organizations to develop appropriate 'culture[s] of asking' instead of relying on funders – or society more broadly – to have 'culture[s] of giving'. Though ACE (2010b, p. 22) may be right that to change practices it is necessary to change cultures, its advice to arts organizations to ask better and to take on more 'civic responsibilities' in a culture that is diminishing taxation (in other words diminishing state-managed giving) seems perversely insufficient to the task, at best naïve, and at worst designed to fail in ways that can then be blamed on arts organizations for 'failing' to master the art of the abracadabra ask. If the 'Big Society' is about dispersing social responsibility, it is cautionary to observe just how flagrantly in this context the onus of responsibility is being placed on the 'needy' rather than the wealthy.

There is also the risk that the act of giving serves the selfish interests of the giver chiefly or rather than the interests of the recipient organization. Writing about philanthropic and charitable foundations in particular, civil society analysts Helmut K. Anheier and Diana Leat observe that, 'At worst, foundations are little more than tax shelters for the privileged to pursue some favoured cause or charity' (2002, p. 29). In a later book, they expand on some of the recent charges of corruption made against US foundations, including insider trading, the self-granting of excessive salaries and severance packages, and 'corporate abuses including use of charitable gifts as bribes to overlook financial improprieties (as in the Enron case)' (2006, pp. 7–8). In the United Kingdom, the Conservative-led coalition government had initially based its argument *for* a cap on tax relief on charitable giving on the grounds that people did and would use charitable giving to dodge paying taxes. In April 2012 – the month between Osborne's announcement of the cap and his u-turn on it – the deputy prime minister and Liberal Democrat leader, Nick Clegg, for example, said, 'If you don't do something about these allowances, which allowed very wealthy rich people to avoid paying income tax altogether, you are effectively asking ordinary taxpayers to subsidise them' (quoted in Chorley, 2012).

As I suggested in the introduction to this chapter, I think that the greatest cumulative risk the emerging UK mixed model of arts funding poses is a capitulation to neoliberal capitalist ideologies, prioritizing individual pursuits of wealth, bespoke experience, pay-off and investment (such as crowdfunding) in a 'free' market; exposing the theatre industry to great insecurity and often conflicting market-oriented priorities; exploiting arts to perform innovation and entrepreneurialism and foster inward investment; contributing to the class stratification of the workforce and the exacerbation of precarious labour; reinforcing networks of privilege (for example through the comparative success of family and friend crowdfunded projects); treating audiences more pervasively as consumers; treating social relations as commodities (for example in the 'experience economy' potential of Punchdrunk's shows); and relying on plucky arts practitioners miraculously to transform cultures not previously given to private donation and sponsorship, however deeply entrenched those cultures might be. In these conditions, the arts' aspiration to achieve any degree of democratic participation, as well as their ability to produce effective progressive critique, are seriously constrained.

Opportunities of arts' mixed economies

All that said, there are some potential opportunities afforded by the arts' shift to a mixed economy model in times of state economic leanness. One such opportunity is the chance simply to survive these trying economic times. Arts organizations may also indeed grow more resilient, as all the funders seem to desire but which arts organizations desire too, and which should not be seen as exclusively the prerogative and domain of neoliberalism. Indeed, arts' response to the need to diversify their sources of funding might be seen as intensely creative. As Shannon Jackson (2011) has explored in *Social Works*, the production and diversification of new lines of support may eventually grow into structures that can provide for organizations and artists; perhaps better yet, they might accrue into networks or ecologies that are systemic rather than structural, in that they remain dynamic and adaptable and resist the kind of institutionalization that can produce dysfunctional or counterproductive bureaucracy. After all, state funding or support is not by definition socially good, so protecting all of it uncritically should not be pursued at any cost. Putative social support systems are considered by some to foster complacency and laziness and are often uneven in their effects, sometimes outright deleterious and sometimes corrupt, for example, as Jackson and others have observed, in the uneven state support offered residents and former residents of New Orleans after Hurricane Katrina. Diversified lines of support may also protect arts organizations from the market vagaries of, for example, one partner failing; if support links are multiple, any individual link may be refreshingly too small to fail the arts organization rather than too big. Diversified lines of support may also protect arts organizations from being expected to represent the interests of one dominant funder, putatively allowing them to choose with whom and in what ways they forge and enact their allegiances. Such partnerships may not only help arts organizations to resist pandering to funders' whims or requests; they may also help arts organizations to influence and lead their funders' organizations. In this perspective, arts organizations are not only not dupes to ideology, they control and influence it.

That said, when asked if I could provide an example where art practice influenced its funder like this, I could not. On the contrary, what comes to mind is the 2012 London Olympics which has many sponsors, but a handful of which claim monopoly control in their respective areas. Of 800 food retailers in the games' 40 venues, McDonalds was the only one with the right to serve chips (except with fish) (Clark, 2012). The only branded food products sold at the games were those of commercial partners (Coca-Cola, McDonald's, Cadbury, Nature Valley and Heineken). Only Visa cards could be used to purchase Olympic and Paralympic tickets and only Visa cash points were available inside games grounds (ibid.). The games also protected sponsors' interests by legislating against so-called 'ambush marketing', where non-sponsoring companies visibly penetrate events, for example on paper flags or t-shirts. London 2012 Olympic delivery chairman Lord Sebastian Coe (Malik, 2012) wrongly reported in a pre-Olympic interview on BBC Radio 4 that 'spectators would not be able to gain entry wearing a Pepsi T-shirt but that they would "probably" get in wearing Nike trainers' (these companies' major rivals were sponsors). Coe was later corrected by Locog (the London Olympic Games Organizing Committee), who said, 'As an individual you are free to wear clothing of your choice ... of course. Including trainers'; nevertheless, Locog did enforce restrictions of 'any objects or clothing bearing political statements or overt commercial identification intended for "ambush marketing"' (ibid.). Sponsorship in this context may be lucrative for games organizers, but definitely restricting for them, commercial competitors, athletes and audiences.

In response to the risk of artists' exploitation I raised above, diversified arts funding need not intrinsically exploit artists. Indeed, Dutch critic and artist Hans Abbing (2004, 2005), amongst others, has argued that the apparent 'security' of extensive public arts funding can work counter-intuitively, giving too many people the false impression that they can survive as artists and perversely growing the number of poor artists. Understood this way, in straightened economic times, diminished circumstances for the arts may be more realistic and do the social good of helping to moderate people's expectations about and desires of careers in the arts, protecting them from the privations of underemployment.

Another one of the potential benefits of arts cuts that can barely be whispered is that they permit the reduction of funding to weaker, 'underperforming' companies as well as companies that might reasonably be expected to garner private sponsorship. They may also allow some 'released' funding to move to emerging companies that have not yet received significant support. In the cuts of 2010, it seems to me certainly the case that companies such as the NT, the RSC and the Almeida, which received mid-level cuts, can and will be able to deploy their elite brand identities to replace that funding with money from private sources. It is also the case that many emerging, innovative theatre and other arts companies and organizations greatly benefited from ACE's redistribution of funds in 2011, companies including Punchdrunk, aerial theatre company Ockham's Razor (which received a 200 per cent increase in funding) and East London's Arcola Theatre (100 per cent increase) as well as several companies which had never previously received regular funding, including children's creative writing centre Ministry of Stories and the Manchester International Festival (see ACE, 2012c).

What I think aspects of the mixed economy model of arts support might most productively at least offer is the opportunity to forge and secure improved social relations with enhanced communication and more even social relations based on dispersed mutual support. Dispersed forms of sponsorship such as crowdfunding can offer new possibilities of potential audience engagement, potential communication and networks of support that can literally enact social interdependence. Multiple partnerships require constructive communication with partners one might never before have contemplated speaking with;

ideally that may produce learning as well as mutual understanding as, perhaps, between Punchdrunk and McQ. Relationships of sponsorship need by no means be patronizing and might be reconsidered as part of a gift economy, requiring little return from the receiver, or indeed as philanthropy, literally, as I noted above, the love of humanity, or social welfare by another name. Though we may be witnessing in the second decade of the twenty-first century in the United Kingdom what is at least a partial erosion of the welfare state, what I might at least hope to witness concurrently is nevertheless an active enactment of *social welfare*, where people continue to invest in what they perceive as social goods such as arts, for example, because they actively want to, not because they are passively required to because their taxes go there. Enacted thus, it might not only be the arts that survive the current economic crisis and possibly thrive in doing so, but also, perhaps, the principles of social welfare.

Conclusion

As I said at the outset of this chapter, I do not want to be an apologist for neoliberal capitalism nor for unthinking and savage cuts to the arts. I do also emphatically want to recognize some of the social, economic and aesthetic risks presented by cuts to state arts funding and by arts' diversified support from private sources and in-kind labour. These risks include the erosion or destruction of structures of arts support, marketization and privatization of the arts, acute instrumentalization of the arts, intensified precarity of arts labour, class stratification of access to the arts, amplified competitiveness to the detriment of collaboration, and intense pressure on artists and arts organizations single-handedly to produce a culture shift in private support for the arts, despite the economically disadvantageous conditions in which they are trying to do so. There is also the broader risk that core cultural values of social democratic citizenship as willing participation in socially (state) organized wealth redistribution are damaged as (some) philanthropists/investors avoid taxation and indulge their own preferred products. I want to be wary of all of these risks and work to minimize the conditions that might most support and enhance them.

However, the Conservative-led coalition government's response to the economic crisis is necessitating shifts in ways that the arts are supported, and I want to imagine and ideally enhance ways that we might see that happening most constructively, socially and artistically. The shift to diversified networks of arts support is not intrinsically bad or neoliberal. It can facilitate arts' survival, enhance their resilience and help them to grow systems of support in the face of declining structures of support, avoid the vagaries of the market, resist instrumentalist deployment by a single powerful funding source, lead rather than be led by their funders and be realistic about what is achievable. Most importantly, I think, at its best, it can help forge resilient, inventive new models of networked artistic, economic and social support that can at least temporarily take up the baton of social welfare and help us envision better futures. Some of the measures that might help realize this future would be: mandating the best endowed companies (such as the NT, the RSC, the Southbank Centre and the ROH) to spread their resources more fully across the arts sector; supporting smaller organizations to collaborate and share resources (for example, management infrastructure such as expertise in human resources, information technology and marketing); and exploring ways of making emerging forms of devolved audience collaboration – be it in a Punchdrunk show or a crowdfunding platform – actively socially engaged.

Afterword

I have sought in this book to investigate contemporary, often explicitly socially engaged art and performance practices in London in particular, in order to test the relationship of these practices to vying contemporary social forces of, on one hand, social democracy and, on the other, rising neoliberal capitalism. I have endeavoured to test the efficacy of this 'social turn' in contemporary art and performance, to test its contribution to an ongoing social commitment to welfare, democracy, social responsibility and social engagement, as well as to test its capitulation to the rising economic and ideological forces of neoliberal capitalism, with its emphases on individualism and market economics.

There is no question that the political context I have surveyed – from around the advent of New Labour in the late 1990s to the Conservative-led coalition government of 2010 on – has grown and continues to grow increasingly neoliberal. Cultural policy increasingly exhorts artists to be entrepreneurs. State funding to the arts has been drastically cut. 'Creative industries' and 'creative cities' policy agendas exacerbate middle-class migration into formerly working-class districts, gradually displaces those districts' former residents and contributes to the erosion of social housing provision and principles of affordable housing and social welfare. As state-led support systems for the arts contract, artists have been compelled to work in increasingly privatized ways in order to sustain their practices, for example, seeking private funding to bankroll their work, occupying independent spaces such as pop-ups in which to show their work, and exploiting the free labour of volunteers to help develop and produce their work.

In some respects, this broader political ascendency of neoliberal capitalism has 'neoliberalized' arts practices and damaged their potential social benefits. Reliance on private funding risks the independence of art and potentially commodifies it. Reliance on free labour in the arts gives those who are independently wealthy privileged access to arts internships' developmental structures and opportunities and to future careers in the arts, reproducing class privilege and plutocracy instead of democracy. The cultivation of creative cities and independent pop-ups risks marketizing and colonizing urban spaces in ways that drive out resident populations, break up their local social networks and risk moving them into greater deprivation. And the cultivation of artists as entrepreneurs risks prioritizing selfish individualism and quantitative value over other qualitative and social values that might importantly be prioritized. In these ways and others, the arts under neoliberal capitalism risk contributing to the accumulating unfairness and inequality of neoliberal capitalist cultures.

However, it has been my pleasure in researching and writing this book to be reminded again and again and again that, despite these enormous, pervasive and wearying pressures of contemporary neoliberal capitalist ideology and policy, artists and arts organizations are by no means entirely 'neoliberalized'. On the contrary, again and again, contemporary arts practices resist and critically respond to the pressures of neoliberal capitalism. They highlight those pressures, but critique them, drawing attention to their damaging social effects. They build alternative structures and networks through which to support their own and others' work and through which to explore collaboration, social or 'folk' connections, social-ism and social welfare. They decline neoliberalism's celebration of commodity, market and product, and explore process and craft. I have been inspired by the practices of, for example, Cornelia Parker, Jeremy Deller, Michael Landy, Grayson Perry, Rachel Whiteread, Lone Twin, Steve McQueen, the Live Art Development Agency, the National Theatre Studio and many other artists and organizations. I have also been inspired by the critical literatures of thinkers such as David Harvey and Richard Sennett, who continue to enumerate the damaging effects of neoliberal capitalism, to highlight and animate its socially progressive alternatives and, especially in Sennett's case, to seek in arts practices models for those alternatives.

It would be naïve to suggest that all contemporary art and performance practices resist neoliberal capitalism, or that they ultimately 'defeat' it. But it may be accurate to say that, at their best, they model ways of critically engaging with it, eluding it, critiquing it, repudiating it and ridiculing it, and they seek and model alternative ways of being which preserve principles of social collaboration and interdependence.

Notes

Introduction: Fair Play

1. Curator Jessica Morgan observes that even that great pioneer of capitalism Adam Smith acknowledged the necessity of 'fellow feeling' to restrain self-interest and, in moderation, to contribute to economic development (Morgan, 2003, pp. 17 and 20). Morgan cites Adam Smith, *Wealth of Nations*, 1776, and *Theory of Moral Sentiments*, 1759.
2. Claire Bishop describes some of Tiravanija's works in detail in 'Antagonism and Relational Aesthetics' (Bishop, 2004); see pp. 55ff. and 67ff.
3. References throughout this paragraph and the next are to this text, so only page numbers will be given for these two paragraphs. In future instances this will not be highlighted with an end note.
4. Artists included in *Common Wealth* at the Tate Modern, 22 October–28 December, 2003, were Jennifer Allora and Guillermo Calzadilla, Thomas Hirschhorn, Carsten Höller and Gabriel Orozco.
5. Bishop, 2004, p. 52. Bishop cites Pine and Gilmore, 1999.
6. Bishop, 2004, p. 66, italics original. Bishop acknowledges that her take on democracy in this context is directly informed by Laclau and Mouffe, 1985.
7. Another approach to redistributing wealth fairly would have been for the government actively and effectively to collect fair taxation, manage greater resource redistribution and stimulate jobs. Polly Toynbee and David Walker note estimates that 'the UK's fifty-four billionaires paid income tax of only £14.7 million in 2006 on fortunes totalling £126 billion. At least thirty-two paid no income tax at all' (Toynbee and Walker, 2009, pp. 17–18). This practice of individuals is matched by the practices of companies including Google, Amazon and Starbucks, all of which were called to appear before the UK's Public Accounts Committee in late autumn 2012 to answer questions about the low corporate taxes they pay in the United Kingdom, despite the enormous trade they turn over here.
8. The slogan was part of the Conservative Party's 2010 election campaign, and appears as a full-page graphic on page vi of their 2010 manifesto (Conservative Party, 2010). The graphic was also available on a t-shirt (see Conservatives, 2012).
9. Data from January 2012 show that applications to English universities had dropped by almost 10 per cent in a year (Shackle, 2012).
10. A deep genealogy of materialists and cultural materialists who have informed my training includes Karl Marx (2012), Raymond Williams (2005), Jonathan Dollimore and Alan Sinfield (1994), Graham Holderness (2001), and Ric Knowles (2004). My 2005 book, *Staging the UK*, likewise attempted a cultural materialist analysis of contemporary theatre culture in the United Kingdom, with a particular emphasis on the ways that contemporary UK identities related to nationality (as British, European, Scottish, global, Welsh, British-Asian, metropolitan and more) were dynamically and multiply produced

through theatre's many cultural and material practices (as genre, festival, infrastructure of buildings, funding patterns, relationships to sites and more).

11. As part of ACE's strategic goal to see 'more people experience and ... inspired by the arts', it commits to 'build[ing] long-term collaborations between arts organisations, cultural partners and local authorities to encourage inspiring, sustainable arts programmes in places where engagement in the arts is low' (ACE, 2012a, pp. 30–1).

1 Labour: Participation, Delegation and Deregulation

1. A version of the show was reportedly originally created in Brighton in 2004 (see Best, 2012).
2. Alison Oddey uses this term in her book, *Re-Framing the Theatrical: Interdisciplinary Landscapes for Performance* (2007, p. 3). Oddey investigates some of the same trends in art practices as I am examining here, but she adopts an 'experiential mode of analysis' (p. 2).
3. Claire Bishop offers a useful, detailed history and analysis of delegated labour as performance in art in her chapter contribution to the book *Double Agent* which accompanied the exhibition of the same name which she co-curated with Mark Sladen at the ICA, London, in 2008. Her analysis focuses much more that I do here on questions of authenticity raised by delegated performance in art (Bishop, 2008).
4. Punchdrunk, 2011, About page. At the time of writing (2011–12), many pages on Punchdrunk's website are navigable through the sole URL www.punchdrunk.org.uk. Therefore, when I cite this webpage I give some further detail in parentheses to aid navigation.
5. Other performances include *Sleep No More* (2003), an adaptation of *Macbeth* produced in a Victorian school; *The Firebird Ball* (2005), produced in a disused factory and fusing the story of Romeo and Juliet and the myth of the Firebird; and *The Masque of the Red Death* (2007/8), produced in Battersea Old Town Hall for a seven-month run which reached an audience of over 40,000 people. In 2009/10, the company took a new version of *Sleep No More* to a school in Boston, Massachusetts, in association with the American Repertory Theatre; its five-month run sold out. It has subsequently been produced in New York.
6. Joseph Beuys is widely attributed with having made the claim that everyone is an artist (see, for example, Bodenmann-Ritter, 2007). The 'social sculpture' Beuys advocated, however, required 'a functioning and *unmediated* public sphere' for the 'exchange of individual opinions with an open public dialogue' rather than the kind of *mediated* performance context I am focusing on here (Mesch, 2007, p. 199, italics added).
7. Users initially had to collect *The Missing Voice* CD along with a portable CD player from the Whitechapel Library in East London, where the walk is designed to start. The audio can now be downloaded directly from Artangel's website in three parts (see Cardiff, 1999).
8. Warner suggests that 'Publics ... lacking any institutional being, commence with the moment of attention' (2002, p. 88).
9. I say almost necessarily because one might possibly find oneself alone in the Tate Modern Turbine Hall at a very quiet moment, but such an opportunity

would be rare, given the Turbine Hall's huge popularity and traffic. In 2010, the Turbine Hall Unilever Series of installations had reportedly attracted over 24 million visitors to Tate Modern since its inception in 2000 (see Wagstaff, 2010, p. 9). During Tino Sehgal's 2012 commission, *These Associations*, it was impossible to experience the Turbine Hall in solitude since Sehgal 'installed' a group there.

2 The 'Artrepreneur': Artists and Entrepreneurialism

1. The neologism 'artrepreneur', thankfully, does not have huge currency but is gaining some. See, for example, the title of Evelyne Brink's *The Artrepreneur: Financial Success for Artistic Souls* (2012) and the Royal College of Arts' student-led 'enterprise society' launched in February 2012, Artrepreneur (FuelRCA, 2012). 'Culturepreneur' has perhaps slightly more currency, including in academic writing such as geographer Bastian Lange's 'From Cool Britannia to Generation Berlin? Geographies of Culturepreneurs and their Creative Milieus in Berlin' (2006).
2. The Brand Partnerships Director for the company Punchdrunk (discussed in more detail in Chapter 4) offers corporate clients 'tailor-made activities that sharpen innate creativity and imagination – taking individuals out of their everyday environment into a truly immersive experience aimed at triggering new ways of looking at the world they work in' (Punchdrunk, 2011, Partnerships page).
3. Six per cent is cited in DCMS *Creative Industries Economic Estimates (Experimental Statistics)*, full statistical release, 9 December 2010 (Burrows and Ussher, 2011, p. 11). Seven per cent was cited by Dame Helen Alexander, Deputy President CBI (2012), and is also suggested by the Work Foundation's *Staying Ahead* (2007, p. 30).
4. This document cites the document *Increasing Voluntary Giving to Higher Education*, Higher Education task force report to Department for Education and Skills, 2004.
5. These include a song-writer, a music publishing agent, an interior decorator and gardener, a clothes designer, a children's wear maker, a joiner and carpenter and a crafts and candle-maker (Gray and Stanworth, 1986, pp. 39–51).
6. She proposes 'that individualization, as manifest in the working practices of the cultural sector, must be separated from neo-liberalization. It is only by investigating individualization-as-lived that we can recognize the possible spaces it opens up for critique of the neo-liberalization of arts and culture' (McRobbie, 2011, p. 80).
7. Successful NEA claimants are also promised business mentoring and a loan of £1000 (see, for example: BBC News 2010a; Department for Work and Pensions, 2012a, 2012b; McGuinness, 2012).
8. They cite Experian, *The Impact of the Downturn on the Creative Industries*, South East England Development Agency, 2009, n.p. cited.
9. I have written at greater length about this work in Harvie, 2006. *Break Down* took place at 499–523 Oxford Street, London, 10–24 February 2001. Commissioned by Artangel, sponsored by *The Times* and part-funded privately, it is documented in Michael Landy, *Michael Landy/Break Down*

(2001a), with a fuller inventory in Michael Landy, *Break Down Inventory* (2001b). See also the documentary *The Man Who Destroyed Everything*, dir. Nadia Haggar (2002).

10. For reviewer Dave Beech, this was one of the piece's weaknesses: 'Landy is not getting rid of his property, he is failing to distinguish between property relations and other relations, such as bonds of love, family, community and sentiment' (2001, p. 31). For me, Landy's 'equal' treatment of all the objects compelled his audience painfully to distinguish between these categories and was, therefore, a strength.
11. Landy was in his late thirties in 2001.
12. For his own part, Landy has acknowledged the influence on his work of auto-destructive Swiss artist, Jean Tinguely (see Landy, 2009), especially the 1960 work *Homage to New York* (see Landy 2007).
13. Sennett emphasizes that, in *The Craftsman*, '*Man* does not, clearly, mean just men' (2009, p. 6, italics original). Where possible I use the word craftsperson to remove its gender specificity, but I use the word 'craftsmanship' in deference to Sennett's important work on this keyword and also because 'craftspersonship' is too cumbersome. Like Sennett, though, I do not mean 'craftsmanship' to refer only to the work of men.
14. Admittedly, my selected focuses within Sennett's analysis of craftsmanship are not likely what he would choose as most important. I select them not to be idiosyncratic but because I think they articulate a core line of concern for sociality running through his book.
15. Sennett repeatedly gives the example of parenting as a learned skill/craft worth doing well (2009, *passim*).
16. The National Theatre developed its use of ground water from its car park to irrigate *FlyTower*.
17. See Veblen, 2007 (1899), ch. VI, 'Pecuniary Canons of Taste', specifically pp. 92–6, and extracts reproduced in Veblen 2005, pp. 60ff.
18. I have written about *Caribs' Leap/Western Deep* at some length in ch. 7, 'Re-imagining the Imperial Metropolis', in Harvie, 2005, pp. 201–14.
19. This book of the exhibition is unpaginated. In order not to clutter this discussion of the work with repeated references to n.p., therefore, all subsequent references to this work are to this book unless otherwise noted.
20. I am grateful to design historian Mary Ann Bolger for a discussion we had on this topic.
21. At the time of writing (July 2012), Royal Mail has not yet agreed to release the stamps.
22. An excellent, broad collection of Perry's work is represented in Klein (2009).

3 Space: Exclusion and Engagement

1. There is a vast critical literature on the spatial operations of power. Foundational texts include Michel Foucault, *Discipline and Punish: The Birth of the Prison* (1995) and Henri Lefebvre, *The Production of Space* (1991).
2. Mulholland cites research conducted by the City Parochial Foundation and the New Policy Institute.

3. Florida describes *Cities and the Creative Class* (2005) as the prequel to *The Rise of the Creative Class* (2008, p. 1); *Who's Your City?: How the Creative Economy is Making Where to Live the Most Important Decision of Your Life* 'provides detailed rankings of the best places to live for everyone: singles, families with children, and empty-nesters alike' (2008, back cover).
4. For example, though they are not describing creative cities directly, Marc Pachter and Charles Landry argue that cities need to 'creat[e] perceptions and images in order to provide profile and to drive international promotion strategies' (2001, p. 62).
5. San Francisco, Boston and Seattle topped the list; Honolulu, Memphis and Louisville came last (Florida, 2005, pp. 177–8).
6. In a section entitled 'How to become a creative city', they recommend, amongst other things, 'making the most of creative individuals' as well as immigrants and intercultural mixing (Landry and Bianchini, 1995, p. 10).
7. Oakley looks in some detail at another example of cultural industries-led urban regeneration: Sheffield's Cultural Industries Quarter, founded in the late 1980s (2009b, pp. 127ff.).
8. See, especially, Peck (2005, 2007) and Rosler (2010, 2011a, 2011b, 2012). For more critique of Florida, see also, for example, Krätke (2012), Brenner, Marcuse and Mayer (2012) and references in Oakley (2009b, pp. 123ff.).
9. Oakley credits the phrase 'immobility regime' to Turner (2007).
10. Peck notes that this outcome 'has been belatedly acknowledged by Florida himself' in *Cities and the Creative Class*. Further for Peck, such cities exacerbate social inequalities by legitimating middle-class privilege. He writes, 'the designated overclass of creatives are held to have *earned* their superior position in the creative city, by virtue of raw talent and creative capital, validated through the market .... The lumpen classes of service and manual workers, on the other hand, are so positioned in the new socioeconomic structure by virtue of their creative deficits .... They must be content with ... the benefit of downward–trickling positive externalities like the opportunity to wait tables for the creative bohemians' (2007, p. 2).
11. For example, see Zukin's influential *Loft Living: Culture and Capital in Urban Change* (1988 [1982]); Lloyd (2010); and on London, Butler (1997) and Butler with Robson (2003).
12. Elements of this discussion draw on Harvie, 2011a.
13. *Seizure* is being moved to Yorkshire Sculpture Park. Its meaning will necessarily shift when dislocated from the specific contexts of a decommissioned housing estate in the Elephant and Castle area of South London. See Higgins (2012).
14. To its credit, the Royal Court's Theatre Local does aim to address both educational and financial issues by offering free workshops and tickets at £10 and on a pay-what-you-like basis if purchased at the venue (see Royal Court, 2012a). I do not have space here to assess the sufficiency of these measures.
15. New legislation criminalized squatting 'in homes and all other residential buildings' in England and Wales from 1 September 2012 (see Ministry of Justice, 2012).
16. For example, the smartphone app the Pop Spot (We Are Pop Up, 2012a) informs users about London pop-up events and locations – usually restaurants and boutiques – and is 'completely dedicated to *unique* experiences,

experiential retail and all things pop up' (We Are Pop Up, 2012b, emphasis added).

17. These figures may be overestimates but growth is virtually certain.
18. Demand might at least be mitigated if governments took concerted action to renovate and rent out homes which are un- or underused in London; the organization Empty Homes reports that there were almost 80,000 empty, or unused, homes in London in October 2010 (see Empty Homes, 2010).
19. This description is from its July 2011 draft.
20. See, for example, paragraphs 47, 50, 159.
21. 'To ensure viability, the costs of any requirements likely to be applied to development, such as requirements for affordable housing, standards, infrastructure contributions or other requirements should, when taking account of the normal cost of development and mitigation, provide competitive returns to a willing land owner and willing developer to enable the development to be deliverable' (DCLG, 2012, p. 41).
22. The London borough of Westminster was reportedly 'most affected by the housing benefit cap'; here 43 per cent of school-age children were anticipated to be affected by the benefit change (see Gentleman, 2012, p. 1).
23. Even in neighbourhoods where the scale of gentrification is minimal, with levels of actual low-income population displacement and middle-income influx being comparatively modest, research suggests that ensuing change tends to privilege middle-class incomers. Even where the middle class are in the minority, their cultural and financial capital tends to change the area as they 'define' areas of gentrification 'in their own image' (Butler with Robson, 2003, p. 8).
24. For a detailed critique of gentrification's displacement effects, see Slater (2012). For historical context on gentrification in London, see Hamnett (2003), especially ch. 7, 'Gentrification and the Middle-Class Remaking of Inner London'. For more context on social housing especially since New Labour in London, see Watt (2009).
25. To those critics who suggest secure tenancy is an unfair privilege that is not 'even' shared by those who own private accommodation, economists point out that home-owners can support their own asset-based welfare (by accumulating wealth in the asset of their home), while those who rent cannot.
26. Additional useful, focused and internationally comparative analysis of neoliberalism's damaging effects on what she calls lower income housing is Glynn, 2009. Another good source on the relationships of neoliberalism to cities is Brenner and Theodore (2002).
27. This approach is advocated by, amongst others, Alan Read (1993). See, for example, the chapter on his work with the Rotherhithe Theatre Workshop, 'Lay Theatre', in *Theatre and Everyday Life: An Ethics of Performance* (1993), pp. 23–57.
28. *House* provoked debate about a huge range of issues including urban relations of race and class; urban development and forced removals; and concurrent and contentious nearby urban development projects such as that at Canary Wharf. I do not have space to go into all of these debates here. For a good indication of many of them, see Lingwood, ed. (1995).
29. The work is well illustrated in Landy (2004).
30. His work is well represented in Creed (2010), and many of the works cited in this section are represented in that book.

31. A short BBC film of the bell-ringing from across the United Kingdom is available at BBC News (2012b).
32. In Lone Twin's 2007 project *Town Crying*, stories, anecdotes and comments submitted by people across the North of England were then cried out by a town crier at such public sites as car boot sales and town squares. Like the company's name, this project's name invokes both the joyousness and pain of communication and sociality (see Metcalfe, 2007).
33. For details on *The Boat Project*'s maiden voyage itinerary, see the document Lone Twin, *The Boat Project:* Maiden Voyage, 7 May–11 August 2012, available at http://www.theboatproject.com/, accessed September 2012.

4 Public/Private Capital: Arts Funding Cuts and Mixed Economies

1. Earlier versions of parts of this chapter were presented at the Irish Theatre History Conference, *Archives, Historiography, Politics – Ten Years On – Performance, Memory, Futures*, at the National University of Ireland, Galway, 25–26 November, 2011 (Harvie, 2011b); at the TaPRA Postgraduate Symposium on Theatre and Alternative Value on 28 January, 2012 (Harvie, 2012a); to the Department of Film, Theatre and Television, University of Reading, 9 February, 2012 (Harvie, 2012b); and at the conference 'Subsidy, Patronage & Sponsorship: Theatre and Performance Culture in Uncertain Times' at the V&A in collaboration with the University of Reading, 21 July, 2012 (Harvie 2012c). My thanks to my hosts in all these contexts, including, in Galway, Lionel Pilkington, Patrick Lonergan and Shelley Troupe; at the TaPRA symposium, Adam Alston, Virginia Elgar and Michael Pearce; and at the University of Reading, Simone Knox, Faye Woods, Graham Saunders and John Bull. Thanks also to other delegates for constructive feedback in those contexts.
2. CEMA began informally in 1939 and was established by Royal Charter in 1940 (see ACE, 2012b).
3. For currency conversion, see Reuters (2012).
4. According to *Measuring Worth*, $1.7 billion in 1999 would have the purchasing power of approximately $2.23 billion in 2010 (see Measuring Worth, 2012b).
5. According to *Measuring Worth*, $17 billion in 2004 would have the purchasing power of approximately $19.6 billion in 2010 (Measuring Worth, 2012b).
6. William J. Baumol and William G. Bowen (1966) famously identified the performing arts' 'cost disease' and tendency to be economically inefficient. The labour-intensiveness of these arts means their comparatively large and growing (with inflation) wage costs will tend to outstrip whatever other efficiencies any given performing arts production might achieve. Tim Donahue and Jim Patterson (2010, pp. 81ff.) offer a richly detailed exploration of theatre finance in the United States and demonstrate how theatre's generally high production costs make it vulnerable to accumulating loss quickly.
7. For an extended discussion of the variety of motivations for publicly funding the arts directly and indirectly and of the merits or problems of such funding, see, for example, Zuidervaart (2011).
8. This chapter focuses on arts funding in England, though many of its issues are shared by the UK's other nations – Northern Ireland, Scotland and Wales – as well as other nations beyond.

9. For an anecdotally rich illustrated history of the Federal Theatre Project, see O'Connor and Brown, eds (1980).
10. £4m was cut in spring 2009 and a further £19m cut was imposed in summer 2009, though it did not have to be implemented until the following year (see ACE, 2010c).
11. Regularly Funded Organizations had infrastructural funding guaranteed for a number of years (with conditions); Grants for the Arts funded and continue to fund project-specific awards.
12. A great short article on theatre and philanthropy is Alston and Daker (2012).
13. 'We know instinctively that the state is often too inhuman, monolithic and clumsy to tackle our deepest social problems', said Conservative Prime Minister David Cameron after election. 'We know that the best ideas come from the ground up, not the top down (BBC, 2010b).
14. For a rich and detailed survey and analysis of arts patronage mostly in the United States, see Garber (2008).
15. Hunt did not address the fact that much US philanthropic 'giving' is effectively indirect taxation permitted through tax incentives. The same scale of tax incentives does not exist in the United Kingdom.
16. The u-turn 'saved' charities £1.5 billion income per year according to Charities Aid Foundation and a commissioned study by Oxford Economics (see Charities Aid Foundation, 2012).
17. I have been unsuccessful in finding details of companies which applied for Catalyst Endowment funding and were unsuccessful in their applications. A request for this information made in July 2012 to ACE under the terms of the Freedom of Information Act was declined in August 2012 on the grounds that applications were submitted to ACE in confidence and, more emphatically, that the information is commercially sensitive and its release might jeopardize the commercial interests of the applying organizations and ACE (see Harvie and Stephenson, 2012).
18. For detailed analysis of individual philanthropic giving in the United States that might be comparatively interesting in this context, see Schanke, ed. (2007).
19. This decline in corporate support was fortunately mitigated by increases in trusts, foundations and individual philanthropy, but impact was nevertheless felt in the arts, 'with just 1% giving to this cause in 2011' (see Hill, 2012).
20. However, there are examples of very large philanthropic gifts. Breeze (2005, p. 55) reports that, in 2005, 'retail entrepreneur Tom Hunter, has recently donated £100m – one-fifth of his wealth – to a range of mainly child-related causes'.
21. I quote David Camps, the head of communications at Barcelona's Museu d'Art Contemporani and co-founder of the Spanish fundraising association, as cited in Burgen, 2012.
22. Donahue and Patterson cite a report in the *Denver Post*, May 2009.
23. Lloyd's assessment is supported by research conducted by the cultural sector agency Arts Quarter (see Nicholls, 2011, p. 10).
24. Crowdfunding sites include Sponsume (2012a), wedidthis (2012), Kickstarter (2012) and Ireland's Fund it (2012a). A helpful survey of crowdfunding sites in Europe and Asia is Judith Staines (2011). A good survey of the field for visual artists is Emily Speed (2011).

25. Figures for both the Southbank and the RSC include additional lottery funding to extend artistic programmes and/or develop major new buildings (see ACE, 2012c).
26. At the time of writing (summer 2012) this is available only in a trial version: National Theatre, Black Play Archive (see NT BPA, 2012a; see also NT BPA 2012b).
27. For a history of the company, see Eglinton (2010).
28. In a 2011 *Time Out* interview Barrett elaborated plans for how the travel company would work: 'You'll get a date, a time and a locker key; turn up at an airport with three days' luggage and follow instructions from there' (McGinn, 2011).
29. Performance Corporation's Artistic Director Jo Mangan commented in 2010, 'They forced us all into this situation of setting up limited companies and professionalising the sector, years ago. None of us wanted to do that originally. Now [with arts funding cuts] it's becoming amateurised ... I don't see any other policy in place' (in Crawley, 2010).
30. Glinkowski cites 'a recent report by the institute of Fiscal Studies'.

Bibliography

Abbing, Hans (2004) *Why Are Artists Poor?: The Exceptional Economy of the Arts* (Amsterdam: Amsterdam University Press)

—— (2005) *Living on the Edge: About Subsidies, Incomes and Numbers of Artists*, Unpublished but in draft on author's website, http://www.sx4all.nl/~abbing/index.htm, accessed August 2012

Ackroyd, Heather, and Dan Harvey (2012) http://www.ackroydandharvey.com/, accessed June 2012

Actorsminimumwage (2011) 'Paid Tribunal Opportunity: You Me Bum Bum Train', 19 June, http://actorsminimumwage.wordpress.com/2011/06/19/paid-tribunal-opportunity-you-me-bum-bum-train/, accessed December 2012

Ad Hoc (2011) http://www.adhoc.eu/, accessed September 2011

Adamson, Glenn (2007) *Thinking Through Craft* (Oxford and New York: Berg)

—— (ed.) (2010) *The Craft Reader* (Oxford and New York: Berg)

Adorno, T. W. (1991) *The Culture Industry: Selected Essays on Mass Culture*, ed. J. M. Bernstein (London: Routledge)

Agrawal, Ajay K., Christian Catalini and Avi Goldfarb (2011) *The Geography of Crowdfunding*, Working paper 16820, NBER Working Paper Series, February (Cambridge, MA: National Bureau of Economic Research), http://www.nber.org/papers/w16820, accessed July 2012

Alexander, Dame Helen [Deputy President CBI] (2012) speaking at 'Creativity and Business: Connectivity, Values and Interventions', *The Culture Capital Exchange/British Library Conference*, London, 12 March

All the Bells (2012) Press release, http://www.allthebells.com/wp-content/uploads/2012/06/ATB-General-PR-140612.pdf, accessed August 2012

Alston, Adam (2012) 'Funding, Product Placement and Drunkenness in Punchdrunk's *The Black Diamond*', *Studies in Theatre & Performance*, 32.2 (June): 193–208

—— and Rebecca Daker (2012) 'Contemporary Theatre "Philanthropy" and the Purchase of Participatory Privilege', *Contemporary Theatre Review*, 22.3: 433–7

Amin, Ash, Doreen Massey and Nigel Thrift (2000) *Cities for the Many Not the Few* (Bristol: Policy)

Anheier, H. K. and D. Leat (2002) *From Charity to Creativity: Philanthropic Foundations in the 21st Century, Perspectives from Britain and Beyond* (Gloucestershire: Comedia in association with the Joseph Rowntree Reform Trust)

—— (2006) *Creative Philanthropy: Towards a New Philanthropy for the Twenty-First Century* (London and New York: Routledge)

Arnott, Jack (2011) 'Punchdrunk? Try petrified – gaming gets the immersive theatre treatment', *Guardian Theatre Blog*, 2 September, http://www.guardian.co.uk/stage/theatreblog/2011/sep/02/punchdrunk-try-terrified, accessed July 2012

Artangel (2011a) Rachel Whiteread, *House*, http://www.artangel.org.uk//projects/1993/house/about_house/about_the_project, accessed October 2011

—— (2011b) Roger Hiorns, *Seizure*, http://www.artangel.org.uk/projects/2008/seizure, accessed October 2011
—— (2011c) Michael Landy, *Break Down*, http://www.artangel.org.uk/projects/2001/break_down, accessed October 2011
—— (2012) 'Artangel Projects 1992–2011', http://www.artangel.org.uk/about_us/project_list_1992_onwards, accessed December 2012
Art Fund (2012) Steve McQueen, *Queen and Country*, http://www.artfund.org/queenandcountry/, accessed August 2012
Arts Council England (2009a) *Theatre Assessment 2009*, 24 August, (London: Arts Council England), available at http://www.artscouncil.org.uk/publication_archive/theatre-assessment/, accessed February 2010
—— (2009b) 'Art in Empty Spaces: Turning Vacant Spaces into Creative Places', 13 August, http://press.artscouncil.org.uk/content/detail.aspx?releaseid800&newsareaid2, accessed October 2012
—— (2010a) *Achieving Great Art for Everyone*, November (London: Arts Council England), http://www.artscouncil.org.uk/media/uploads/achieving_great_art_for_everyone.pdf, accessed December 2012
—— (2010b) *Endowments in the Arts*, December (London: Arts Council England), available at http://www.artscouncil.org.uk/publication_archive/endowments-arts/, accessed August 2012
—— (2010c) 'Arts Council Implements £19 million cuts to 2010/11 budget', 18 June, http://press.artscouncil.org.uk/Press-Releases/Arts-Council-England-implements-19-million-cuts-to-2010-11-budget-412.aspx, accessed November 2011
—— (2011a) 'Details Unveiled for £100m Scheme to Boost Private Giving to Culture', 29 September, http://www.artscouncil.org.uk/news/details-unveiled-100-million-catalyst-scheme-boost/, accessed November 2011
—— (2011b) 'Register for Nationwide Fundraising Master Classes', 19 May, http://www.artscouncil.org.uk/news/register-nationwide-mas/, accessed November 2011
—— (2011c) 'Details Unveiled for £100m Scheme to Boost Private Giving to Culture', 29 September, http://www.artscouncil.org.uk/news/details-unveiled-100-million-catalyst-scheme-boost/, accessed November 2011
—— (2011d) '£55 million fund announced to help cultural organisations build endowments', 4 July, http://www.artscouncil.org.uk/news/55-million-fund-announced-help-cultural-organisati/, accessed November 2011
—— (2012a) *The Relationship Between the Arts Council and Funded Organisations: How the Arts Council Works with National Portfolio Organisations and Major Partner Museums*, April (London: Arts Council England), http://www.artscouncil.org.uk/media/uploads/pdf/FINALrelationship_framework_1904.pdf, accessed July 2012
—— (2012b) 'The History of the Arts Council: 1940–45', http://www.artscouncil.org.uk/who-we-are/history-arts-council/1940-45/, accessed August 2012
—— (2012c) 'Spreadsheet of National Portfolio Organizations', National Portfolio Funding Programme, http://www.artscouncil.org.uk/funding/apply-for-funding/national-portfolio-funding-programme/, accessed July 2012
—— (2012d) Catalyst Arts, http://www.artscouncil.org.uk/funding/apply-for-funding/strategic-funding/grant-programmes/catalyst-arts/, accessed July 2012

—— (2012e) *Catalyst Arts: Endowments: How We Will Manage the Grant*, June, http://www.artscouncil.org.uk/media/uploads/pdf/Catalyst_endowment_how_manage_your_grant_June2012.pdf, accessed August 2012

—— (2012f) *Arts Council England Grant-in-Aid and Lottery Annual Report and Accounts 2011/12*, July (London: The Stationary Office), available at http://www.official-documents.gov.uk/document/hc1213/hc02/0283/0283.pdf, accessed August 2012

—— (n.d). *National Portfolio Facts and Figures*, 'National Portfolio Funding by Region and Value', http://www.artscouncil.org.uk/media/uploads/npo_by_region_and_value_pie_charts_290311.pdf, accessed December 2012

Arts Quarter (2012) News, http://www.artsquarter.co.uk/news.html, accessed July 2012

Ashery, Oreet and Larissa Sansour (2010) *Falafel Road*, http://www.falafelroad.blogspot.co.uk/, accessed August 2012

Aspden, Peter (2012) 'Childish Fun and Games', *Financial Times*, 27 July, http://www.ft.com/cms/s/2/4b20dc0e-d67c-11e1-bd9c-00144feabdc0.html#axzz25V9BbvzC, accessed August 2012

Atavar, Michael (2012) http://www.creativepractice.com/, accessed August 2012

Atkinson, R., and G. Bridge (2005) *Gentrification in a Global Context: The New Urban Colonialism* (London: Routledge)

Baker, Bobby (1997) *Daily Life Ltd*, http://dailylifeltd.co.uk/previous-work/table-occasions-1997/, accessed August 2012

Barnett, Laura (2012a) 'You Me Bum Bum Train Gives Actors a Bad Ride, Says Union', *Guardian*, 13 July, http://www.guardian.co.uk/stage/2012/jul/13/you-me-bum-bum-train-equity, accessed December 2012

—— (2012b) 'Lone Twin's Ship That Hockey Sticks Built', *Guardian*, 2 May, appeared online on 1 May, http://www.guardian.co.uk/culture/2012/may/01/lone-twin-boat-project, accessed August 2012

Bauman, Zygmunt (2002) Foreword, 'Individually, Together', in Ulrich Beck and Elisabeth Beck-Gernsheim, *Individualization: Institutionalized Individualism and Its Social and Political Consequence* (London: Sage), pp. xiv–xix

Baumol, William J., and William G. Bowen (1966) *Performing Arts – The Economic Dilemma: A Study of Problems Common to Theater, Opera, Music, and Dance* (New York: Twentieth Century Fund)

BBC News Devon (2012) 'Olympic Nowhereisland "Invaded" in Devon by Swimmers', *BBC News Devon*, 10 August, http://www.bbc.co.uk/news/uk-england-devon-19199274, accessed October 2012

BBC News (2004) 'Saatchi mulls £6.25m shark offer', 23 December, http://news.bbc.co.uk/2/hi/entertainment/4120893.stm, accessed June 2011

—— (2007) 'The Downturn in Facts and Figures', UK, 21 November, http://news.bbc.co.uk/1/hi/7073131.stm, accessed August 2012

—— (2010a) 'Iain Duncan Smith Announces "Enterprise Allowance"', Politics, 5 October, http://www.bbc.co.uk/news/uk-politics-11479291, accessed December 2012

—— (2010b) 'Cameron and Clegg Set out "Big Society" Policy Ideas', Politics, 18 May, http://news.bbc.co.uk/1/hi/uk_politics/8688860.stm, accessed 14 July 2012

—— (2011) 'What Future for Social Housing', BBC News, Politics, 29 July, http://www.bbc.co.uk/news/uk-politics-14327691, accessed September 2011

—— (2012a) 'Child Poverty Down as Household Income Drops', UK, 14 June, http://www.bbc.co.uk/news/uk-18436795, accessed December 2012
—— (2012b) 'Mass Bell-Ringing Heralds Olympics Opening', 27 July, http://www.bbc.co.uk/news/entertainment-arts-19001529, accessed August 2012
—— (2012c) 'Tax Relief Limit on Charity To Be Axed in Fresh U-turn', News, 31 May, http://www.bbc.co.uk/news/uk-politics-18278253, accessed July 2012
BBC Radio 4 (2010) 'Grayson on His Bike', tx 7 November, http://www.bbc.co.uk/programmes/b00vkw55, accessed June 2012
Beck, Ernest (1989) 'Nicholas Serota', *Artnews*, 88.3 (March)
Beck, Ulrich (1999) *World Risk Society* (Cambridge: Polity Press)
Beck, Ulrich, and Elisabeth Beck-Gernsheim (2002) *Individualization: Institutionalized Individualism and Its Social and Political Consequence* (London: Sage)
Beech, Dave (2001) 'Michael Landy', *Art Monthly*, 244: 30–1
—— (2008) 'Include Me Out! Dave Beech on Participation in Art', *Art Monthly*, 315 (April)
Belleflamme, Paul, Thomas Lambert and Armin Schwienbacher (2012) 'Crowdfunding: Tapping the Right Crowd', 25 April. CORE Discussion Paper No. 2011/32, available at SSRN: http://ssrn.com/abstract1578175 or http://dx.doi.org/10.2139/ssrn.1578175, accessed July 2012
Benhamou, Françoise (2000) 'The Opposition between Two Models of Labour Market Adjustment: The Case of Audiovisual and Performing Arts Activities in France and Great Britain over a Ten-Year Period', *Journal of Cultural Economics*, 24: n.p.
Bennett, Rosemary (2010) 'Budget 2010: 13,000 Families Hit as Housing Benefit Capped at £1,100 a Week', *The* Times, 25 March, http://business.timesonline.co.uk/tol/business/economics/budget/article7074953.ece, accessed October 2011
Berman, Marshall (1983) *All That is Solid Melts into Air: The Experience of Modernity* (London: Verso)
Best, Jason (2012) 'You Me Bum Bum Train' *The Stage*, 25 July, http://www.thestage.co.uk/reviews/review.php/36865/you-me-bum-bum-train, accessed December 2012
Beveridge, William (1942) *Report of the Inter-Departmental Committee on Social Insurance and Allied Services* (London: HMSO)
Bey, Hakim (1991) *T.A.Z.: The Temporary Autonomous Zone, Ontological Anarchy, Poetic Terrorism* (New York: Automedia)
Billing, Johanna, Maria Lind and Nilsson Lars (eds) (2007) *Taking the Matter into Common Hands: Contemporary Art and Collaborative Practices* (London: Black Dog)
Bingham, Juliet (ed.) (2010) *Ai Weiwei: Sunflower Seeds* (London: Tate Publishing)
Bird, Jon (1995) 'Dolce Domum', in James Lingwood, ed., *Rachel Whiteread: House* (London: Phaidon in association with Artangel), pp. 110–24
Bishop, Claire (2004) 'Antagonism and Relational Aesthetics', *October* 110: 51–79
—— (2005) *Installation Art: A Critical History* (London: Tate Publishing)
—— (ed.) (2006a) *Participation: Documents of Contemporary Art* (London and Boston, MA: Whitechapel and MIT Press)
—— (2006b) 'The Social Turn: Collaboration and its Discontents', *ArtForum*, 44.6 [XLIV.6]: 178–83
—— (2008) 'Outsourcing Authenticity? Delegated Performance in Contemporary Art', in Claire Bishop and Silvia Tramontana (eds), *Double Agent* (London: ICA), pp. 110–25

—— (2012) *Artificial Hells: Participatory Art and the Politics of Spectatorship* (London: Verso)

—— and Phil Collins (2008) 'Staging a Terrain of Shared Desire' [Interview with Phil Collins], in Claire Bishop and Silvia Tramontana (eds), *Double Agent* (London: ICA), pp. 28–33

—— and Mark Sladen (2008) 'Introduction', in Claire Bishop and Silvia Tramontana (eds), *Double Agent* (London: ICA) pp. 8–11

—— and Silvia Tramontana (eds) (2008), *Double Agent* (London: ICA)

Bishop, Peter, and Lesley Williams (2012) *The Temporary City* (London: Routledge)

Blair, Tony (2007) 'Blair's Speech on the Arts in Full', 6 March, *Guardian*, http://www.guardian.co.uk/politics/2007/mar/06/politicsandthearts.uk1, accessed July 2012

Bodenmann-Ritter, Clara (2007) 'Every Man an Artist: Talks at Documenta V by Joseph Beuys', in Claudia Mesch and Viola Michely (eds), *Joseph Beuys; The Reader* (London: I. B. Tauris), pp. 189–97

Bourriaud, Nicolas (2002 [1998]) *Relational Aesthetics*, trans. Simon Pleasance and Fronza Woods with Mathieu Copeland (Dijon: Les presses du réel)

Bowlby, John (1973) *Separation* (New York: Basic Books)

Boyle, Danny (2012) *Isles of Wonder*, London. See Youtube 'Opening Ceremony: London 2012 Olympic Games', 27 July, http://www.youtube.com/watch?v4As0e4de-rI, accessed December 2012

Breeze, Beth (2005) 'Special Report: The Return of Philanthropy', *Prospect*, January, pp. 52–5

Brenner, Neil, Peter Marcuse and Margit Mayer (eds) (2012) *Cities for People, Not for Profit: Critical Urban Theory and the Right to the City* (London and New York: Routledge)

Brenner, Neil, and Nik Theodore (eds) (2002) *Spaces of Neoliberalism: Urban Restructuring in North America and Western Europe* (Oxford: Blackwell)

Bridge, Gary, and Sophie Watson (eds) (2010) *The Blackwell City Reader*, 2nd edn (Oxford:Wiley-Blackwell)

Brink, Evelyne (2012) *The Artrepreneur: Financial Success for Artistic Souls* (UK: Papy Publishing)

British Museum (2011) Grayson Perry, *The Tomb of the Unknown Craftsman*, British Museum, 6 October 2011 to 26 February 2012, http://www.britishmuseum.org/whats_on/exhibitions/grayson_perry/introduction.aspx, accessed June 2012

British Vogue (2012) 'Karl's Selfridges Pop-up Store', *British Vogue*, 25 July, available at http://www.vogue.co.uk/news/2012/07/25/karl-lagerfeld-unveils-selfridges-pop-up-store/gallery#, accessed August 2012

Brooks, Arthur C. (2006) 'Non-profit Firms in the Performing Arts', in Victor A Ginsburgh and David Throsby (eds), *Handbook of the Economics of Art and Culture* (Amsterdam: Elsevier), pp. 473–506

Brown, Ralph (2007) 'Promoting Entrepreneurship in Arts Education', in Colette Henry (ed.), *Entrepreneurship in the Creative Industries: An International Perspective* (Cheltenham: Edward Elgar), pp. 126–41

Brown, Wendy (2005 [2003]) 'Neoliberalism and the End of Liberal Democracy', rev. edn, in Wendy Brown, *Edgework: Critical Essays in Knowledge and Politics* (Princeton, NJ: Princeton University Press), pp. 37–60; original version (2003) in *Theory and Event*, 7.1: 1–23

Burchell, Graham, Colin Gordon and Peter Miller (eds) (1991) *The Foucault Effect: Studies in Governmentality: With Two Lectures by and an Interview with Michel Foucault* (London: Harvester Wheatsheaf)

Burgen, Stephen (2012) 'Spanish Culture Industry Becomes Bank Casualty', Guardian.co.uk, 29 June, http://www.guardian.co.uk/world/2012/jun/29/spanish-culture-industry-bank-collapse-casualty, accessed 12 July 2012

Burrows, Helen, and Kitty Ussher (2011) *Risky Business* (London: Demos), http://demos.co.uk/files/Risky_business_-_web.pdf?1320841913, accessed November 2011

Butler, Robert (2007) 'Grassing the Flytower', National Theatre, April, http://www.nationaltheatre.org.uk/?lid24226, accessed June 2012

Butler, Tim (1997) *Gentrification and the Middle Classes* (Aldershot: Ashgate)

—— with Garry Robson (2003) *London Calling: The Middle Classes and the Remaking of Inner London* (Oxford: Berg)

Cabinet Office (2011) *10, The Official Site of the British Prime Minister's Office*, Policy, Our Vision, http://www.number10.gov.uk/policy/cabinet-office/, accessed October 2011

—— (2012) 'Big Society – Overview', http://www.cabinetoffice.gov.uk/content/big-society-overview, accessed December 2012

Caird, Jo (2010) 'Punchdrunk Presents Night Chauffeur to Launch Stella Artois Black', *What's On Stage*, 5 November, http://www.whatsonstage.com/news/theatre/off-west+end/E8831288960898/Punchdrunk+Presents+The+Night+Chauffeur+to+Launch+Stella+Artois+Black.html, accessed July 2012

Callon, Michel, John Law and Arie Rip (eds) (1986) *Mapping the Dynamics of Science and Technology* (London: Macmillan)

Cameron, David, MP (2010) Speech to the CBI, 25 October, www.epolitix.com/latestnews/article-detail/newsarticle/primeminister-cbi-speech-in-full/, accessed November 2011

Cardiff, Janet (1999) *The Missing Voice (Case Study B)* (London: Artangel), http://www.artangel.org.uk//projects/1999/the_missing_voice_case_study_b/download_listen/part_1, accessed June 2011

Carrell, Severin, and Charlotte Higgins (2012) 'Bells Toll Across UK as Martin Creed's Army of Ringers Welcome Olympics', Guardian.co.uk, 27 July, http://www.guardian.co.uk/culture/2012/jul/27/bells-toll-martin-creed-olympics, accessed August 2012

Castells, Manuel (2010 [1996]) *The Rise of the Network Society, The Information Age: Economy, Society, and Culture*, Volume 1, 2nd edn (Oxford: Wiley-Blackwell)

Catalyst (2012) http://catalyst.artscouncil.org.uk/, accessed 11 July 2012

Chamberlain, Vassi (2010) 'Oh! What a night: Louis Vuitton's lavish bash', *London Evening Standard*, 26 May, http://www.standard.co.uk/lifestyle/oh-what-a-night-louis-vuittons-lavish-bash-6473839.html, accessed July 2012

Chandrasekhar, Indu (2012) 'You Me Bum Bum Train: The Volunteering Experience of a Lifetime', *Telegraph*, 14 September, http://www.telegraph.co.uk/culture/theatre/theatre-reviews/9535160/You-Me-Bum-Bum-Train-the-volunteering-experience-of-a-lifetime.html, accessed December 2012

Chapman, Cheryl (2011) 'Budget welcomed as genuine boost to philanthropy but with calls for government to do more', *Philanthropy UK*, 24 March, http://www.philanthropyuk.org/news/2011-03-24/budget-welcomed-genuine-boost-philanthropy-calls-government-do-more, accessed July 2012

Charities Aid Foundation (2012) 'Charity Tax cap will cost society up to £1.5 billion a year', 10 May, https://www.cafonline.org/media-office/press-releases/2012/charity-tax-cap-cost-society.aspx, accessed August 2012

Chorley, Matt (2012) 'Nick Clegg: Charity Tax U-turn Means Ordinary Taxpayers Will Subsidise Rich People's Donations', Eagle Eye, iPolitics, *The Independent Blogs*, 31 May, http://blogs.independent.co.uk/2012/05/31/clegg-charity-tax-u-turn-means-ordinary-taxpayers-will-subsidise-rich-peoples-donations/, accessed March 2013

Clapp, Susannah (2006) 'A Damn Good Show', *Observer*, 29 October, http://www.guardian.co.uk/stage/2006/oct/29/theatre, accessed May 2011

Clark, Emma (2012) 'McDonald's Force Olympic Bosses to Ban All Other Restaurants from Selling Chips... Unless They're Served with Fish', *Daily* Mail, 11 July, http://www.dailymail.co.uk/news/article-2172168/London-Olympics-2012-McDonalds-force-Olympics-bosses-ban-restaurants-selling-chips-unless-FISH.html, accessed August 2012

Clifton, Nick (2008) 'The "Creative Class" in the UK: An Initial Analysis', *Geogr. Ann. B*, 90.1: 63–82

Compendium (2011a) 'Quick Facts – United Kingdom', *Compendium: Cultural Policies and Trends in Europe*, http://www.culturalpolicies.net/web/countries.php?pcid1490, accessed November 2011

—— (2011b) 'Quick Facts – Germany', *Compendium: Cultural Policies and Trends in Europe*, http://www.culturalpolicies.net/web/countries.php?pcid1190, accessed November 2011)

—— (2011c) 'Quick Facts – Ireland', *Compendium: Cultural Policies and Trends in Europe*, http://www.culturalpolicies.net/web/countries.php?pcid1240, accessed November 2011

Conservative Party (2010, April) *Invitation to Join the Government of Britain: The Conservative Party Manifesto 2010* (London: Conservative Party), available at http://www.conservatives.com/~/media/Files/Activist%20Centre/Press%20and%20Policy/Manifestos/Manifesto2010, accessed December 2012

Conservatives (2012) Shop, http://shop.conservatives.com/product97203/were-all-in-this-together-mens-t-shirt.aspx, accessed December 2012

Cooke, P., and C. De Laurentis (2008) *The Index of Knowledge Economies in the European Union: Performance Rankings of Cities and Regions*, Regional Industrial Research Report 41 (Cardiff: Centre for Advanced Studies, Cardiff University)

Cooper, Yvette MP (2010) 'Women Bear Brunt of Budget Cuts', 5 July, http://www.yvettecooper.com/women-bear-brunt-of-budget-cuts, accessed November 2012

Crawley, Peter (2010) 'Funding Cuts Exceed Expectations', *Irish Theatre Magazine*, February, http://www.irishtheatremagazine.ie/News/Current/funding-cuts, accessed July 2012

Creative Clyde (2011) 'Creative Collaboration on the Clyde', 19 June, http://www.creativeclyde.com/news--events/news/creative-collaboration-on-the-clyde, accessed August 2012

—— (2012) 'About Creative Clyde', http://www.creativeclyde.com/about, accessed August 2012

Creed, Martin (2002) in *Art Now: Interviews with Modern Artists*, ed. Illuminations (London and New York: Continuum), pp. 94–111

—— (2010) *Works* (London: Thames & Hudson)

—— (2012) *All the Bells*, http://www.allthebells.com/, accessed August 2012

Curtis, Polly (2012) 'Will the Housing Benefit Cap Cause the "Social Cleansing" of London?' Guardian.co.uk, 24 April, http://www.guardian.co.uk/politics/reality-check-with-polly-curtis/2012/apr/24/housing-housing-benefit, accessed August 2012

Davey, Alan (2010) 'Foreword', *Endowments in the Arts*, December (London: Arts Council England), pp. 3–4

—— (2011) 'Foreword [Part 1]: Supporting Growth in the Arts Economy', in Fleming and Erskine, *Supporting Growth in the Arts Economy*, July (London: ACE), pp. 1–2, available at http://www.artscouncil.org.uk/media/uploads/pdf/creative_economy_final210711.pdf, accessed August 2011

—— (2013) Chief Executive's Report, *Arts Council England Grant-in-Aid and Lottery Annual Report and Accounts 2011/12*, London: The Stationary Office, 5–6 July, available at http://www.official-documents.gov.uk/document/hc1213/hc02/0283/0283.pdf, accessed August 2012

Davis, Mike, and Daniel Bertrand Monk (2007) 'Introduction', in Mike Davis and Bertrand Monk (eds), *Evil Paradises: Dreamworlds of Neoliberalism* (New York: The New Press), pp. ix–xvi

Debord, Guy (1994 [1967]) *The Society of the Spectacle*, trans. Donald Nicholson-Smith (New York: Zone Books)

Deller, Jeremy (2012a) *Joy in People* (London: Hayward Publishing)

—— (2012b) http://www.jeremydeller.org/, accessed August 2012.

Dench, Geoff, Kate Gavron and Michael Young (2006) *The New East End: Kinship, Race and Conflict* (London: Profile)

Department for Communities and Local Government [DCLG] (2011a) Local Authority Housing Statistics, England: 2010–11: Housing Strategy Statistical Appendix and Business Plan Statistical Appendix, 30 November, http://www.communities.gov.uk/publications/corporate/statistics/lahousing201011, accessed August 2012

—— (2011b) National Planning Policy Framework, summary, http://www.communities.gov.uk/publications/planningandbuilding/draftframework, accessed September 2011

—— (2011c) Localism Bill, http://www.communities.gov.uk/localgovernment/decentralisation/localismbill/, accessed September 2011

—— (2012) *National Planning Policy Framework*, March (London: Department for Communities and Local Government), http://www.communities.gov.uk/documents/planningandbuilding/pdf/2116950.pdf, accessed August 2012

Department for Culture, Media and Sport [DCMS] (1998) *Creative Industries Mapping Document* (London: DCMS) available at http://webarchive.nationalarchives.gov.uk/+/http://www.culture.gov.uk/reference_library/publications/4740.aspx, accessed August 2012

—— (2001) *Creative Industries Mapping Document*, 2nd edn. (London: DCMS) available at http://webarchive.nationalarchives.gov.uk/+/http:/www.culture.gov.uk/reference_library/publications/4632.aspx/, accessed August 2012

—— (2006) *Developing Entrepreneurship for the Creative Industries: The Role of Higher and Further Education* (London: DCMS)

—— (2008) *Creative Britain: New Talents for the New Economy*, 22 February (London: DCMS), available at http://webarchive.nationalarchives.gov.uk/+/http://www.culture.gov.uk/images/publications/CEPFeb2008.pdf, accessed August 2012

—— (2010) 'Culture Secretary announces action plan to boost philanthropy', 8 December, http://www.culture.gov.uk/news/media_releases/2010/7631.aspx, accessed July 2012

—— (2011) *Catalyst Arts: Endowments, Guidance for Applicants*, updated 19 December (London: DCMS), http://www.artscouncil.org.uk/media/uploads/pdf/catalyst_arts_endowments_guidance_16-12-11.pdf, accessed 12 July 2012

—— (2012a) 'Michael Portillo announces £56 million endowment grants', 20 June, http://www.culture.gov.uk/news/media_releases/9145.aspx, accessed July 2012

—— (2012b) 'Catalyst Endowment Awards, June 2012', http://www.culture.gov.uk/images/publications/CatalystSuccessfulApplicantsUne2012.pdf, accessed July 2012

—— (n.d.) 'Why Is the National Lottery Being Used to Fund the London 2012 Olympic and Paralympic Games?', http://www.culture.gov.uk/what_we_do/national_lottery/4223.aspx, accessed November 2011

Department for Education and Skills (2004) *Increasing Voluntary Giving to Higher Education*, Higher Education task force report (London: DfES)

Department for Work and Pensions [DWP] (2012a) 'Aspiring Entrepreneurs Helped to Kick-Start New Businesses', 17 October, http://www.dwp.gov.uk/newsroom/press-releases/2012/oct-2012/dwp106-12.shtml, accessed December 2012

—— (2012b) 'Advisers and Intermediaries; Updates; New Enterprise Allowance (NEA)', 31 October, http://www.dwp.gov.uk/adviser/updates/new-enterprise-allowance/, accessed December 2012

—— (2012c) 'Universal Credit', http://www.dwp.gov.uk/policy/welfare-reform/universal-credit/, accessed November 2012

—— (2012d) *Benefit Cap (Housing Benefit) Regulations 2012: Impact Assessment for the Benefit Cap* (London: DWP), 16 July, http://www.dwp.gov.uk/docs/benefit-cap-wr2011-ia.pdf, accessed November 2012

—— (2012e) 'Philanthropy and Fundraising', http://www.culture.gov.uk/what_we_do/arts/8405.aspx, accessed August 2012

De Peuter, G. and N. Dyer-Witheford (2006) 'A Playful Multitude? Mobilising and Counter-Mobilising Immaterial Game Labour', *Fibreculture*, 5: n.p.

De Salvo, Donna (2002) 'Making *Marsyas*', in Anish Kapoor, *Marsyas* (London: Tate Publishing), pp. 12–17

Dibdin, Thom (2011) 'Scottish Performance Art Company Wound Up', *The Stage*, 15 December, http://www.thestage.co.uk/news/newsstory.php/34690/scottish-performance-art-company-wound-up accessed August 2012

Dillon, Brian (2008) 'Fissures', *Roger Hiorns: Seizure* (London: Artangel). Rpt at http://www.artangel.org.uk/projects/2008/seizure/brian_dillon_fissures/page_1 and four following pages, accessed June 2010

Dollimore, Jonathan, and Alan Sinfield (1994 [1985]) *Political Shakespeare: Essays in Cultural Materialism*, 2nd edn (Manchester: Manchester University Press)

Donahue, Tim, and Jim Patterson (2010) *Stage Money: The Business of the Professional Theater* (Columbia, SC: University of South Carolina Press)

Dorling, Daniel (2011) *Injustice: Why Inequality Persists* (Bristol: Polity Press)

Dorment, Richard (2007) 'A Glimpse into the Abyss', *The Daily Telegraph*, 9 October

Economist, The (2012) 'Raising Capital Online: The New Thundering Herd', *The Economist* 16 June (New York, print edition), available at http://www.economist.com/node/21556973, accessed July 2012

Eglinton, Andrew (2010) 'Reflections on a Decade of Punchdrunk Theatre', *Theatre Forum*, 37 (1 June): 47–55

Eisenberg, Christiane, Rita Gerlach and Christian Handke (eds) (2006) *Cultural Industries: The British Experience in International Perspective* (Berlin: Humboldt University Berlin)

Electric Hotel (2012) http://www.electrichotel.co.uk/bookings.htm, accessed November 2012

Empty Homes (2010) Statistics, How Many Homes are Empty, Table 615, downloadable from http://www.emptyhomes.com/statistics-2/, accessed October 2010

Espinoza, Elizabeth (2010) 'Punchdrunk and Stella Artois: A Match Made in Corporate Heaven?', *Backstage Blog, Stage*, 15 November, http://blogstage.backstage.com/2010/11/punchdrunk-and-stella-artois-a-match-made-in-corporate-heaven-1.html, accessed July 2012

European Commission (2010) *Unlocking the Potential of the Cultural and Creative Industries* (Brussels: COM)

Eyre, Ben (2012) 'Award winners illustrate a "new blueprint for corporate engagement" with the arts', *Philanthropy UK*, 1 June, http://www.philanthropyuk.org/news/2012-06-01/award-winners-illustrate-new-blueprint-corporate-engagement-arts, accessed July 2012

Eyre, Hermione (2011) 'How Punchdrunk Theatre Troup [*sic*] Is Taking over the World', *London Evening Standard*, 2 September, http://www.standard.co.uk/lifestyle/esmagazine/how-punchdrunk-theatre-troup-is-taking-over-the-world-6439364.html, accessed July 2012

Fenton, Alex (2011) *Housing Benefit Reform and the Spatial Segregation of Low-Income Households in London* (Cambridge: Cambridge Centre for Housing and Planning Research), January, http://www.cchpr.landecon.cam.ac.uk/Downloads/hb_reform_london_spatial_implications-cchpr2011.pdf, accessed August 2012

Fitzpatrick, Suzanne, and Mark Stephens (eds) (2008) *The Future of Social Housing* (London: Shelter)

Fleming, Tom, and Andrew Erskine (of Tom Fleming Creative Consultancy) (2011) *Supporting Growth in the Arts Economy*, July (London: Arts Council England), available at http://www.artscouncil.org.uk/media/uploads/pdf/creative_economy_final210711.pdf, accessed August 2011

Florida, Richard (2002) *The Rise of the Creative Class and How It's Transforming Work, Leisure, Community and Everyday Life* (Basic Books: Cambridge)

—— (2005) *Cities and the Creative Class* (New York: Routledge)

—— (2008) *Who's Your City?: How the Creative Economy is Making Where to Live the Most Important Decision of Your Life* (New York: Basic Books)

—— (2011) Creative Class, Clients, http://www.creativeclass.com/richard_florida/clients/, accessed September 2011

Flounders, Eric (1993) Letter to the Editor, *Independent*, 5 November, Rpt in *Rachel Whiteread: House*, ed. James Lingwood (London: Phaidon in association with Artangel, 1995)

FlyTower (2007) 10 May – 17 June, http://www.youtube.com/watch?vFlulkni8bgE, accessed June 2012

Folly for a Flyover (2012) http://www.follyforaflyover.co.uk/, accessed November 2012

Forgan, Dame Liz (2012) 'Chair's Report', *Arts Council England Grant-in-aid and Lottery Annual Report and Accounts 2011/12*, July (London: The Stationary Office), pp. 4–5, http://www.official-documents.gov.uk/document/hc1213/hc02/0283/0283.pdf, accessed August 2012

Foucault, Michel (1991) 'Governmentality', in Graham Burchell, Colin Gordon and Peter Miller (eds), *The Foucault Effect: Studies in Governmentality: With Two Lectures by and an Interview with Michel Foucault* (London: Harvester Wheatsheaf, 1991), pp. 87–104

—— (1995) *Discipline and Punish: The Birth of the Prison*, trans. Alan Sheridan (New York: Vintage Books)

Fourth Plinth (2012) http://www.london.gov.uk/fourthplinth/, accessed December 2012

FuelRCA (2012) 'A Entrepreneurs Launch', http://fuel.rca.ac.uk/videos/rca-artrepreneurs-launch, accessed July 2012

Fund It (2012a) http://www.fundit.ie/browse, accessed July 2012

—— (2012b) 'Performance, Misterman', http://www.fundit.ie/project/misterman-1, accessed November 2011

Garber, Marjorie (2008) *Patronizing the Arts* (Princeton, NJ: Princeton University Press)

Gardner, Lyn (2006) 'An Offer They Can't Refuse', *Guardian*, 20 June, http://www.guardian.co.uk/stage/2006/jun/20/theatre2, accessed July 2012

Garner, Jr., Stanton B. (2008) 'Introduction: Is There a Doctor in the House? Medicine and the Making of Modern Drama', *Modern Drama*, 51.3: 311–28

Garratt, Sheryl (2010) 'Punchdrunk theatre company opens Louis Vuitton's new Bond Street store', *Telegraph*, 24 June, http://www.telegraph.co.uk/culture/theatre/7843548/Punchdrunk-theatre-company-opens-Louis-Vuittons-new-Bond-Street-store.html, accessed July 2012

Gentleman, Amelia (2012) 'Housing Benefit Cap Forces Families to Leave Central London or Be Homeless', *Guardian*, 17 February, main section, p. 1, http://www.guardian.co.uk/society/2012/feb/16/housing-benefit-cap-families-central-london, accessed August 2012

Give It Back, George (2012a) Website, http://giveitbackgeorge.org/, accessed August 2012

—— (2012b) Twitter feed, GIB_George https://twitter.com/GIB_George, accessed August 2012

Gleadell, Colin (2012) 'How Damien Hirst Tried to Transform the Art Market', *Telegraph*, 21 March, http://www.telegraph.co.uk/culture/art/art-features/9157252/How-Damien-Hirst-tried-to-transform-the-art-market.html#, accessed July 2012

Glinkowski, Paul (2007) 'Reflections on 21st-Century Philanthropy and on the Role of Trusts and Foundations in Supporting the Arts in the United Kingdom', in Paul Glinkowski, *Good Foundations: Trusts & Foundations and the Arts in the United Kingdom*, Volume 2: *An Overview* (London: Laurence King), pp. 11–44

—— ed. and compiler (2008) *The Art of Giving: The Artist in Public and Private Funding: An Interpretative Summary of a Conference Organised by Tate Britain and Wimbledon College of Art, University of the Arts London, supported by the Rootstein Hopkins Foundation* (London: Research at Wimbledon)

Glusker, Anne (2006) 'The Best Seats for this Play Are Moving Fast', *New York Times*, 17 December, http://www.nytimes.com/2006/12/17/theater/17glus.html, accessed May 2011

Glyn, Andrew, and Stewart Wood (2001) 'New Labour's Economic Policy', in Andrew Glyn (ed.), *Social Democracy in Neoliberal Times: The Left and Economic Policy since 1980* (Oxford: Oxford University Press), pp. 200–22

Glynn, Sarah (ed.) (2009) *Where the Other Half Lives: Lower Income Housing in a Neoliberal World* (London: Pluto Press)

Gray, Colin, and John Stanworth (1986) *Allowing for Enterprise: A Qualitative Assessment of the Enterprise Allowance Scheme*, June (London: Small Business Research Trust)

Greater London Authority (2011) *The London Plan: Spatial Developments Strategy for Greater London*, 22 July (London: Greater London Authority), http://www.london.gov.uk/publication/londonplan, accessed September 2011

Greenblatt, Stephen (1994 [1985]) *Political Shakespeare: Essays in Cultural Materialism*, 2nd edn (Manchester: Manchester University Press)

Gregg, Melissa (2011) *Work's Intimacy* (Cambridge: Polity Press)

Groves, Nancy (2011) 'You Me Bum Bum Train', *What's On Stage*, 9 December, http://www.whatsonstage.com/reviews/theatre/london/E8831323437594/You+Me+Bum+Bum+Train.html, accessed December 2012

Guardian (2010) G2 section, *Guardian*, 'Is There No End to the Pop-up Revolution?', 12 October

—— (2012) 'Rich List Reveals Record Fortunes for Britain's Wealthiest', *The Guardian*, 29 April, http://www.guardian.co.uk/business/2012/apr/29/rich-list-record-fortunes-britain, accessed August 2012

Gunnell, Barbara (2011) 'One Leaf that David Cameron Should Take out of Thatcher's Book', *Guardian*, 6 January, http://www.guardian.co.uk/commentisfree/2011/jan/06/new-enterprise-allowance-david-cameron, accessed August 2012

Gunnell, Barbara, and Martin Bright (2011) *Make a Job Don't Take a Job: Building the Creative Society* (London: New Deal of the Mind), http://www.thecreativesociety.co.uk/wp-content/uploads/2011/02/the-creative-society-make-a-job-report.pdf, accessed August 2012

Hackworth, Jason (2007) *The Neoliberal City: Governance, Ideology, and Development in American Urbanism* (Ithaca, NY, and London: Cornell University Press)

Haggar, Nadia (dir.) (2002) *The Man Who Destroyed Everything*, tx. BBC 4, 2 March, 7pm

Halford, Bethany (2009) 'Concocting a Crystalline Lair', *Chemical and Engineering News*, 5 January

Hall, Tim, and Phil Hubbard (1998) *The Entrepreneurial City: Geographies of Politics, Regime and Representation* (Chichester: John Wiley & Sons)

Hamnett, Chris (2003) *Unequal City: London in the Global Arena* (London: Routledge)

Hancox, Simone (2013) *Global Art in an Age of Global Performance: Complicity and Critique* (PhD Thesis, Queen Mary University of London)

Harvey, David (1988 [1982]) Foreword to Sharon Zukin, *Loft Living: Culture and Capital in Urban Change* (London: Radius), pp. ix–xii

—— (1995 [1989]) *The Condition of Postmodernity: An Enquiry into the Origins of Cultural Change* (Oxford: Wiley-Blackwell)

—— (2005) *A Brief History of Neoliberalism* (Oxford: Oxford University Press)

—— (2007) 'Neoliberalism as Creative Destruction', *Annals of the American Academy of Political and Social Science*, Volume 610, March, NAFTA and Beyond: Alternative Perspectives in the Study of Global Trade and Development: 22–44

—— (2011 [2010]) *The Enigma of Capital and the Crises of Capitalism*, updated edn (London: Profile Books)

Harvie, Jen (2003) 'Nationalizing the "Creative Industries"', *Contemporary Theatre Review*, 13.1, special issue on Contemporary British Theatre: Playwrights, Politics, Performance: 15–32

—— (2005) *Staging the UK* (Manchester: Manchester University Press)

—— (2006) 'Witnessing Michael Landy's *Break Down*: Metonymy, Affect, and Politicised Performance in an Age of Global Consumer Capitalism', *Contemporary Theatre Review*, 16.1 Special issue on Globalisation and Theatre: 62–72

—— (2009a) *Theatre & the City* (Basingstoke: Palgrave MacMillan)

—— (2009b) 'Agency and Complicity in a "Special Civic Room": London's Tate Modern Turbine Hall', in DJ Hopkins, Shelley Orr and Kim Solga (eds), *Performance and the City* (Basingstoke: Palgrave Macmillan), 204–21

—— (2011a) 'Democracy and Neoliberalism in Art's Social Turn and Roger Hiorns's *Seizure*', *Performance Research*, 16.2: 113–23

—— (2011b) 'Public/Private Capital: Arts Funding and Mixed Economies', Keynote presented at 'Irish Theatre History Conference – Archives, Historiography, Politics – Ten Years On – Performance, Memory, Futures', at the National University of Ireland, Galway, 25–26 November

—— (2012a) 'Public/Private Capital: Arts Funding and Mixed Economies', Keynote presented at TaPRA Postgraduate Symposium on Theatre and Alternative Value, 28 January, London

—— (2012b) 'Public/Private Capital: Arts Funding and Mixed Economies', paper presented to the Department of Film, Theatre and Television, University of Reading, 9 February

—— (2012c) 'Public/Private Capital: Arts Funding and Mixed Economies', paper presented at conference *Subsidy, Patronage & Sponsorship: Theatre and Performance Culture in Uncertain Times* at the V&A in collaboration with the University of Reading, 21 July, London

—— and Stephenson (2012) Personal email to the author from Debbie Stephenson, Senior Officer, Freedom of Information, Arts Council England, National Office, 7 August

Healey, Helen (2011) Ed Whiting in interview with Helen Healey, 'Micro-philanthropy', *a-n.co.uk*, April, http://www.a-n.co.uk/jobs_and_opps/article/1196856, accessed July 2012

Hemming, Sarah (2011) 'Audience on Show', *Financial Times*, 2 December, http://www.ft.com/cms/s/2/0a1ee5d0-1b3c-11e1-8b11-00144feabdc0.html#axzz2FOuS7gSM, accessed December 2012

Henley, Jon (2007) 'Cracked! Tate Modern's Dramatic New Installation', *Guardian*, 10 October

Henry, Colette (ed.) (2007) *Entrepreneurship in the Creative Industries: An International Perspective* (Cheltenham: Edward Elgar)

Hewitt + Jordan [Andy Hewitt and Mel Jordan], (2004) *I Fail To Agree* (Sheffield: Site Gallery)

—— (2012) *SHOWFLAT*, http://www.hewittandjordan.com/archive/showflat.html, accessed September 2012

Higgins, Charlotte (2007) 'Overthrow the Tyranny of Targets: Minister's Message for the Arts', *Guardian*, 6 July

—— (2009) 'Immersive Theatre – Tired and Hackneyed Already?' *Guardian On Culture Blog*, 7 December, http://www.guardian.co.uk/culture/charlottehigginsblog/2009/dec/07/theatre-punchdrunk?INTCMPSRCH, accessed June 2011

—— (2010) 'Arts Funding Cut 30% in Spending Review', *Guardian*, 20 October, http://www.guardian.co.uk/politics/2010/oct/20/arts-cuts-spending-review-council, accessed July 2012

—— (2012) 'Roger Hiorns' Turner Prize-nominated Artwork, Seizure Escapes Demolition', Guardian.co.uk, 6 July, available at http://www.guardian.co.uk/artanddesign/2012/jul/06/roger-hiorns-seizure-demolition-yorkshire, accessed August 2012; rpt, *Guardian*, 7 July 2012, main section, p. 14

Higgs, Peter, Stuart Cunningham and Hasan Bakhshi (2008) *Beyond the Creative Industries: Mapping the Creative Economy in the United Kingdom* (London: NESTA, February)

Hill, Nicola (2011) 'Donations fall but animal welfare giving goes up, Charity Market Monitor shows', *Philanthropy UK*, 15 July, http://www.philanthropyuk.org/news/2011-07-15/donations-fall-animal-welfare-giving-goes-charity-market-monitor-shows, accessed July 2012

—— (2012) 'Corporate Donations to Arts Fall by 7% but Individual Philanthropy Rises', *Philanthropy UK*, 1 March, http://www.philanthropyuk.org/news/2012-03-01/corporate-donations-arts-fall-7-individual-philanthropy-rises, accessed July 2012

HM Government (2011) *Giving White Paper*, May (London: TSO [The Stationary Office]), http://www.cabinetoffice.gov.uk/sites/default/files/resources/giving-white-paper2.pdf, accessed July 2012

HM Revenue & Customs (2012) On Gift Aid, 'Giving to Charity Through Gift Aid', http://www.hmrc.gov.uk/individuals/giving/gift-aid.htm, accessed August 2012

Holden, John (2007) *Publicly-Funded Culture and the Creative Industries* (London: ACE)

Holderness, Graham (2001) *Cultural Shakespeare: Essays in the Shakespeare Myth* (Hatfield: University of Hertfordshire)

Höller, Carsten (2006) *Test Site* (London: Tate Publishing)

Holtom, Helen (2010) 'A Story in Progress – What Ever Happened to the National Review of Live Art?' *Axis: The Online Resource for Contemporary Art*, April, http://www.axisweb.org/dlForum.aspx?ESSAYID18086, accessed August 2012

Home Live Art [HLA] (2012a) http://www.homeliveart.com/, accessed September 2012

—— (2012b) *The Alternative Village Fete*, http://homeliveart.com/current-projects/142-the-alternative-village-fete, accessed September 2012

Homes and Communities Agency (2011) *2011–15 Affordable Homes Programme – Framework*, February (London: Homes and Communities Agency), http://www.homesandcommunities.co.uk/sites/default/files/our-work/affordable-homes-framework.pdf, accessed August 2012

Hopkins, DJ, Shelley Orr and Kim Solga (eds) (2009) *Performance and The City* (Basingstoke: Palgrave Macmillan)

Huber, Evelyne, and John D. Stephens (2001) 'The Social Democratic Welfare State', in Andrew Glyn (ed.), *Social Democracy in Neoliberal Times: The Left and Economic Policy since 1980* (Oxford: Oxford University Press), pp. 276–311

Hunt & Darton Café, http://huntanddartoncafe.com/, accessed August 2012

Hunt, Jeremy (DCMS) (2010) 'Philanthropy keynote speech', *European Association for Philanthropy & Giving Conference*, London, 8 December, http://www.culture.gov.uk/news/ministers_speeches/7633.aspx, accessed July 2012

Imrie, Rob, Loretta Lees and Mike Raco (eds) (2009) *Regenerating London: Governance, Sustainability and Community in a Global City* (London: Routledge)

Institute for the Art and Practice of Dissent at Home, The [IAPDH] (2012) http://www.twoaddthree.org/home/, accessed September 2012

Jackson, Shannon (2011) *Social Works: Performing Art, Supporting Publics* (New York and London: Routledge)

James, Oliver (2007) *Affluenza* (London: Vermilion)

—— (2008) *The Selfish Capitalist* (London: Vermilion)

Jeffreys, Tom (2012) 'Marcus Coates – Vision Quest at Elephant and Castle Shopping Centre', *Spoonfed*, 12 April, http://www.spoonfed.co.uk/spooners/tom-699/marcus-coates-vision-quest-at-elephant-and-castle-shopping-centre-6701/, accessed September 2012

Jenkins, Patrick, and Brooke Masters (2012) 'Finance: London's Precarious Position', *ft.com*, 29 July, http://www.ft.com/cms/s/0/6547a42c-d7d1-11e1-80a8-00144feabdc0.html#axzz2FOuS7gSM, accessed December 2012

Johnson, Boris (2010) 'Boris Johnson Won't Accept "Kosovo-style" Social Cleansing', *BBC London Radio*, 28 October, http://www.bbc.co.uk/news/uk-politics-11643440, accessed September 2011

—— (2011) 'Foreword', Greater London Authority, *The London Plan: Spatial Developments Strategy for Greater London*, 22 July (London: Greater London Authority), pp. 5–7, http://www.london.gov.uk/publication/londonplan, accessed September 2011

Jones, Jonathan (2007) 'Salcedo Causes a Rift at Tate Modern', *Guardian Unlimited*, 8 October, http://www.guardian.co.uk/artanddesign/2007/oct/08/art3, accessed March 2013

—— (2012) 'Will You Ring Creed's Bell to Mark the Start of the Olympics?', Guardian.co.uk, 26 July, http://www.guardian.co.uk/artanddesign/jonathanjonesblog/2012/jul/26/ring-bell-martin-creed-olympics, accessed August 2012

Kapoor, Anish (2002) *Marsyas* (London: Tate Publishing)

Kattwinkel, Susan (ed.) (2003) *Audience Participation: Essays on Inclusion in Performance*, Contributions in Drama and Theatre Studies, Number 101 (Westport, CT: Praeger)

Keay, Douglas (1987) 'Aids, education and the year 2000!' [interview with Margaret Thatcher], *Woman's Own*, 31 October, pp. 8–10. An excerpt is available on the Margaret Thatcher Foundation website, www.margaretthatcher.org/speeches/displaydocument.asp?docid106689, accessed October 2008

Kennedy, Maev (2012) 'London 2012 Cultural Festival's Free Events Draw Almost 10m People', Guardian.co.uk, 6 August, http://www.guardian.co.uk/culture/2012/aug/06/london-2012-cultural-festival-events, accessed August 2012

Kennedy, Roger G., and David Larkin (2009) *When Art Worked* (New York: Rizzoli International Publications)

Kester, Grant H. (2004) *Conversation Pieces: Community and Communication in Modern Art* (Berkeley, CA: University of California Press)
Kick Starter (2012) http://www.kickstarter.com/, accessed July 2012
Kinsella, Ana Rose (2012) 'Inside Karl Lagerfeld's Selfridges Soirée', *Elle*, 25 July, available at http://www.elle.com/news/fashion-style/karl-lagerfeld-selfridges-olympic-pop-up-party, accessed August 2012
Kintrea, Keith (2008) 'Social Housing and Spatial Segregation', in Suzanne Fitzpatrick and Mark Stephens (eds), *The Future of Social Housing* (London: Shelter), pp. 69–83
Klein, Jacky (2009) *Grayson Perry* (London: Thames & Hudson)
Klein, Naomi (2007) *The Shock Doctrine: The Rise of Disaster Capitalism* (London: Penguin)
Knell, John, and Matthew Taylor (2011) *Arts Funding, Austerity and the Big Society: Remaking the Case for the Arts*, February (London: Royal Society for the Arts), http://www.thersa.org/__data/assets/pdf_file/0011/384482/RSA-Pamphlets-Arts_Funding_Austerity_BigSociety.pdf , accessed June 201
Knowles, Ric (2004) *Reading the Material Theatre* (Cambridge: Cambridge University Press)
Koester, Cathy (ed.) (2006) *Creative Nation: Advancing Britain's Creative Industries* (London: Smith Institute)
Kong, Lily, and Justin O'Connor (eds) (2009) *Creative Economies, Creative Cities: Asian-European Perspectives*, The GeoJournal Library Volume 98 (Dordrecht: Springer)
Kötting, Andrew, and Iain Sinclair (2012) *Swandown*, http://swandown.info/, accessed August 2012
Krätke, Stefan (2012) 'The New Urban Growth Ideology of "Creative Cities"', in Neil Brenner, Peter Marcuse and Margit Mayer (eds), *Cities for People, Not for Profit: Critical Urban Theory and the Right to the City* (London and New York: Routledge), pp. 138–49
Laclau, Ernesto, and Chantal Mouffe (1985) *Hegemony and Socialist Strategy: Towards a Radical Democratic Politics* (London: Verso)
Laing, Barry (2011) 'Lone Twin – Avowals of Hope and Labours of Love', in David Williams and Carl Lavery (eds), *Good Luck Everybody, Lone Twin: Journeys Performances Conversations* (Aberystwyth: Performance Research Books), pp. 155–60
Lamont, Tom (2012) 'Marcus Coates: "Eventually Something Serious Comes Through"', *Observer*, 8 April, http://www.guardian.co.uk/artanddesign/2012/apr/08/marcus-coates-artist-elephant-castle, accessed September 2012
Landry, Charles, and Franco Bianchini (1995) *The Creative City* (London: Demos), pp. 28–9, available at http://www.demos.co.uk/publications/thecreativecity, accessed October 2012
Landy, Michael (2001a) *Break Down* (London: Artangel)
—— (2001b) *Break Down Inventory* (London: Ridinghouse)
—— (2004) *Semi-Detached* (London: Tate Publishing)
—— (2007) *H2NY* (New York and London: Alexander & Bonin and Thomas Dane Gallery)
—— (2009) 'Heavy Meta: Landy and Tinguely in the Dump', in Laurence Sillars (ed.), *Joyous Machines: Michael Landy and Jean Tinguely* (Liverpool: Tate Liverpool), pp. 131–4

Lange, Bastian (2006) 'From Cool Britannia to Generation Berlin? Geographies of Culturepreneurs and their Creative Milieus in Berlin', in Christiane Eisenberg, Rita Gerlach and Christian Handke (eds), *Cultural Industries: The British Experience in International Perspective* (Berlin: Humboldt University of Berlin). Available online: http://edoc.hu-berlin.de/conferences/culturalindustries/proc/culturalindustries.pdf, accessed July 2012

Latour, Bruno (1995) *Reassembling the Social – An Introduction to Actor-Network-Theory* (Oxford: Oxford University Press)

—— (1998a) 'On Actor Network Theory: A Few Clarifications', *Nettime.org*, Part 1, p. 11 January, http://www.nettime.org/Lists-Archives/nettime-l-9801/msg00019.html, accessed December 2012

—— (1998b) 'On Actor Network Theory: A Few Clarifications', *Nettime.org*, Part 2, p. 11 January, http://www.nettime.org/Lists-Archives/nettime-l-9801/msg00020.html, accessed December 2012

Law, Jonathan, and John Smullen (eds) (2008) *A Dictionary of Finance and Banking* (Oxford: Oxford University Press)

Lazzarato, Maurizio (1996) 'Immaterial Labour', in Paolo Virno and Michael Hardt (eds), *Radical Thought in Italy: A Potential Politics* (Minneapolis, MN: University of Minnesota Press), pp. 133–50

Leat, Diana (2012) 'Government, Foundations and the Big Society: Will You Be My Friend?', in Armine Ishkanian and Simon Szreter (eds), *The Big Society Debates: A New Agenda for Social Welfare?* (Cheltenham: Edward Elgar), pp. 128–38

Lees, Loretta, Tom Slater and Elvin Wyly (2008) *Gentrification* (New York and London: Routledge)

Leeser, Rachel (2011) *Focus on London 2011: Poverty: The Hidden City* (London: GLA Intelligence Unit), http://data.london.gov.uk/documents/focus-on-london-2011-poverty.pdf, accessed November 2012

Lefebvre, Henri (1991) *The Production of Space*, trans. Donald Nicholson-Smith (Oxford: Basil Blackwell).

—— (2003 [1970]) *The Urban Revolution*, trans. Robert Bononno (Minneapolis, MN, and London: University of Minnesota Press)

Léger, Marc James (2011) 'Introduction: Doing the Unexpected, Creating the Present', in Marc James Léger (ed.), *Culture and Contestation in the New Century* (Bristol: Intellect), pp. 7–20

Lightig, Toby (2007) 'The Play's Location's the Thing', *Guardian Theatre Blog*, 9 March, http://www.guardian.co.uk/stage/theatreblog/2007/mar/09/theplayslocationsthething, accessed May 2011

Lind, Maria (2007) 'The Collaborative Turn', in Johanna Billing, Maria Lind and Lars Nilsson (eds), *Taking the Matter into Common Hands: Contemporary Art and Collaborative Practices* (London: Black Dog), pp. 15–31

Lingwood, James (ed.) (1995) *Rachel Whiteread: House* (London: Phaidon Press in association with Artangel)

—— (2008) 'The Impregnation of an Object: Roger Hiorns in Conversation with James Lingwood', Artangel, July, available at www.artangel.org.uk//projects/2008/seizure/a_conversation_with_roger_hiorns/q_a#, accessed August 2012

Live Art Development Agency, http://www.thisisliveart.co.uk/, accessed December 2012

Living Places (2011) http://www.living-places.org.uk, accessed September 2011

Lloyd, Richard (2010 [2006]) *Neo-Bohemia: Art and Commerce in the Postindustrial City*, 2nd edn (New York: Routledge)

Lobel, Brian (2011) *Purge*, http://www.blobelwarming.com/purge/, accessed August 2012

Local Data Company (2010) 17 September, www.localdatacompnay.com/news-and-media/2010/9/17/hsbc-one-in-eight-town-centre-shops-empty-report-finds.html

—— (2012) Shop Vacancy, September 2012 (GB), http://www.localdatacompany.com/knowledge accessed November 2012

London 2012 Festival (2012) http://festival.london2012.com/about/culturalolympiad/cultural-olympiad.php, accessed August 2012

London's Poverty Profile (2011a) Inequality, http://www.londonspovertyprofile.org.uk/indicators/topics/inequality/, accessed October 2011

—— (2011b) 'Housing Costs Risk Piling Pressure on Outer-London Services', News, http://www.londonspovertyprofile.org.uk/news/housing-costs-risk-piling-pres/, accessed October 2011

Lone Twin (2012) *The Boat Project:* Maiden Voyage, 7 May–11 August 2012, available at http://www.theboatproject.com/, accessed September 2012

Lotringer, Sylvère (2004) 'Foreword: We, the Multitude', in Paolo Virno, *A Grammar of the Multitude: For an Analysis of Contemporary Forms of Life*, trans. Isabella Bertoletti, James Cascaito and Andrea Casson (Los Angeles, CA: Semiotext(e)), pp. 7–19

Louise, Dany (2012) 'Endowment Funding – a Catalyst for Conformity?', a-n.co.uk, 22 June, http://www.a-n.co.uk/artists/article/2273109/1818356, accessed July 2012

Lowe, Stuart (2011) *The Housing Debate* (Bristol: Policy Press)

MacGregor, Neil (2010) *A Report for the Secretary of State for Culture, Olympics, Media and Sport on the Role Endowments Could Play in DCMS Funded Museums and Galleries* (London: DCMS), http://www.culture.gov.uk/images/publications/Endowments_paper_20101208.pdf, accessed July 2012

Malik, Shiv (2012) 'London 2012: Coe Sparks Olympics Sponsorship Row', *Guardian*, 20 July, http://www.guardian.co.uk/sport/2012/jul/20/coe-olympics-sponsorship-row, accessed August 2012

Mallen, Siobhan (2010) 'All the Secrets Behind McQ's Spectacular Show: EXCLUSIVE INTERVIEW', *Grazia*, 23 February, http://www.graziadaily.co.uk/fashion/archive/2012/02/23/all-the-secrets-behind-mcqs-spectacular-show--exclusive.htm, accessed July 2012

Manchester International Festival (2012) Punchdrunk, *The Crash of the Elysium*, http://mif.co.uk/event/the-crash-of-the-elysium-a-punchdrunk-show-for-children-aged-6-12/, accessed July 2012

Mandelson, Peter (2008) Letter to the *Guardian*, 12 January, http://www.guardian.co.uk/politics/2008/jan/12/tonyblair.labour, accessed December 2012

Marini, Charikleia (2013) 'Employing a Derelict Space for Performance', in *Re-Defining Urban Space Through Performance* (PhD thesis, Queen Mary, University of London)

Markusen, Ann (2006) 'Urban Development and the Politics of a Creative Class: Evidence from the Study of Artists', *Environment and Planning, A* 38.10: 1921–40

Marmion, Patrick (2010) 'You Me Bum Bum Train: The Very Zenith of Thespian Cool Is "One-on-one" Theatre', *Mail Online*, 14 July, http://www.dailymail.co.uk/tvshowbiz/reviews/article-1293433/You-Me-Bum-Bum-Train-The-zenith-thespian-cool-one-theatre.html, accessed December 2012

Marmot Review Team (2010) *Fair Society, Healthy Lives: The Marmot Review: Strategic Review of Health Inequalities in England post-2010*, February, available at http://www.ucl.ac.uk/gheg/marmotreview/FairSocietyHealthyLives, accessed February 2010

Martin, Randy (2006) 'Artistic Citizenship: Introduction', in Mary Schmidt Campbell and Randy Martin (eds), *Artistic Citizenship: A Public Voice for the Arts* (New York and London: Routledge), pp. 1–22

Marx, Karl (2012 [1859]) *A Contribution to the Critique of Political Economy* (Charleston, SC: Forgotten Books)

Marx, Karl, and Friedrich Engels (1998) *The Communist Manifesto: A Modern Edition* (London and New York: Verso)

Massey, Doreen (1995) 'Space-Time and the Politics of Location', in James Lingwood, ed., *Rachel Whiteread: House* (London: Phaidon in association with Artangel), pp. 34–49

Mauss, Marcel (2002) *The Gift: The Form and Reason for Exchange in Archaic Societies* (London: Routledge Classics)

McAlpine, Kenny, and Andrew Nicoll (2012) '£460k on Migrants-only Footie Pitch in Woods', *The Scottish Sun*, 7 February, http://www.thescottishsun.co.uk/scotsol/homepage/news/4112307/460k-on-migrants-only-footie-pitch-in-woods.html, accessed November 2012

McGinn, Caroline (2011) 'Punchdrunk Isn't Just Theatrical Any More', *Time Out*, 11 July, http://www.timeout.com/london/theatre/article/2547/punchdrunk-isnt-just-theatrical-any-more, accessed July 2012

McGuinness, Feargal (2012) 'New Enterprise Allowance', *Briefing Paper for Members of Parliament* (London: House of Commons Library), 23 November, available at www.parliament.uk/briefing-papers/SN05878.pdf, accessed December 2012

McMaster, Brian (2008) *Supporting Excellence in the Arts*, December (London: DCMS)

McQueen, Steve (2009) *Giardini* (London: British Council)

—— (2010) *Queen and Country* (London: British Council in association with The Art Fund, Imperial War Museum, Manchester International Festival)

McRobbie, Angela, (2011) '"Everyone is Creative": Artists as Pioneers of the New Economy?', in Marc James Léger (ed.), *Culture and Contestation in the New Century* (Bristol: Intellect), pp. 77–92

Measuring Worth (2012a) 'UK Compare', http://www.measuringworth.com/ukcompare/, accessed August 2012

—— (2012b) 'Index', http://www.measuringworth.com/index.php, accessed August 2012

Mesch, Claudia (2007) 'Institutionalizing Social Sculpture: Beuys' *Office for Direct Democracy through Referendum* Installation (1972)', in Claudia Mesch and Viola Michely (eds), *Joseph Beuys: The Reader* (London: I. B. Tauris), pp. 198–217

Mesch, Claudia, and Viola Michely (eds) (2007) *Joseph Beuys: The Reader* (London: I. B. Tauris)

Metcalfe, David (ed.) (2007) *Town Crying: A Lone Twin Project* (Newcastle upon Tyne: Forma Arts and Media)

Miessen, Markus, and Shumon Basar (eds) (2006) *Did Someone Say Participate? An Atlas of Spatial Practice* (Cambridge, MA: MIT Press)
Milgrom, Melissa (2010) *Still Life: Adventures in Taxidermy* (Boston, MA: Houghton Mifflin Harcourt)
Millar, John Douglas (2012) 'Polemic: Art Workers', *Art Monthly*, 355 (April): 34
Miller, Phil (2011) 'Police Called after Scots Arts Company Wound Up', *Herald Scotland*, 13 December, http://www.heraldscotland.com/news/home-news/police-called-after-scots-arts-company-wound-up.16139975, accessed August 2012
Milliard, Coline (2008) 'Roger Hiorns: *Seizure*', *Art Monthly*, October
Ministry of Justice (2012) 'Squatting New Criminal Offence', 31 August, http://www.justice.gov.uk/news/features/squatting-new-criminal-offence, accessed November 2012
Montague, Sir Adrian (2012) *Review of the Barriers to Institutional Investment in Private Rented Homes*, London: Department for Communities and Local Government, August, http://www.communities.gov.uk/documents/housing/pdf/2204242.pdf, accessed August 2012
Moody, Michael (2011) 'A Hippocratic Oath for Philanthropists', in Donelson R. Forsyth and Crystal L. Hold (eds), *For the Greater Good of All: Perspectives on Individualism, Society, and Leadership*, Jepson Studies in Leadership (New York: Palgrave Macmillan), pp. 143–65
Morgan, Jessica (2003) 'Introduction', in Jessica Morgan (ed.), *Common Wealth* (London: Tate Publishing), pp. 15–33
—— (2006) 'Turbine Höller', in Carsten Höller, *Test Site* (London: Tate Publishing), pp. 11–15
Morgan, Polly (2012) http://pollymorgan.co.uk/, accessed August 2012
Morris, Nigel, and Andrew Grice (2012) '"Charity tax" scrapped in third Budget U-turn in four days', *The Independent*, 31 May, http://www.independent.co.uk/news/uk/politics/charity-tax-scrapped-in-third-budget-uturn-in-four-days-7808368.html#, accessed 11 July 2012
Morrison, Blake (2008) 'Waving Goodbye', in Grayson Perry, *Unpopular Culture: Grayson Perry Selects from the Arts Council Collection* (London: Hayward Publishing), pp. 13–16
Morton, Alex (2012) *Ending Expensive Social Tenancies: Fairness, Higher Growth and More Homes*, 20 August (London: Policy Exchange), http://www.policyexchange.org.uk/images/publications/ending%20expensive%20social%20tenancies.pdf, accessed August 2012
Morton, John (dir.) (2012) 'Loose Ends', *Twenty Twelve* series 2, episode 7, tx BBC Two, 24 July, 10.00pm
Moss, Stephen (2011) 'The Death of a Housing Ideal', *Guardian*, 4 March, section G2, p. 6, http://www.guardian.co.uk/society/2011/mar/04/death-housing-ideal accessed September 2012
Muir, Gregor (2009) *Lucky Kunst: The Rise and Fall of Young British Art* (London: Aurum Press)
Mulholland, Hélène (2009) 'London Has Highest Rates of Poverty and Inequality in UK', *Guardian*, 19 May, available at http://www.guardian.co.uk/politics/2009/may/19/london-poverty, accessed September 2011
Mullins, Charlotte (2004) *Rachel Whiteread* (London: Tate)
Nancy, Jean-Luc (2000 [1996]) *Being Singular Plural*, trans. Robert D. Richardson and Anne E. O'Byrne (Stanford, CA: Stanford University Press)

National Endowment for the Arts (2012) 'National Endowment for the Arts Appropriations History', http://www.arts.gov/about/Budget/AppropriationsHistory.html, accessed August 2012

National Theatre (2010) 'Press Release: The National Theatre announces a £10 million gift from Lloyd Dorfman for NT Future', 28 October, available at http://www.nationaltheatre.org.uk/document/the-national-theatre-announces-a-%C2%A310-million-gift-from-lloyd-dorfman, accessed August 2012

—— (2012) 'The National Theatre Around the World', http://www.nationaltheatre.org.uk/69625/american-associates/the-national-theatre-around-the-world.html, accessed July 2012

—— (n.d.a) *National Theatre Annual Report 2010–2011* (London: National Theatre), available at http://www.nationaltheatre.org.uk/68098/annual-reportreview/annual-report-1011.html, accessed July 2012

—— (n.d.b) *Financial Statements, 2010–2011* (London: National Theatre) available at http://www.nationaltheatre.org.uk/68098/annual-reportreview/annual-report-1011.html, accessed July 2012

National Theatre Black Theatre Archive (2012a) http://www.blackplaysarchive.org.uk/, accessed August 2012

—— (2012b) http://microsites.nationaltheatre.org.uk/70327/black-plays-archive/the-black-plays-archive.html, accessed August 2012

National Theatre of Scotland [NTS] (2012) Home Glasgow, http://www.nationaltheatrescotland.com/content/default.asp?pagehome_showHome_Glasgow, accessed November 2012

National Trust (2011) 'Government Reforms Threaten Green Spaces', September, http://www.nationaltrust.org.uk/main/w-chl/w-countryside_environment/w-planning-landing.htm, accessed September 2011

Nesbitt, Judith (2004) 'Everything Must Go', in Michael Landy, *Semi-Detached* (London: Tate Publishing), pp. 12–23

New Deal of the Mind (2009) *Do It Yourself: Cultural and Creative Self-Employment in Hard Times: A New Deal of the Mind Report for Arts Council England*, June (London: New Deal of the Mind), http://www.thecreativesociety.co.uk/wp-content/uploads/2011/02/NDotM_ACE1.pdf, accessed December 2012

—— (2010) *Creative Survival in Hard Times: A New Deal of the Mind Report for Arts Council England*, March (London: New Deal of the Mind), http://www.thecreativesociety.co.uk/wp-content/uploads/2011/02/Creative_Survival_NDotM_for_ACE_march_2010_FINAL.pdf, accessed December 2012

Newcastle City Council (2012) *Newcastle City Council Budget Proposals 2016*, 22 November, http://www.newcastle.gov.uk/your-council/budget-and-annual-report/budget-proposals-2016, accessed December 2012

Nicholls, John (2011) *Hidden Wealth Research Project*, July, updated findings April 2010–June 2011 (London: Arts Quarter), http://www.artsquarter.co.uk/hwrp.html, accessed 12 July 2012

—— (2012a) *Implementation of the Philanthropy in the Arts Agenda: Findings from the 2012 Arts Quarter Survey*, Report Summary, April (London: Arts Quarter LLP)

Nowhereisland (2012a) http://nowhereisland.org/, accessed August 2012

—— (2012b) Resident Thinkers, http://nowhereisland.org/resident-thinkers/, accessed August 2012

—— (2012c) School Info, http://nowhereisland.org/embassy/school-info/, accessed August 2012

—— (2012d) Embassy, http://nowhereisland.org/embassy/, accessed August 2012

NRLA (2012) archive, http://www.bris.ac.uk/theatrecollection/liveart/liveart_NRLA.html, accessed August 2012

Oakley, Kate (2009a) *'Art Works': Cultural Labour Markets*, Creativity, Culture and Education Literature Review Series (London: Arts Council England)

—— (2009b) 'Getting Out of Place: The Mobile Creative Class Takes on the Local. A UK Perspective on the Creative Class', in Justin O'Connor and Lily Kong (eds), *Creative Economies, Creative Cities: Asian-European Perspectives*, The GeoJournal Library Vol. 98 (Dordrecht: Springer), pp. 121–34

O'Connor, John, and Lorraine Brown (eds) (1980) *The Federal Theatre Project: 'Free, Adult, Uncensored'* (London: Eyre Methuen)

O'Connor, Justin (2010) *The Cultural and Creative Industries: A Literature Review*, Creativity, Culture and Education Literature Review Series, 2nd edn (London: Arts Council England), November (ACE Creative Partnerships), http://www.creativitycultureeducation.org/wp-content/uploads/CCE-lit-review-creative-cultural-industries-257.pdf, accessed October 2012

O'Connor, Justin, and Lily Kong (2009a) 'Introduction', in Lily Kong and Justin O'Connor (eds), *Creative Economies, Creative Cities: Asian-European Perspectives*, The GeoJournal Library Volume 98 (Dordrecht: Springer), pp. 1–5

Oddey, Alison (2007) *Re-Framing the Theatrical: Interdisciplinary Landscapes for Performance* (Basingstoke: Palgrave Macmillan)

Ormerod, Katherine (2012) 'Lim in London: Phillip Lim's Selfridges Pop Up', *Graziadaily.co.uk*, 22 May, http://www.graziadaily.co.uk/fashion/archive/2012/05/22/lim-in-london--phillip-lims-selfridges-pop-up.htm, accessed August 2012

Osborne, George, MP (2011) 'Chancellor Announces Tax Breaks for Philanthropists', March, DCMS, http://www.culture.gov.uk/news/news_stories/7979.aspx, accessed 11 July 2012

—— (2012) 'Autumn Statement 2012 to the House of Commons by the Rt Hon George Osborne, MP, Chancellor of the Exchequer', 5 December, available on *HM Treasury*, UK Economy, http://www.hm-treasury.gov.uk/as2012_statement.htm, accessed December 2012

Oxford Reference Online, Oxford University Press, http://www.oxfordreference.com/views/ENTRY.html?subview+Main&entryt20.e1189, accessed via British Library, 5 April 2012

Pachter, Marc, and Charles Landry (2001) *Culture at the Crossroads: Culture and Cultural Institutions at the Beginning of the 21st Century* (Bournes Green: Comedia)

Painter, Joe (1998) 'Entrepreneurs Are Made, Not Born: Learning and Urban Regimes in the Production of Entrepreneurial Cities', in Tim Hall and Phil Hubbard (eds), *The Entrepreneurial City: Geographies of Politics, Regime and Representation* (Chichester: John Wiley & Sons), pp. 259–73

Parker, Cornelia (1991) *Cold Dark Matter: An Exploded View* (London: Chisenhale Gallery)

—— (2000) *Cornelia Parker* (Boston, MA: Institute of Contemporary Art)

—— (2001) *Cornelia Parker* (Torino: hopefulmonster)

—— (2007) *Never Endings* (Birmingham: Ikon Gallery)

Payton, Robert L., and Michael Moody (2008) *Understanding Philanthropy: Its Meaning and Mission* (Bloomington, IN: Indiana University Press)

Peck, Jamie (2005) 'Struggling with the Creative Class', *International Journal of Urban and Regional Research*, 29.4 (December): 740–70
—— (2007) 'The Creativity Fix', *Fronesis*, 24, rpt. in Eurozine, 28 June, http://www.eurozine.com/articles/2007-06-28-peck-en.html, accessed August 2011
Perry, Grayson (2002) *Guerrilla Tactics* (Amsterdam/Rotterdam: Stedelijk Museum/NAi Publishers)
—— 'Unpopular Culture' (2008a) in Grayson Perry, *Unpopular Culture: Grayson Perry Selects from the Arts Council Collection* (London: Hayward Publishing), pp. 7–11
—— (2008b) *Unpopular Culture: Grayson Perry Selects from the Arts Council Collection* (London: Hayward Publishing)
—— (2011) *The Tomb of the Unknown Craftsman (*London: British Museum Press)
Pharoah, Cathy (2011) *Charity Market Monitor 2011*, cited in Nicola Hill, 'Donations fall but animal welfare giving goes up, Charity Market Monitor shows', *Philanthropy UK*, 15 July 2011, http://www.philanthropyuk.org/news/2011-07-15/donations-fall-animal-welfare-giving-goes-charity-market-monitor-shows, accessed 12 July 2012
Pilkington, Ed, Lizzy Davies and Henry McDonald (2010) 'Hard times: How the recession is affecting arts funding around the globe', *Guardian*, 19 February, available at http://www.guardian.co.uk/culture/2010/feb/19/arts-funding-global-recession, accessed July 2012
Pine II, B. Joseph, and James H. Gilmore (1999) *The Experience Economy: Work Is Theatre and Every Business a Stage* (Boston, MA: Harvard Business School Press)
—— (2011 [1999]) *The Experience Economy: Work Is Theatre and Every Business a Stage*, updated edn (Boston, MA: Harvard Business School Press)
Phillips, Adam, and Barbara Taylor (2009) *On Kindness* (London: Hamish Hamilton)
Potts, Jason (2011) *Creative Industries and Economic Evolution*, New Horizons in Institutional and Evolutionary Economics series (Cheltenham: Edward Elgar)
Press Association (2012a) 'Thousands March in Trade Unions' Anti-cuts Demonstration', *Guardian*, 20 October, http://www.guardian.co.uk/politics/2012/oct/20/trade-unions-anti-cuts-demonstration, accessed December 2012
—— (2012b) 'London 2012: Big Ben to Chime for Three Minutes to Mark Olympic Opening', Guardian.co.uk, 24 July, http://www.guardian.co.uk/sport/2012/jul/24/london-2012-big-ben-olympic, accessed August 2012
Punchdrunk (2011) www.punchdrunk.org.uk, accessed May 2011
—— (2012a) Key Holder scheme, http://www.punchdrunk.org.uk/key_holder/, accessed July 2012
—— (2012b) *Under the Eiderdown*, http://www.punchdrunk.org.uk/documents/UTE_Booklet.pdf, accessed July 2012
—— and Arcola (2012) *Uncommercial Traveller*, http://artinemptyspaces.org.uk/projects/uncommercial-traveller, accessed October 2012
Quine, Michael (1998) 'The Theatre System of the United Kingdom', in H. van Maanen and S. E. Wilmer (eds), *Theatre Worlds in Motion: Structures, Politics and Developments in the Countries of Western Europe* (Amsterdam and Atlanta, GA: Rodopi), pp. 668–720
Quinn, Susan (2008) *Furious Improvisation: How the WPA and a Cast of Thousands Made High Art out of Desperate Times* (New York: Walker)

Ragsdale, Diane (2011) *Rethinking Cultural Philanthropy: Towards a More Sustainable Arts and Culture Sector*, London: Royal Society for the Arts, February, http://www.thersa.org/__data/assets/pdf_file/0005/384485/RSA-Rethinking_Cultural_Philanthropy-Diane_Ragsdale.pdf, accessed June 2011

Ramesh, Randeep (2010a) 'Healthy Living Is Cut Short by 17 Years for Poorest in Britain', *Guardian*, 10 February, http://www.guardian.co.uk/society/2010/feb/10/equality-poverty-health-society, accessed February 2010

—— (2010b) 'Spending Review 2010: Key Points at a Glance: Social Housing', Guardian.co.uk, 20 October, http://www.guardian.co.uk/politics/2010/oct/20/spending-review-2010-key-points, accessed August 2012

—— and Juliette Jowit (2012) 'Government confirms U-turn on charity tax', *Guardian*, 31 May, http://www.guardian.co.uk/society/2012/may/31/government-confirms-u-turn-charity-tax, accessed July 2012

—— and Peter Walker (2012) 'London Council Seeks to Move Benefit Claimants from Capital', *Guardian*, 24 April, http://www.guardian.co.uk/society/2012/apr/24/london-borough-benefit-claimants-outside-capital?intcmp239, accessed November 2012

Rancière, Jacques (2007) 'The Emancipated Spectator', *ArtForum*, March, pp. 270–81

—— (2009) *The Emancipated Spectator*, trans. Gregory Elliott (London: Verso)

Rayner, Jay (2011) 'Restaurant Review: Brixton Village', *The Observer*, 9 October, available at http://www.guardian.co.uk/lifeandstyle/2011/oct/09/jay-rayner-brixton-village-unit, accessed August 2012

Read, Alan (1993) *Theatre and Everyday Life: An Ethics of Performance* (London: Routledge)

—— (2011) 'Preface in the Company of Kindness', in David Williams and Carl Lavery (eds), *Good Luck Everybody: Lone Twin: Journeys Performances Conversations* (Aberystwyth: Performance Research Books), pp. 7–11

Reeling, Gideon (2012) brochure, http://gideonreeling.co.uk/WebFriendly Brochure.pdf, accessed July 2012

Reeve, Michael (2010) MykReeve on flickr, 30 November, http://www.flickr.com/photos/mykreeve/5215571319/, accessed July 2012

Reid, Benjamin, Alexandra Albert and Laurence Hopkins (2010) *A Creative Block? The Future of the UK Creative Industries*, report for the Work Foundation, December (London: The Work Foundation and the DCMS)

Reuters (2012) 'Currency Conversion', http://uk.reuters.com/business/currencies/, accessed August 2012

Ridout, Nicholas (2008) 'Performance in the Service Economy: Outsourcing and Delegation', in Claire Bishop and Silvia Tramontana (eds), *Double Agent* (London: ICA), pp. 126–31

Roche, Jennifer (2006) 'Socially Engaged Art, Critics and Discontents: An Interview with Claire Bishop', *Community Arts Network Reading Room*, July, http://www.communityarts.net/readingroom/archivefiles/2006/07/socially_engage.php, accessed June 2010

Rogers, Simon (2011a) 'Arts Council Cuts Listed: Get the Data', *Guardian Data Blog*, 30 March, http://www.guardian.co.uk/news/datablog/2011/mar/30/arts-council-cuts-list-funding, accessed Nov. 2011

—— (2011b) 'Arts Council Funding: Get the Full Decision List', *Guardian Data Blog*, 30 March, http://www.guardian.co.uk/news/datablog/2011/mar/30/

arts-council-funding-decisions-list, accessed July 2012 and see links to data, https://docs.google.com/spreadsheet/ccc?key0AonYZs4MzlZbdFVPUnpQcWwxOG5seUd4ckFkTEltTXc&hlen#gid2, accessed July 2012

Rosler, Martha (2010) 'Culture Class: Art, Creativity, Urbanism, Part I', *e-flux*, 21 (December), http://www.e-flux.com/journal/view/190, accessed November 2011

—— (2011a) 'Culture Class: Art, Creativity, Urbanism, Part II', *e-flux*, 23 (March), http://www.e-flux.com/journal/view/219, accessed November 2011

—— (2011b) 'Culture Class: Art, Creativity, Urbanism, Part III', *e-flux*, 25 (May), http://www.e-flux.com/journal/view/231, accessed November 2011

—— (2012) 'The Artistic Mode of Revolution: From Gentrification to Occupation', *e-flux*, 33 (March), http://www.e-flux.com/journal/the-artistic-mode-of-revolution-from-gentrification-to-occupation/, accessed March 2012

Royal Court, Theatre Local (2010) http://royalcourttheatre.com/season/theatre-local, accessed August 2012

—— (2011) http://www.royalcourttheatre.com/season/theatre-local-peckham, accessed August 2012

—— (2012a) http://www.royalcourttheatre.com/season/theatre-local-peckham-2012, accessed August 2012

—— (2012b) 'Press Release: Theatre Local to Return to Peckham This Summer', 5 April, http://www.royalcourttheatre.com/news/articles/theatre-local-to-return-to-peckham-this-summer/, accessed August 2012

Sadler's Wells (2012) http://www.sadlerswells.com/show/Electric-Hotel, accessed November 2012

Salcedo, Doris (2007) *Shibboleth* (London: Tate Publishing)

Sampson, Adam (Shelter Chief Executive) (2008) Foreword, in Suzanne Fitzpatrick and Mark Stephens (eds), *The Future of Social Housing* (London: Shelter), pp. 3–4

Schanke, Robert A. (ed.) (2007) *Angels in the American Theater: Patrons, Patronage, and Philanthropy*, Theater in the Americas (Carbondale, IL: Southern Illinois University Press)

Schmidt Campbell, Mary and Randy Martin (eds) (2006) *Artistic Citizenship: A Public Voice for the Arts* (New York and London: Routledge)

Schneider, Christiane (ed.) (2002) *Rachel Whiteread* (London: Haunch of Venison)

Schumpeter, Joseph A. (1994) *Capitalism, Socialism and Democracy*, rev. edn (London: Routledge)

Scotland World Class (2011) 'Creative Collaboration on the Clyde', in *World Class Scotland: A Place for Business* (Stirling: World Class Publishing), available at http://www.scotlandworldclass.com/images/chapters/2011/08%20Clyde%20Waterfront.pdf, accessed August 2012

Scott, John, and Gordon Marshall (2009) *A Dictionary of Sociology* (Oxford: Oxford University Press), *Oxford Reference Online*, Oxford University Press, http://www.oxfordreference.com/views/ENTRY.html?subview+Main&entryt88.e730, accessed via British Library, 5 April 2012

Searle, Adrian (2008) 'Don't Forget Your Wellies...', *Guardian*, 4 September, http://www.guardian.co.uk/artanddesign/2008/sep/04/art, accessed June 2010

Searle, Adrian, Jonathan Jones, Charlotte Higgins and Skye Sherwin (2010) 'The Tate Modern at 10', *Guardian*, 4 May, http://www.guardian.co.uk/artanddesign/2010/may/04/tate-modern-10th-anniversary, accessed March 2013

Selfridges & Co. (2012) 'Christian Louboutin Launches a Spectacular Anniversary Pop Up Shop at Selfridges London', 21 February, available at http://style.selfridges.com/whats-in/christian-louboutin-launches-spectacular-anniversary-pop-shop-selfridges-london, accessed August 2012

Sennett, Richard (1998) *The Corrosion of Character: The Personal Consequences of Work in the New Capitalism* (New York: W. W. Norton)

—— (2006) *The Culture of the New Capitalism* (New Haven, CT, and London: Yale University Press)

—— (2009 [2008]) *The Craftsman* (London: Penguin Books) (originally published by Yale University Press and Allen Lane [London])

Sennett, Richard, Grayson Perry, Ian Bostridge and Marina Warner (2008) 'Amateurism, Art and Absorption', *Crafts*, 214 (September/October): 52–5

Shackle, Samira (2012) 'UK University Applications down 8.7 Per Cent as Fees Rise', *New Statesman*, 30 January, http://www.newstatesman.com/blogs/the-staggers/2012/01/applications-fees-students, accessed December 2012

Shelter (2012) 'The Housing Crisis', http://england.shelter.org.uk/campaigns/why_we_campaign/the_housing_crisis, accessed August 2012

Shipman, Tim (2011) 'Parts of Our Society Are Not Broken but Sick – the Prime Minister's Verdict on Riot UK', *Mail Online*, 11 August, http://www.dailymail.co.uk/news/article-2024709/David-Cameron-UK-riots-Parts-society-broken-sick.html, accessed October 2011

Sholette, Gregory (2011) *Dark Matter: Art and Politics in the Age of Enterprise Culture* (London and New York: Pluto Press)

Sillars, Laurence (ed.) (2009) *Joyous Machines: Michael Landy and Jean Tinguely* (Liverpool: Tate Liverpool)

Simmonds, Tristan, Martin Self and Daniel Bosia (2006) 'Woven Surface and Form', *Architectural Design*, 76.6: 82–9

Slater, Tom (2012) 'Missing Marcuse: On Gentrification and Displacement', in Neil Brenner, Peter Marcuse and Margit Mayer (eds), *Cities for People, Not for Profit: Critical Urban Theory and the Right to the City* (London and New York: Routledge), pp. 171–96

Slyce, John (2004) 'Temporary Monumental: Visibility, Labour, Value, and Procedure in the Projects of Michael Landy', in Michael Landy, *Semi-Detached* (London: Tate Publishing), pp. 50–63

Smith, Chris (1998) *Creative Britain* (London: Faber & Faber)

—— MP, Secretary of State for Culture Media and Sport (2000) in Smith Institute, *The New Entrepreneurs: Seminar 2: Cultural Entrepreneurship*, a seminar held on 23rd June 1999, 11 Downing Street, London (London: Smith Institute), pp. 3–7

Soros, George (1998) *The Crisis of Global Capitalism: Open Society Endangered* (London: Little Brown)

Southbank Centre (2011) *Annual Review 2010/11* (London: Southbank Centre), http://ticketing.southbankcentre.co.uk/sites/default/files/documents/21743_Annual_Review.pdf, accessed August 2012

Space Makers Agency (2011) http://spacemakers.org.uk/, accessed September 2011

—— (n.d.) 'Brixton Village', http://spacemakers.org.uk/projects/brixton/, accessed August 2012

Sparrow, Andrew and agencies (2012) 'Social Homes Funding Plan "Blindingly Obvious", Says Housing Minister', Guardian.co.uk, 20 August, http://www.

guardian.co.uk/society/2012/aug/20/sell-social-housing-fund-homes, accessed August 2012

Speed, Emily (2011) 'How to Get Crowd-funding', *a-n.co.uk*, January, http://www.a-n.co.uk/knowledge_bank/article/1002915/77173, accessed July 2012

Sponsume (2012a) http://www.sponsume.com/, accessed July 2012

—— (2012b) 'Belarus Free Theatre', http://www.sponsume.com/project/belarus-free-theatre, accessed July 2012

—— (2012c) *GO TRAVIATA*, http://www.sponsume.com/project/go-traviata-0, accessed July 2012

Staines, Judith (2011) 'Crowdfunding for the Arts, Updated', culture360,org, 7 September, http://culture360.org/news/crowdsourced-funding-for-the-arts/, accessed July 2012

Stevenson, Angus (ed.) (2010) *Oxford Dictionary of English, Oxford Reference Online*, Oxford University Press, http://www.oxfordreference.com/views/ENTRY.html?subviewMain&entryt140.e0268460, accessed via British Library, 5 April 2012

Stevenson, Mark (2012) of the company Honda Dream Factory, speaking at 'Creativity and Business: Connectivity, Values and Interventions', *The Culture Capital Exchange/British Library Conference* (London), 12 March

Summerton, J. (2001) 'Framing Pictures: Creative Thinking about Creative Workers', *Arts Professional*, 11 (October)

Sunday Times, The (2012) 'The Sunday Times Rich List', *The Sunday Times*, 29 April

Szreter, Simon, and Armine Ishkanian (2012) 'Introduction: What Is Big Society? Contemporary Social Policy in a Historical and Comparative Perspective', in Armine Ishkanian and Simon Szreter, eds, *The Big Society Debates: A New Agenda for Social Welfare?* (Cheltenham: Edward Elgar), pp. 1–24

Theatre Delicatessen (2012a) About Us, http://www.theatredelicatessen.co.uk/about-us/, accessed November 2012

—— (2012b) Working with Property Developers, http://www.theatredelicatessen.co.uk/about-us/working-with-property-developers/, accessed November 2012

Thornton, Neil (2012) 'Christian Louboutin's Selfridges Pop-up Store', FashionBeans, http://www.fashionbeans.com/2012/christian-louboutin-pop-up-store-strides-into-selfridges/, accessed August 2012

Thorpe, Vanessa (2012) 'Newcastle's Arts Groups Face up to a Future Without Public Funding', *Observer*, 9 December, http://www.guardian.co.uk/culture/2012/dec/09/newcastle-arts-groups-face-funding-cut, accessed December 2012

Thrift, Nigel (2008) *Non-Representational Theory: Space/Politics/Affect* (Abingdon: Routledge)

Time Out (2012) 'We Take a Ride on the Mysterious You Me Bum Bum Train', *The Time Out London Blog*, 15 June, http://now-here-this.timeout.com/2012/06/15/we-take-a-ride-on-the-mysterious-you-me-bum-bum-train/, accessed December 2012

Todolí, Vincente (2007) 'Director's Foreword', Doris Salcedo, *Shibboleth* (London: Tate Publishing), pp. 7–9

Townsend, Chris (ed.) (2004) *The Art of Rachel Whiteread* (London: Thames & Hudson)

Toynbee, Polly, and David Walker (2009 [2008]) *Unjust Rewards: Ending the Greed That is Bankrupting Britain*, rev. edn (London: Granta)

Turner, B. (2007) 'The Enclave Society: Towards a Sociology of Immobility', *European Journal of Social Theory*, 10.2: 287–303

UK Uncut (2012) http://www.ukuncut.org.uk/, accessed December 2012
Vaizey, Ed, MP (2011) 'Foreword [Part 2]: Supporting Growth in the Arts Economy', in Tom Fleming and Andrew Erskine, *Supporting Growth in the Arts Economy*, July (London: ACE), p. 3, available at http://www.artscouncil.org.uk/media/uploads/pdf/creative_economy_final210711.pdf, accessed August 2011
van Maanen, H., and S. E. Wilmer (eds) (1998) *Theatre Worlds in Motion: Structures, Politics and Developments in the Countries of Western Europe* (Amsterdam and Atlanta, GA: Rodopi)
Veblen, Thorstein (2005) *Conspicuous Consumption*, Great Ideas series (London: Penguin Books)
—— (2007 [1899]) *The Theory of the Leisure Class* (Oxford: Oxford University Press)
Vidler, Anthony (1995) 'A Dark Space', in James Lingwood (ed.), *Rachel Whiteread: House* (London: Phaidon in association with Artangel), pp. 62–72
Virno, Paolo (2004) *A Grammar of the Multitude: For an Analysis of Contemporary Forms of Life*, Foreword by Sylvère Lotringer, trans by Isabella Bertoletti, James Cascaito and Andrea Casson (Los Angeles, CA: Semiotext(e))
Virno, Paolo, and Michael Hardt (eds) (1996) *Radical Thought in Italy: A Potential Politics* (Minneapolis, MN: University of Minnesota Press)
Vogel, Carol (2006) 'Swimming with Famous Dead Sharks', *The New York Times*, 1 October, p.3, http://www.nytimes.com/2006/10/01/arts/design/01voge.html?pagewanted1&ei5088&en6fcefeb8359f9748&ex1317355200&partnerrssnyt&emcrss, accessed June 2011
Wagstaff, Sheena (2010) 'Foreword', in Juliet Bingham (ed.), *Ai Weiwei: Sunflower Seeds* (London: Tate Publishing), pp. 7–9
War Horse (2012) produced by National Theatre, http://warhorseonstage.com/show, accessed July 2012
Ward, Ossian (n.d.) 'Jeremy Deller: Joy in People', *Time Out*, n.d., http://www.timeout.com/london/feature/2330/jeremy-deller-joy-in-people, accessed June 2012
Warner, Michael (2002) *Publics and Counterpublics* (New York: Zone Books)
Watney, Simon (1995) 'On *House*, Iconoclasm & Iconophobia', in James Lingwood (ed.), *Rachel Whiteread: House* (London: Phaidon in association with Artangel), pp. 96–109
Watt, Paul (2009) 'Social Housing and Regeneration in London', in Rob Imrie, Loretta Lees and Mike Raco (eds), *Regenerating London: Governance, Sustainability and Community in a Global City* (London: Routledge), pp. 212–33
We Are Pop Up (2012a) http://www.wearepopup.com/thepopspot/, accessed August 2012
—— (2012b) http://www.wearepopup.com/, accessed August 2012
We Did This (2012) http://www.wedidthis.org.uk/, accessed July 2012
Whelan, Gregg, and Gary Winters with David Williams (2011) 'People Together Doing Something', in David Williams and Carl Lavery (eds), *Good Luck Everybody: Lone Twin: Journeys Performances Conversations* (Aberystwyth: Performance Research Books), pp. 27–39
Whiting, Ed (2011) 'Crowdfunding the Arts – Who's with Us?', Guardian.co.uk, 11 March, http://www.guardian.co.uk/culture/culture-cuts-blog/2011/mar/11/crowdfunding-arts-wedidthis, accessed July 2012

Wilkes, James (2008) 'Roger Hiorns: *Seizure*', *Studio International*, 22 December, http://www.studio-international.co.uk/sculpture/hiorns.asp, accessed June 2010

Wilkinson, Richard, and Kate Pickett (2010 [2009]) *The Spirit Level: Why Equality Is Better for Everyone*, rev. edn (London: Penguin)

Williams, David (ed.) (2012) *The Lone Twin Boat Project* (Dartington Hall, Devon: Chiquita Books)

Williams, David, and Carl Lavery (eds) (2011) *Good Luck Everybody: Lone Twin: Journeys Performances Conversations* (Aberystwyth: Performance Research Books)

Williams, Gilda (2008) 'Roger Hiorns: Artangel at Harper Road', *ArtForum*, 47.4 (December)

Williams, Raymond (2005 [1980]) *Culture and Materialism: Selected Essays* (London, Verso)

Wintour, Patrick (2012) 'Cameron Backs Plan to Abolish Social Housing Rent Subsidy for Higher Earners', *Guardian*, 19 May, http://www.guardian.co.uk/society/2012/may/19/social-housing-income-cap-shapps, accessed August 2012

Witham, Barry B. (2003) *The Federal Theatre Project: A Case Study* (Cambridge: Cambridge University Press)

Work Foundation (2007) *Staying Ahead: The Economic Performance of the UK's Creative Industries*, June (London: The Work Foundation and the DCMS)

Wright, Stephen (2004) 'The Delicate Essence of Artistic Collaboration', *Third Text*, 18.6 (November): n.p.

Wu, Chin-Tao (2002) *Privatising Culture: Corporate Art Intervention since the 1980s* (London and New York: Verso)

Wyly, E., and D. Hammel (2005) 'Mapping Neoliberal American Urbanism', in R. Atkinson and G. Bridge (eds), *Gentrification in a Global Context: The New Urban Colonialism* (London: Routledge), pp. 18–38

Young, James E. (2004) 'Rachel Whiteread's Judenplatz Memorial in Vienna', in Chris Townsend (ed.), *The Art of Rachel Whiteread* (London: Thames & Hudson), pp. 162–72

Zerihan, Rachel (2009) *One to One Performance*, Live Art Development Agency Study Room Guide (London: Live Art Development Agency, n.d. [2009]), http://www.thisisliveart.co.uk/resources/Study_Room/guides/Rachel_Zerihan.html, accessed December 2012

Zuidervaart, Lambert (2011) *Art in Public: Politics, Economics, and a Democratic Culture* (Cambridge: Cambridge University Press)

Zukin, Sharon (1988 [1982]) *Loft Living: Culture and Capital in Urban Change* (Baltimore, MD: Johns Hopkins University Press)

—— (2010) *The Naked City: The Death and Life of Authentic Urban Places* (Oxford: Oxford University Press)

Index

Printed and bound by CPI Group (UK) Ltd, Croydon, CR0 4YY